MAKING THE MOST OF YOUR INTERNSHIP

A Strategic Approach

Ryan K. Gower
Michael A. Mulvaney

SAGAMORE
PUBLISHING

Publishers: Joseph J. Bannon and Peter L. Bannon
Director of Sales and Marketing: William Anderson
Director of Development and Production: Susan M. Davis
Director of Technology: Christopher Thompson
Production Coordinator: Amy S. Dagit

ISBN print edition: 978-57167-657-3
ISBN ebook: 978-1-57167-656-6
LCCN: 2012942242

Sagamore Publishing LLC
1807 N. Federal Dr.
Urbana, IL 61801
www.sagamorepub.com

For Tracey, Evan, Grace, and Adin.
You are my reason for being and my hope for tomorrow.
—RG

To my wife, Megan, for her love, support,
and patience throughout all my endeavors.
—MM

CONTENTS

Section II: Internship Selection

Section III: Managing the Internship Experience

PREFACE

The Foundation of the Book

A capstone experience of a majority of academic programs in recreation, sport, and tourism industries is the internship. Designed as an opportunity to mesh classroom-based instruction with on-the-job experiences, the internship seeks to establish a mutually beneficial relationship among the student, the agency, and academic institution. For students, the internship provides "real-world" exposure to the field, strengthens their resume, and allows them to examine the "ins and outs" of a professional agency and chosen service sector (i.e., public, commercial, and nonprofit, etc.). Agencies that employ interns are able to get a first-hand look at the on-the-job performance within the pipeline of future professionals in a cost-effective manner. Finally, the internship allows the academic institution to further integrate the student's intellectual and theoretical development with application-based experiences while promoting and fostering relationships with relevant agencies and practitioners.

Recognizing the prominence and value of the internship experience, this book aims to serve as a resource for the internship planning, selection, and management processes. Drawing from a variety of theoretically grounded sources, personal experiences in the advisement and supervision of interns and internship programs, and student and practitioner-based feedback, *Making the Most of Your Internship: A Strategic Approach* provides a comprehensive and up-to-date coverage of vital strategies associated with the internship. The book adopts an action-oriented approach by focusing on the "how-to" aspects of the internship experience while stressing the important and influential role of the internal (i.e., needs, constraints, interests, etc.) and external (i.e., trends, issues, job-related factors, etc.) environments in the internship planning, selection, and management phases.

The book's purpose is to point the way toward the student thinking strategically about the tasks associated with the internship. A key tenet of *Making the Most of Your Internship: A Strategic Approach* is the contention that the internship is not an isolated activity that occurs without regard to the student's previous coursework, experiences, interests, or future career plans. Rather, the internship represents a key piece in the student's overall career. Guided by this framework, *Making the Most of Your Internship: A Strategic Approach* encourages the student through a variety of readings, examples, testimonials, and activities, to be intentional about the integration of their past, present, and future experiences and interests into the planning, selecting, and managing of their internship experiences.

The Audience for the Book

The primary audience for this book is undergraduate students who have aspirations to complete an internship experience in the recreation, sport, and tourism industries. More specifically, it is intended as a desk aid to help instructors prepare students for the internship and as a text for students. *Making the Most of Your Internship: A Strategic Approach* should also be of interest to recreation, sport, and tourism professionals who engage in their own career planning, supervise interns, or have an interest in developing an internship program for their agency.

Overview of the Contents

Making the Most of Your Internship: A Strategic Approach represents a collection of strategies, tips, personal stories and advice from students and professionals, exercises, activities, and case studies. Taken collectively, this information provides a comprehensive framework for the student's successful and strategic engagement in the internship experience. The chapters are organized in a linear sequence starting with the steps and strategies associated with the internship planning processes and ending with a discussion of post internship activities including, career planning, job searching, and salary negotiation. It is also worth mentioning that while we expect that several will want to follow the sequence outlined in this book, it is also likely that others might wish to adapt their approach to meet specific student and/or course demands. Regardless of the sequence, it is our hope that the book's content will provide you with a comprehensive resource that can be utilized before, during, and after the internship experience.

Making the Most of Your Internship: A Strategic Approach is divided into three sections related to the internship experience: planning, selecting, and managing. Section one consists of chapters one, two, and three. It provides a conceptual overview of the internship experience as well as the processes associated with internship planning.

Chapter one serves as an introduction to the internship experience. It positions the internship in the context of experiential learning while highlighting the outcomes of the experience. A discussion of the specific student, university, and agency benefits are also provided. In Chapter two, the individual assessment is presented including procedures for completing the self, task, and agency analyses. Chapter three focuses on the strategic connection between the individual assessment and the development of career and internship goals and objectives. A variety of examples, exercises, and testimonials are provided to assist the student in developing these goals and strategic direction.

Section two of the book comprises chapters four through seven. They are unified by a common direction—internship selection. Chapter four sets the stage for the internship selection phase with a description of the search process, including an overview of the recruitment process for students and agencies;

tips for beginning the internship search process; keys to finding the "perfect fit"; strategies for discovering internship opportunities; and internship search sources and best practices. Chapter five picks up where Chapter four left off with a detailed overview of resume and cover letter development. Specifically, the content and format of a cover letter are presented with several examples and testimonials provided to aid the student in the development of this important application document. Next, the resume and its essential components are discussed with special attention paid to the creation of a resume that is specific to recreation, sport, and tourism industries in its organization and format. Similar to the cover letter discussion, a variety of resume examples and testimonials are presented. The interview process, the different types, stages, and preparation strategies are reviewed in Chapter six. Chapter seven begins with an overview of the internship selection process (from the agency's perspective) and insight on what the student can expect following the interview. The chapter concludes with tips on managing the internship offer and making and communicating the final decision to the agency.

Section three consists of Chapters eight through twelve that cover, respectively, strategies and tips on managing the internship experience and life following the internship. Specifically, Chapter eight provides an overview of the internship experience, including the five common stages—anticipation, disillusionment, confrontation, competence, and culmination. Chapter nine highlights the strategic role of networking in, and following, the internship. Truths about networking, the value of networking, identifying where to network, and instructions on how to network are provided. Chapter 10 encourages students to start (if they haven't already) thinking about life after the internship. Specifically, the role and importance of individual-centered career planning is discussed. Information on career choice and interest inventories is provided as well as strategies to manage early career problems. Chapter 11 focuses on preparing for the next step—employment in the field. Definitions and responsibilities among the agency, academic institution, site-supervisor, and student in securing a job are discussed. Chapter 11 also identifies common myths associated with the job search process as well as the tips for landing that first full-time employment. Finally, Chapter 12 presents a detailed orientation on the salary negotiation process. The chapter begins with an overview of salary negotiation leading to a description of the essential elements needed in successful salary negotiating.

Ancillary materials accompany the book. These materials provide slides to accompany each chapter of the text. An example syllabus for a pre-internship course, many application-level exercises and examples and handouts from the text, and activities based on or meant to improve student understanding of each chapter are also provided.

ACKNOWLEDGMENTS

As those who have gone through the process know, writing a text is a very time-consuming and involved process. I'd like to gratefully acknowledge the following people.

First and foremost, I'd like to thank my wife, Tracey, for her partnership in this text and in life. In her own right, Tracey is a talented educator who has supervised hundreds of student interns. Her insight, perspective, and good nature contributed greatly to the book. I'd also like to acknowledge my children, Evan, Grace, and Adin James. Thanks for letting Daddy spend a few extra hours at the office! The three of you are and always will be the best part of my life.

I'd also like to thank my coauthor, Dr. Michael Mulvaney. You helped make the process more enjoyable, and without the accountability of a good colleague like you, I am not sure the text would have ever been finished. I hope this is the first of many projects we complete together.

The staff at Sagamore Publishing deserves recognition here. Although she has now moved on to new adventures, Mrs. Elaina Tucker-Buhs, who was one of my talented undergraduate students, first brought the idea of an internship text to me, and I am grateful for her confidence in my abilities. Dr. Bannon, Mr. Sanders, and Mrs. Davis have extended us every courtesy, and have been wonderful to work with. Thank you all.

Finally, I'd like to acknowledge a man who forever changed the course of my life, Dr. Jim Brademas. For some reason, while I was one of his student interns, he saw something special in me and invited me to join him as a graduate assistant. He taught me everything he knew about internships and opened doors for me that I never even knew existed. He gave me my first experiences as a coordinator of student internships and even introduced me to my wife. Jim, you have been, and remain, a gentleman and a scholar. Thank you.

—Ryan

An internship is clearly a group effort of agency professionals, students, and faculty working together to advance the field of recreation, sport, and tourism. Without this passion for professional growth and development, the internship as we know it would be nonexistent. In this regard, a deep amount of gratitude is directed toward the recreation, sport, and tourism professionals and their agencies; the students; and the faculty and their university support systems that promote these opportunities.

Specific to this project, I would like to thank my employer, Eastern Illinois University. Eastern Illinois University has provided resources and support to complete this text. Through EIU's increasing support and recognition for the value of the internship experience, they have demonstrated their belief in the future of our profession and its increasing importance to society.

I would also like to thank Sagamore Publishing for their ongoing support, assistance, and patience throughout the project. Textbook writing is a process involving several stages and resources. Sagamore's staff provided an ideal level of autonomy and support as we worked through the textbook's development and I thank them for their guidance.

Finally, I am indebted to my wife, Megan, for her loving support and willingness to tackle this challenge with me. Her caring nature, encouragement, and patience have been instrumental in completing this project. Many thanks and much love go out to her. My faithful Labrador companion, Atticus, has also played a significant role with this project by providing me with a bit of "balance" and perspective in life. His cheerful demeanor and demand for attention have provided much needed opportunities for relaxation and reflection, and I thank him for these experiences. To my parents, Richard and Dianne, thank you for your loving guidance. Your tireless efforts and encouraging words put me in position to pursue my dreams, and I am forever indebted to you. I will always remember that my accomplishments would not be possible without your selfless acts.

—Mike

ABOUT THE AUTHORS

RYAN K. GOWER is a lecturer and the Director of Undergraduate Studies in the Department of Recreation, Sport and Tourism at the University of Illinois at Urbana-Champaign. As the former internship coordinator, Dr. Gower has over 13 years of experience in guiding and directing student internships. He has given numerous presentations and invited lectures on the topic and has a strong interest in researching the impact of internship experiences on student learning and self-concept. Dr. Gower's research interests include enhancing our understanding of interactions with public recreation agencies with an emphasis on exploring customer satisfaction and the impact on pricing service, future use, and perceptions of staff competency. Dr. Gower received his Ph.D. from the University of Illinois at Urbana-Champaign with an emphasis in experiential education. Prior to earning his Ph.D., he worked as an academic advisor at the University of Illinois and remains passionate about helping students navigate the academy in pursuit of their academic, professional, and personal goals.

MICHAEL A. MULVANEY is an assistant professor in the Department of Recreation Administration at Eastern Illinois University. Dr. Mulvaney is a member of the National Recreation and Park Association, the Illinois Park and Recreation Association, and several regional park and recreation associations. Dr. Mulvaney's areas of research include human resource management functions in public park and recreation agencies, management and organization of public park and recreation agencies, learning and the use of learning technologies in employee training, and planning processes in park and recreation agencies. Dr. Mulvaney also has extensive experience on the development and testing of the effectiveness of various modes of instruction and their relationship to student learning of park and recreation concepts. Publications authored include journal articles, technical reports, and several national and international presentations. Dr. Mulvaney received a Ph.D. from the University of Illinois. Prior to obtaining his Ph.D., Dr. Mulvaney was employed with the Decatur Park District (Decatur, Illinois) in a variety of capacities, including facility management, fitness, programming, and special recreation.

Section 1

INTERNSHIP PLANNING

Chapter 1

Benefitting from the Internship Experience

Overview

Congratulations! If you are reading this book, you will soon be participating in what has the potential to be one of the most memorable experiences in your life—an internship. The process of searching for and completing an internship is a challenging yet rewarding experience. Done thoughtfully and carefully, this internship can set the stage for your emerging professional career. It is important, however, that you begin this process with an understanding of what experiential learning is, why the internship is a part of your undergraduate curriculum, and what benefits you (and the sponsoring agency and your university) can hope to realize in the weeks ahead. In short, this chapter is designed to help you understand the purpose of the internship experience.

Let's Get Started

Before you go any further in your readings, take a few moments to jot down your thoughts on the following questions:

- Why are you completing an internship?

- Name three things that you hope to gain as a result of your experience?

- What are you most afraid of about the internship?

Hang on to your responses for the next few weeks. As you will soon discover, if you are to have a positive experience, it is going to require a great deal of reflection, insight, and careful planning.

The Internship as Experiential Learning

Experiential learning has a long-standing history in American higher education. Early pioneers in education realized that carefully designed experiences outside of the traditional classroom could have tremendous educational impact. Such experiences, today commonly referred to as a co-op, internship, practicum, or service learning, are designed to assist students in bridging academia and their chosen profession. They do this by exposing students to new situations that force students to reflect and apply materials learned in the classroom while simultaneously developing professional competencies that might be difficult to impart in traditional classroom settings (Kiser & Partlow, 1999; Sweitzer & King, 1995). Due to the pioneering works and efforts of stewards like Herman Schneider and John Dewey, along with countless other early progressive educators, experiential learning has become an accepted educational pedagogy and plays a prominent and vital role in the education and development of college-aged students (Beauchamp, 1982; Gryski, Johnson, & O'Toole, 1987). These stewards recognized that students learn more effectively when they are placed in real-life settings in which they can test, apply, and better understand knowledge acquired in traditional settings (Beauchamp, 1982; Dewey, 1938; Kolb, 1984).

Perhaps the simplest definition of experiential learning is any hands-on experience that yields learning (Kiser & Partlow, 1999). The basic premise of experiential learning is that the student is learning from a work or life experience. David Kolb, a leading expert in the field of experiential learning, indicated that experiential learning involves a "direct encounter with the phenomena being studied rather than merely thinking about the encounter, or only considering the possibility of doing something about it" (Kolb, 1984, p. 42). Internships are not just a facet of service industry curriculums, as they have become popular additions to many programs of study. Hoffmann (2003) quoted a professor in business administration as saying,

> Teaching management outside a business setting is just like teaching swimming without putting students in the water…it's true, I've been teaching for almost a quarter of a century, but I've yet to meet another professor who took a course in how to be a professor. We learned by doing, not by watching from the sidelines. If business schools don't ensure that all students, management students in particular, get this type of exposure through a required practicum of some form or fashion before they graduate, then we have failed them. …Many educators entertain the assumption, a false one, that with enough knowledge about how to do something one can do it. Well, folks, if you believe that works, read everything you can about flying and go jump off a tall building. (p. 2)

It is important for you to realize that participating in an internship does not guarantee that you will have an enjoyable or meaningful educational experience. If you hope to have a positive experience, you must engage in careful planning and deliberation. The design and implementation of the experience is critical if the desired outcomes are to be reached. Chapters 2 and 3 will help you in the beginning stages of this planning process. Done properly, an internship can be the single most significant experience of your undergraduate career. Recognizing the potential for significant learning through internships, the National Park and Recreation Association's (NRPA) Council on Accreditation of Parks, Recreation, Tourism, and Related Professions (COAPRT) considers an internship experience a crucial aspect of a quality curriculum.

Internships Defined

The term *internship* is one that is used rather loosely to describe a number of different types of experiences. Despite the inconsistencies in usage, in this text internships will be operationally defined as a single-term, off-campus, work-based learning experience. In an internship, students are not sent off to survive the workplace alone but are instead supervised by a faculty representative of the college or university in conjunction with an agency supervisor. You might be interested to know that internships can be paid or unpaid and academic credit of varying amounts are awarded by the educational institution for participation in the internship experience as long as the experience is related to the student's major. In many programs of study, internships are a capstone experience, taking place in the senior year or at the end of traditional academic study. Most internships are full-time experiences, often referred to as *block placements*, where the student engages in the work-based learning experience to the exclusion of other academic classes. Preliminary studies suggest that student perception of the quality of their experience is greatly enhanced when they are fully immersed into an organization through a full-time internship (Gower, 2008). While concurrent classes are not typically acceptable as they could be a distraction to the working/learning process, an orientation course (you might be reading this book as a requirement of this class) is generally required before the onset of the internship experience (Gower, 2006). Less common in practice are *concurrent placements*, where students complete a designated number of hours each day with the host work agency and then attend traditional courses (Linn, 1999). Why is this important for you to know? The term *internship* is one that is used loosely and carries different meanings. When you are searching and applying for internships, you will want to be sure that all parties (you, the agency, and your faculty sponsor) all have the same expectations and understandings.

Did You Know?

Many employers require students to receive academic credit for an internship and use the award of such credit to justify not paying the student for their efforts. Why? The Fair Labor Standards Act (FLSA) requires that employers compensate employees for activities that primarily benefit the employer. The exception is internships, which the law considers to be an apprenticeship primarily for the benefit of the student. This book will provide you with many helpful suggestions to help you ensure that you do benefit from the internship. Don't fall into the trap of thinking of yourself as "inexpensive labor." The law clearly states that if you are not being paid, the internship should primarily benefit you. For more information about the FLSA, check out the Department of Labor website at www.dol.gove/whd/regs/compliance/whdfs71.htm.

Outcomes of the Internship

It would be normal for you to be wondering what you could expect to gain from an internship. You've just learned that you will likely be working full time, probably for 10 to 16 weeks, for an agency that might or might not be paying you. What's in it for you? You will be glad to know that much of the literature on internships has focused on the benefits students derive from such experiences. The findings of these studies, however, have been varied and diverse. Qualitative studies, in particular, have been extremely supportive of internship experiences. Self-report data from students who have completed an internship and the faculty members who supervise them reveal a deep conviction that the experience is valuable and that the benefits of the experience are varied and highly individualized (Gryski et al., 1987). By contrast, a number of quantitative studies have found mixed or even negative results. These studies, which by and large have been outcome assessments, have found little impact of the experience on technical skills and have even linked experiences to a lack of confidence and trust in the agency (O'Hare & Collins, 1997). John Dewey (1938), considered by many to be the father of experiential education, noted that poorly designed experiences might be mis-educative and even detrimental to future student development. So will you benefit from this internship or not? The overwhelming majority of research suggests that there are positive outcomes from internship experiences, and this research is supported by student and supervisor testimony.

As you prepare for the internship, it is important for you to know how all of the parties involved—yourself as the intern, the university who sponsors you, and the hiring agency—benefit from a good internship placement. While you might be most curious about what you can take away from this experience, it is equally important to understand the desires of the agency and the university and to recognize that internships are not solely intended to benefit students.

Student Benefits from the Internship

The literature is replete with support for student development through internship experiences. You can hope to benefit from your internship in at least two ways. *Pragmatic benefits* are those benefits that will have a direct impact on the knowledge, skills, and abilities necessary to gain entry into your chosen profession. *Personal benefits*, on the other hand, may improve your ability to perform on the job, but most directly impact your self-image and attitude. Among the pragmatic benefits are (a) increased postgraduation employment rate (Fletcher, 1989; Gualt, Redington, & Schlager, 2000), (b) higher starting salaries (Fletcher, 1989; Gualt et al., 2000), (c) more rapid promotion (Gualt et al., 2000), (d) development and refinement of technical skills (Fletcher, 1989; Gualt et al., 2000; Petrillose & Montgomerey, 1997), (e) problem solving and critical thinking (Parks, 2003; Petrillose & Montgomerey, 1997), (f) career exploration (Gualt et al., 2000; Petrillose & Montgomerey, 1997), (g) communication skills (Hensen, 2003; Parks, 2003), and (h) teamwork (Parks, 2003; Petrillose & Montgomerey, 1997). The personal benefits of the internship experience are (a) enhanced self-esteem (Fletcher, 1989; Gualt et al., 2000), (b) development of a professional and social ethic (Gualt et al., 2000), and (c) positive attitude and responsibility (Parks, 2003).

A close examination of the research has shown that students who have participated in an internship are at a distinct advantage over their peers who do not (Gualt et al., 2000; Moriarty, 2000; Southall, Nagel, LeGrande, & Han, 2003). For example, according to a 2008 study conducted by the National Association of Colleges and Employers (NACE, 2008), about 36% of new college hires had been former interns in their organization. Likewise, 48% of employers reported that they offer higher starting salaries to applicants who have had an internship experience compared to applicants who have not. Similarly, Coco (2000) claims that individuals who have had an internship experience have a significant "head start" and as a result are promoted more rapidly than those who have not.

The internship experience also aids in the development and refinement of technical skills and builds your professional résumé (Marlin-Bennett, 2002; Williams, Sternber, Rashotte, & Wagner, 1993). Students who have participated in internships have also had the opportunity to refine skills learned in the classroom and apply and practice them in a real-world setting. By developing these job skills, students become more attractive to employers who are looking for hires that are ready to begin work with less on-the-job training. Simply put, the inclusion of the experience and the skills you acquire on your internship can bolster your résumé and makes you more appealing for hire.

Another pragmatic benefit of the internship experience is the ability to develop problem solving and critical thinking skills (Beauchamp, 1982; Langford & Cates, 1995; Phillips, 1978). As analytical skills are frequently among the top three skills/traits listed as preferable by employers, the opportunity to develop these skills in an internship setting will again give you a distinct advantage as you search for full-time employment at the conclusion of the experience.

The internship can also provide you with a realistic preview of the industry before full-time employment is secured. The experience may help you determine if the industry holds appeal for full-time employment and could even raise awareness of opportunities and niches that may have been previously unknown. This allows for a more efficient and productive job search and presumably a better fit once employment is secured.

Caution Advised!

It is dangerous for a student to consider his/her experience in a single organization to be representative of the entire profession. Different agencies have unique cultures and characteristics that may contribute to your overall satisfaction or dissatisfaction with your experience. When things are going well, and especially when they are not, spend some time identifying what is and is not working and why. Don't give up on the profession as the result of one bad placement. You may just need to find a larger/smaller organization or a manager with a different vision of service delivery.

Students who have participated in internship experiences have also been found to develop superior communication (interpersonal) skills (Langford & Cates, 1995). Commonly referred to as "soft skills," these skill sets are frequently more desirable to service sector employers than "technical capabilities or higher grade point averages" (Langford & Cates, 1995, p. 13). Through the internship, you will likely be given the opportunity to develop these communication skills and learn to work collaboratively with a diverse clientele. Developing and demonstrating these skills to prospective employers will make you more attractive to employers than those who have yet to demonstrate their capabilities in this regard (Langford & Cates, 1995).

The development of these skills is also extremely valuable to your overall self-concept. One of the most frequently cited findings in the literature is the ability of the internship to enhance self-esteem (Dressler & Keeling, 2004; Petrillose & Montgomery, 1997). In fact, students who have completed these experiences have been found to be more comfortable in professional settings, more aware of their professional capabilities, and more confident in interview settings (Dressler & Keeling, 2004).

A personal benefit that accrues from internship experiences is the development of a personal and social ethic. By confronting problems and understanding these problems in the context of professional application, you may quickly establish a personal code of ethics. Often these ethical standards are as a result of being placed in compromising or undesirable situations and, at times, are a result of seeing a social need that is not being addressed. Studies have also shown that students who participate in internships have better attitudes and are more eager to accept responsibility and criticism, recognizing that such input is necessary to learn and grow (Lemieux & Allen, 2007).

University Benefits from the Internship

A smaller portion of the experiential learning literature has addressed the impact that internships can have on the educational institution. This research, along with our many years of experience in higher education, suggests that there are at least four benefit areas for programs that include internships in their curriculum: (a) high student satisfaction with experience, (b) the opportunity for feedback on the curriculum, (c) building collaborative relationships with industry, and (d) recruitment of new students.

Students participating in internship experiences are typically very positive about their encounters (Diambra, Cole-Zakrzewski, & Booher, 2004; Gryski et al., 1987; Wonacott, 2002). In today's economic climate, institutions of higher education are under increased pressure to develop meaningful and enjoyable academic experiences for their students. For this reason, many programs of study elect to have a student internship serve as the capstone academic requirement required for graduation. In doing this, faculty and administrators can be comfortable knowing that as their students graduate, they are likely to leave with a positive final experience and an enhanced appreciation for the materials that have been presented in the classroom. Therefore, secondary benefits that might accrue from internship experiences could be alumni and potential donors expressing a positive impression of their academic program.

Internships also allow university administrators the unique ability to evaluate the effectiveness of their curriculum. Through conferences with students and site supervisors, areas of deficiency may become apparent and changes can be made to the curriculum to better prepare future students. By learning more about where the students go and what they do in their careers, the educational institution can make more informed decisions about its policies and curricula (Hull, Mather, Christopherson, & Young, 1994).

Placing students in professional environments also allows for increased communication between institutions of higher education and agencies of professional practice. When this occurs, it is likely that both parties will benefit. The university may benefit by identifying applied research laboratories for future studies or student engagement or by finding new consumers of the knowledge that they produce. The university may come to a better understanding of how it can serve the community and its profession through teaching, research, and service (Gryski et al., 1987).

Finally, universities can benefit from internship experiences by using them as a recruiting tool for new students. The excitement of having the opportunity to earn college credit for dynamic experiential learning encounters is attractive to prospective students. When prospective students are afforded the opportunity to see where former students in a particular program of study find employment, it may facilitate an interest in the academic program. Let's face it—there are some pretty amazing jobs in the recreation, sport, and tourism fields. And since potential benefits of an internship include higher postgraduation employment rates and higher starting salaries, educational institutions may be able to advertise these employment rates and placement locations to recruit and retain talented students (Grubb, 1995; Gryski et al., 1987).

Agency Benefits from the Internship

The agency that supports the student through the internship program is also likely to experience several benefits. Among these agency benefits are (a) skilled labor at an inexpensive rate, (b) infusion of creativity, and (c) an opportunity to groom potential hires (Freeze, 1997; Morrow, 1995).

Think About It

You should recognize that one of the most significant benefits agencies receive from hosting an intern is the infusion of creativity you bring and your critical perspective. Think about the tools/resources you have that your employers may not:

- first-hand experience with programs,

- technology and social media expertise, and

- digital media skills.

Also, if you find yourself wondering "why do they do it this way, it would be so much easier if we just..." don't keep it to yourself. Speak up! Your ability to see things differently is one of the biggest values you bring.

Students who are or have participated in internships or cooperatives are often extremely attractive to employers because of the talents and skills that they bring to the organization and the relatively low cost of securing their employment. While cooperative experiences are always paid, many internships are not. Internships that are paid may be compensated at a level well below minimum wage by providing a stipend to the student to compensate them for their efforts. In this way, agencies are able to infuse their organization with talent and help at a relatively low cost (Coco, 2000; Morrow, 1995).

Student interns are also attractive to employers because of the creativity, energy, and information that they bring with them to the organization. Students often arrive with the latest information from the academic world, a better understanding of the technological tools to increase efficiency and effectiveness, or an outside perspective that challenges conventional thinking (Gryski et al., 1987). This can help organizations find new operational standards, maintain relevance, or reach new clientele (Morrow, 1995).

Don't Sell Yourself Short!

Many soon-to-be college graduates have feelings of anxiety about entering the working world. The overall lack of confidence in their ability to perform and produce is usually unfounded. Students today fail to realize the value they add to the organizations they will be joining. While you and your peers may be well versed in video editing, uploading to YouTube, and using the host of social media tools, those who hire you may not be. Many of the tools you use in your leisure are yet to be fully integrated into the workforce—always look for creative ways to use the things you know in an unconventional way.

A final benefit to the agency is the ability to prescreen potential hires (Coco, 2000; Dennis, 1996). Many agencies hire from within and are more likely to select a former intern for an open position due to an established track record (NACE, 2008). A growing number of agencies no longer hire at entry-level positions, but instead use internships, practicum, or cooperatives as a way of training, screening, and ultimately grooming those they will bring into the agency (Freeze, 1997; Ramos, 1997). By using internships and cooperatives as a prescreening tool, agencies are able to test the capabilities and fit of the individual before they extend a full-time offer and minimize the chance that the hire will be a poor one (Gualt et al., 2000).

Summary

This chapter clearly illustrates a number of valuable benefits that you can potentially realize as you complete your internship experience. However, as John Dewey (1938) noted, not all experiences have the same educative value. If you do not approach the internship experience thoughtfully, understanding and communicating your personal and professional goals, and recognizing the needs and goals of the other parties involved, it is likely that you will be less than satisfied at the conclusion of the internship. The remainder of the text is designed to provide you with tangible steps you can take to ensure that your internship will be an instrumental start to a lifetime of continued learning experiences.

Chapter 1 Essentials

- An internship has the potential to be a powerful educational experience—or not—depending on the manner in which you approach it.

- Much of this text will help you focus on and explore your personal and career interests, but it is important to remember that internships are not all about you.

- Understanding why the sponsoring agency seeks to host an intern is important for several reasons:

    - It should give you ideas for key areas to address in an interview. Talk less about what you want to accomplish for yourself and focus on explaining what you can accomplish for them.

    - When completing your internship you will invariably be assigned duties and tasks that are not highly desirable. Remember that your internship is a symbiotic partnership that must benefit you, your sponsoring agency and your school. You must be willing to contribute to the partnership if it is to be successful.

- As you are completing your internship keep in constant communication with the Internship Coordinator at your school.

    - Let them know about areas your class work has supported you, or deficiencies you feel may need to be addressed.

    - Take time to introduce them to influential professionals that you meet. Supporting your school in this way helps them better prepare young professionals, and ultimately increases the value of your diploma!

Discussion Questions

1. Why are you completing an internship? What resources are available to help you obtain your desired outcomes?

2. Recognizing that all three parties involved in an internship have certain needs and expectations, what are things that you could do to help the internship be beneficial to the university, the organization, and yourself?

3. Is an internship really necessary? List at least three things you can do/learn through an internship that would be difficult to do/learn in a traditional classroom setting.

4. Do a little independent research on the School-to-Work Opportunities Act of 1994. How might it impact your internship experience?

Opportunity or Obligation?

Jason is a junior undergraduate student majoring in recreation and is beginning to think about his internship and the experiences associated with this experiential learning opportunity. His academic advisor has informed him that the internship must be completed with an approved recreation-based agency, and it must be at least 12 weeks in length (40 hours per week). The internship course/experience is 12-credit academic course and is a requirement for his major. Depending on the agency, the internship may or may not be a paid experience. Per university policy, Jason is also not allowed to hold any other (outside) employment during the internship experience.

As Jason begins the internship planning process, he shares the internship and its requirements with his parents. During the discussion, Jason's parents inquire about the potential of the agency hiring him at the conclusion of the internship. Jason responds, "It does happen with some students, but it is not a guarantee."

Concerned about the financial commitment required for the internship and the uncertainty of employment following the experience, Jason's parents express concern over the utility of the internship experience. In particular, they ask, "Why not just go out and get a part-time job with the agency? At least you will be guaranteed to make some money, and it could lead to a job with the agency down the road. In fact, the internship sounds like a part-time job, but with little to no pay. And, to top it off, we will have to pay university tuition for you to work there! This 'free' labor that is labeled an internship just doesn't make sense to us."

1. What do you think of issues presented by Jason's parents? Are they valid? Do they have merit?

2. As you reflect on the internship experience, how would you respond to Jason's parents?

3. Is there a difference between part-time employment and an internship experience? If so, how are they different?

References

Beauchamp, G. (1982). Curriculum theory: Meaning, development, and use. *Theory Into Practice, 21*(1), 23–29.

Botter, R. (2010). Internship Insights: A Report From the National Internship and Co-Op Study. *NACE Journal,* Vol. 70 Issue 3, p26-28.

Coco, M. (2000). Internships: A try before you buy arrangement. *S.A.M. Advanced Management Journal, 65*(2), 41–43.

Dennis, A. (1996). The benefits of using college interns in a firm. *Journal of Accountancy, 181,* 889–892.

Dewey, J. (1938). *Experience and education.* New York: Macmillan.

Diambra, J., Cole-Zakrzewski, K., &. Booher, J. (2004). A comparison of internship stage models: Evidence from intern experiences. *Journal of Experiential Education* (27) 2, 191–212.

Dressler, S., & Keeling, A. (2004). Student benefits of cooperative education. In R. K. Coll & C. Eames (Eds.), *International handbook for cooperative education: An education.* Boston, MA: WACE.

Fletcher, J. K. (1989). Student outcomes: What do we know and how do we know it? *Journal of Cooperative Education, 26*(1), 26–33.

Freeze, V. (1997). Work study programs give employers a sneak preview. *Workforce,* 19–20.

Gualt, J., Redington, J., & Schlager, T. (2000). Undergraduate business internships and career success: Are they related? *Journal of Marketing Education, 22*(1), 45–53.

Gower, R. (2006). *Internships in recreation, sport, and tourism: A student guide.* Champaign, IL: Stipes.

Gower, R. (2008) *Internships in recreation, sport, and tourism: Exploring student perceptions* (Doctoral dissertation). Retrieved from http://vufind.carli.illinois.edu/vfuiu/Record/uiu_5779097/Holdings

Grubb, W. (1995). The sub-baccalaurete labor market and the advantages of cooperative education. *Journal of Cooperative Education, 30*(2), 6–19.

Gryski, G. S., Johnson, G. W., & O'Toole, T. L., Jr. (1987).Undergraduate internships: An empirical review. *Public Administration Quarterly, 11*(1), 150–170.

Hensen, K. T. (2003). Foundations for learner-centered education: A knowledge base. *Education, 124*(1), 5–16.

Hull, G., Mather, J., Christopherson, P., & Young, C. (1994). Quality assurance in social work education: A comparison of outcome assessments across the continuum. *Journal of Social Work Education, 30*(3), 388–396.

Kiser, J., & Partlow, C. (1999) Experiential learning in hospitality education: An exploratory study. *Journal of Hospitality and Tourism Management, 11*(23), 70–74.

Kolb, D. (1984). *Experiential learning: Experience as the source of learning and development.* Upper Saddle River, NJ: Prentice Hall.

Langford, D., & Cates, C. (1995). Developing general education skills through co-operative education. *Proceedings of the World Conference on Co-operative Education,* 129-137. Kinston, Jamaica: World Association of Cooperative Education.

Lemieux, C. M., & Allen, P. D. (2007). Service learning in Social Work education: The state of knowledge, pedagogical practicalities, and practice conundrums. *Journal Of Social Work Education, 43*(2), 309–325.

Linn, P. (1999). Learning that lasts a lifetime. *Liberal Education, 85*(3), 26–34.

Marlin-Bennett, R. (2002). Linking experiential and classroom education: Lessons learned from the American University-Amnesty International USA Summer Institute on Human Rights. *International Studies Perspectives, 3*(4), 384–395.

Moriarty, E. (2000). Hands-on experience key for students in VCU program. *Sports Business Journal, 3*(34), 2000.

Morrow, E. P. (1995). An intern can help you. *Insurance Sales,* 60–69.

O'Hare, T., & Collins, P. (1997). Development and validaton of a scale for measuring social work practices. *Journal of Research on Social Work Practices, 7*(2), 228–239.

Parks, D. K. (2003). *An examination of cooperative education students' learning outcomes* (Doctoral dissertation). Valdosta State University, Georgia.

Petrillose, M. J., & Montgomery, R. (1997). An exploratory study of internship practices in hospitality education and industry's perception of the importance of internships in the hospitality curriculum. *Journal of Hospitality and Tourism Education, 9*(4), 46–51.

Phillips, J. (1978). An employer evaluation of a cooperative education program. *Journal of Cooperative Education, 14*(2), 104–120.

Ramos, E.(1997). Internship program from start to finish. *Folio: the Magazine for Magazine Management,* 38–39.

Southall, R., Nagel, M., LeGrande, D., & Han, P. (2003) Sport management practica: A metadiscrete experiential learning model. *Sports Marketing Quarterly, 12*(1), 27–36.

Sweitzer, H. F., & King, M. A. (1995) The internship seminar: A developmental approach. *National Society for Experiential Education Quarterly, 21*(1), 22–25.

Williams, W., Sternber, R., Rashotte, C., & Wagner, R. (1993). Assessing the value of cooperative education. *Journal of Cooperative Education, 28*(2), 32–55.

Wonacott, M. (2002). *The impact of work-based learning on students.* (Report No. EDO CE 02 242). Columbus, OH: Eric Digest. ERIC Clearinghouse on Adult Career and Vocational Education.

Chapter 2

Completing the
Individual Assessment

Overview

Too often, students pursue internships with agencies simply because the agency was well advertised and marketed or because other students have worked there in the past. It makes little sense for a student to choose an internship agency simply out of the site's convenience (i.e., location, near friends, family, etc.). This convenience approach can be minimized through the completion of an individual assessment. The individual assessment will allow you to research and secure internship opportunities with agencies that are more closely aligned with your professional and career development needs.

This chapter will discuss the most comprehensive and sophisticated approach to completing the individual assessment. This assessment consists of three forms of analyses: self, tasks, and agency (Noe, 2007). These analyses will assist you in determining your areas of weakness as well as areas in need of improvement, what you must learn/develop in order to become a competent professional, and what is your preferred working environment (i.e., agency culture, its resources available for interns, and its placement rate).

As you begin the individual assessment process, it is important to keep several things in mind. First, the assessment requires time and reflection to be completed properly. It is not an activity that can be completed in a few minutes. Second, the assessment is an activity that can be repeated throughout one's career as your interests, needs, job scope, and so forth change. Finally, the three analyses (self, task, and agency) should be completed simultaneously since they interrelate highly with one another (Wexley & Latham, 2002).

The Individual Assessment

The following sections examine the three elements of the individual assessment: self-analysis, task(s) analysis, and agency analysis. Figure 2.1 illustrates the individual assessment process.

The Self-Analysis

The self-analysis focuses on the individual. The analysis should seek to address two issues. First, the analysis should identify areas of weakness or improvement within the individual. From personal reflection to reviews of previous academic and professional experiences, you should analyze your performance to assess what areas require further development. Next, the self-analysis should include an assessment of personal factors and their role in the internship experience.

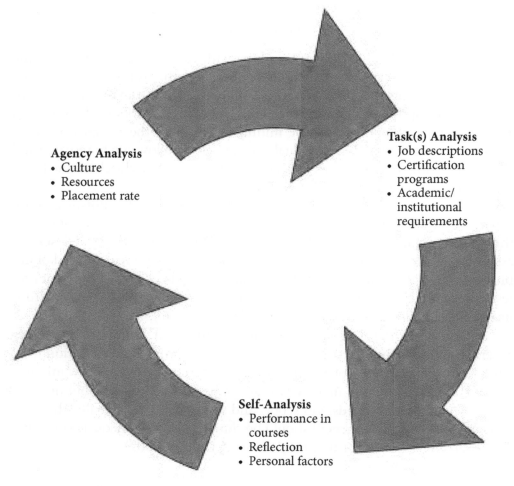

Agency Analysis
- Culture
- Resources
- Placement rate

Task(s) Analysis
- Job descriptions
- Certification programs
- Academic/ institutional requirements

Self-Analysis
- Performance in courses
- Reflection
- Personal factors

Figure 2.1. The Individual Assessment

Review previous performance. You should review previous performance data to identify any recurring trends or areas of weakness. Performance data can be obtained from academic courses and previous performance appraisals.

Performance in academic courses can provide you with valuable insight into professional development needs. Areas of improvement can be identified by reviewing scores and grades obtained from specific projects within courses and by the overall course grades. To complete this analysis, you should complete an academic course performance chart (see Figure 2.2). Through the completion of the academic course performance chart, you can identify categories or areas of deficiency. For example, the student in Figure 2.2 appears to need improvement within the areas of programming, classroom behaviors (or on-the-job behaviors), planning, and foundational leisure knowledge. Using this assessment data as a guide, the student could prioritize these areas as key (development) needs within their internship experience.

Previous performance appraisal data can also be used in the self-analysis. To assess developmental needs through the performance appraisal process, your performance inadequacies must be determined by reviewing the scores and/or rankings from previous performance appraisal reviews. Based upon the areas of weakness, as identified by the scores and/or rankings, you can identify areas in need of improvement and further development.

Reflection. Another way of collecting self-assessment data is through personal reflection. Personal reflection can be formal, such as interviews with supervisors, coworkers, and academic advisors, or a more informal approach (i.e., individual reflection of professional experiences, challenges, and weaknesses associated with the chosen career path) can be adopted. Regardless of the approach, the purpose is to gather information on problems and/or weaknesses perceived by the student.

Personal factors. In addition to the identification of performance deficiencies, you are also likely to face the reality of situational constraints and social support. Situational constraints include issues such as budgetary support, time, geographical location, and so forth. Social support refers to the student's ability to obtain assistance and/or support from family, friends, and other nonwork related individuals (Cohen, 1990). Taken collectively, the situational constraints and the availability of social support associated with the internship site are vital determinants of student performance and motivation. Numerous studies have found if the student has the knowledge, skills, attitudes, behavior, and overall fit needed to perform but does not have the needed budgetary support and social support, his/her performance will suffer.

Course/Project	Course Grade/Project Score	Student Self-Appraisal of Performance 1 = Below Standard 2 = Meets Standard 3 = Exceeds Standard	Student Reflections and/or Instructor Comments	Category
REC 4740 Special Events Evaluation Project	75 (out of 100)	2	Instructor: Student displayed adequate command of survey design process. Could use a bit more development in data analysis phase. Student: I really enjoyed this experience; unfortunately, the project came at a very busy time of the semester for me and I was unable to invest as much time as I would have liked. I really feel I have a solid understanding of the process, but think a bit more practice w/event evaluation would help push me "over the top."	Event Planning & Evaluation
REC 1780 Exam III	79 (out of 100)	2	Instructor: Unable to locate comments. Student: The exam was an assessment of various leisure service providers (public, non-profit, TR, etc.). I took this course when I was a freshman and believe my knowledge in this area has improved, but I still struggle with	Foundational (Leisure) Knowledge

Figure 2.2. Sample Academic Course Performance Chart

			understanding the differences between a nonprofit and public sector agency.	
REC 2290 Programming Course	D	1	Instructor: Student needs to improve work in the areas of program design, delivery, and implementation. Student: I am weak in this area. I took this course my sophomore year and really struggled. I have also had my summer camp supervisors inform me that I need a better understanding of program design particularly when deciding what activity to use for a certain age group. I need my internship to really enhance my skill in this area.	Programming
REC 3250 Sports Marketing Course	C-	1	Instructor: Unable to locate comments. Student: I think my grade and performance was directly impacted by my attendance and inattentiveness in class. It was an evening class and I had worked all day at my part-time job, which made for a bad experience on my end. I have since learned from my (scheduling) mistake, but failed to gain much insight into marketing. More development and practice is definitely needed here.	Classroom Behaviors
REC 4830 Administration Course	B	3	Instructor: Student displayed strong command of content associated with course	Management

Figure 2.2. (cont.)

			(i.e., personnel, risk management, policy development, etc.) Student: I really enjoyed the content in this course. I was able to use some of these skills in my summer job and would like to pursue jobs with these administrative tasks—planning, personnel management, risk management policy development, and training.	
REC 4600 Facility Planning Project	32 (out of 50)	1	Instructor: Student failed to connect capital master plan and design of facility. Student also needs improvement in site map interpretation. Student: I am in complete agreement with the instructor. I need more work with capital master plans and site map interpretation. Although I did not enjoy these activities, I realize I need them for my future career.	Planning
REC 4850 Finance Project	85 (out of 100)	3	Instructor: Unable to locate any instructor comments. Student: I loved this course project. I did well and felt I developed a solid understanding of the various elements associated with the business plan activity. Would enjoy implementing this type of project with my internship agency.	Financial Management
REC 1780 Leisure Philosophy Paper	33 (out of 50)	2	Instructor: Course completed at previous institution and unable	Foundational (Leisure) Knowledge

Figure 2.2. (cont.)

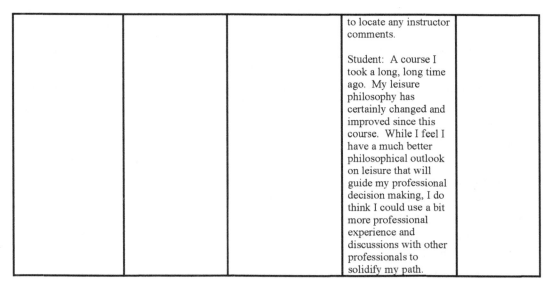

| | | | to locate any instructor comments.

Student: A course I took a long, long time ago. My leisure philosophy has certainly changed and improved since this course. While I feel I have a much better philosophical outlook on leisure that will guide my professional decision making, I do think I could use a bit more professional experience and discussions with other professionals to solidify my path. | |

Figure 2.2. (cont.)

In assessing the situational constraints and social support opportunities, you should consider the following:

- **Perform a review of your personal budget.** Determine the parameters of the budgetary resources by answering the following questions: What are my financial limitations? How much money do I have available to me each week, month, and so forth? What are my expected expenses?

- **Inventory existing resources.** Resources, such as an automobile, bike, needed equipment for your career path (i.e., hiking gear, suits, laptop, etc.), should be considered. What are possible equipment needs for the internship that you do not currently own?

- **Consider lodging.** Where will I stay during my internship? Is housing a common provision for internship opportunities in my area of interest? What are my options (i.e., staying with family, friends, etc.)?

- **Consider any geographical location limitations.** Are there geographical areas where I am unable or unwilling to intern?

In summary, the self-analysis involves determining whether you have an adequate understanding of the content and skill sets within your existing academic and professional experiences. By using a combination of academic performance data, previous performance appraisals, and personal reflection, you can make an astute assessment of the areas in need of further development. For example, if a student is performing satisfactorily in certain areas (i.e., budgeting, marketing, event planning, etc.), those areas are given a lower priority within the upcoming internship experience compared to those areas where the student is not performing satisfactorily.

It is important to note that the self-analysis alone does not provide a complete picture of the student's development needs. For example, consider the student who displays high levels of performance in a majority of areas he or she has been exposed to during his or her academic and professional career. The student's grades on projects and performance appraisals in the areas of programming, budgeting, communications and marketing, and leadership have been well above standard. However, the student, who is interested in a career in special events, has received little to no exposure in the planning of festivals and special events. Thus, the student will require development in areas beyond the scope of his or her existing academic and professional experiences. Specifically, the student will need to ensure the internship experience will expose him or her to all of the tasks associated with the chosen career path.

Reflect and Review

1. Schedule an appointment to meet with your academic advisor or a faculty who you have worked with in the past.

2. Prior to the meeting, complete the following:

   a. Complete the academic course performance chart (see Figure 2.2).

   b. Write a half-page reflection that summarizes your professional experiences, perceived challenges and/or concerns associated with your future career. The reflection paper should also identify any areas in need of further development (i.e., finance, communications, personnel management, etc.).

   c. Reflect on your situational constraints and social support opportunities. Review your personal budget, identify your existing resources (i.e., automobile, laptop, bike, equipment, etc.), and consider any geographical limitations and/or lodging needs related to your internship.

3. Share your academic course performance chart, reflection paper, and situational constraints with your academic advisor and/or identified faculty member. Discuss your reactions to the data and work toward the development of three to five priorities related to addressing the identified areas of concern/weakness.

The Task Analysis

The task analysis is conducted to determine the content needed within the professional setting to successfully perform the job. For the student, this addresses the question, "What are the knowledge, skills, and abilities (beyond my current knowledge, skills, and abilities) that are necessary to be a competent recreation professional?" This analysis serves as a supplement to the self-analysis by moving beyond the identification of existing performance deficiencies to the exposure of those areas that are currently missing from the student's list of experiences but are essential components of the job within their given career path.

The task analysis for the internship generally involves three steps.

1. To select a job to be analyzed, spend considerable time reviewing job postings and job descriptions for positions that are of interest to you. These jobs should be positions that you have aspirations of filling upon completion of your internship.

    Beyond job descriptions, you should also review the content outlines associated with professional certification programs, such as the Certified Park and Recreation Professional. Many of these professional certifications have utilized job analyses of recreation, sport, and tourism professionals in determining the content for the certification. In addition, a review of academic accreditation standards can also be helpful in determining the needed knowledge, skills, and abilities for your professional area of interest.

2. Once the job(s) have been identified and the certification/accreditation information has been reviewed, you should develop a preliminary list of tasks performed on the job. In completing this process, you should carefully review the job descriptions, certification content outlines, and accreditation standards and extract and organize key tasks and responsibilities into categories or content areas. For example, a section of a convention center manager job description may state the position requires the individual to prepare and monitor the budget, recommend purchase of supplies and equipment, manage payroll budgets, develop rental/reservation fee structures, process check requests and requisitions, and complete other financial paperwork. Taken collectively, these tasks could be categorized

into a content area, such as financial management. It is likely that this process of categorization of specific tasks will result in the creation of four to seven content areas (e.g., financial management, communications, rentals/ reservations, safety, personnel management, organizational planning, etc.) and will assist you in organizing the tasks into more manageable chunks or sections.

"**WHEN THE INSTRUCTOR ASKED EACH OF US** to complete this thing called the self-assessment, I thought it was going to be one of those pointless, academic exercises. Busy work, plain and simple. I was partly right—it kept me busy, as it was time consuming. However, I was wrong about it being pointless. Although some of the tasks I identified were not surprising to me, there were several tasks and even two content areas that I hadn't really thought about being important for my future career interests. For example, I always felt I needed more hands-on experiences with programming and budgeting, but until I reviewed several job descriptions and the content outline for the CPRP, I had not thought about how important marketing and communications would be for me in my future job. It really made me think about where I might want to go for an internship. As a bonus, it also gave me some great questions to ask during my internship interviews as I was able to ask about opportunities to develop these skill sets."

3. It is also recommended that you validate or confirm your identified and categorized list of tasks. This can be achieved by having a group of individuals with expertise in the job (i.e., job incumbents, supervisors, faculty, etc.) review your list. A helpful strategy for you to employ at this time is the completion of a task statement rating form. Figure 2.3 provides a sample task statement rating form for a student with an interest in an athletic supervisor position. The tasks are inserted into the form and rated based upon the task's importance, its frequency performed, and the student's perceived level of mastery. Once completed, you can use this form to prioritize the list of tasks. For example, tasks that are important (to the position), are frequently performed, and have low levels of self-appraisal (by the student) would be given a higher development priority compared to the less important and infrequently performed tasks (or tasks in which the student has a higher level of perceived skill level).

TASK STATEMENT RATING FORM

Student Name: _____

Job Type of Interest: **Athletics Supervisor for public park and recreation agency**

Job Titles/Certifications Reviewed: **CPRP content outline, 2 adult athletics coordinator position announcements, 1 youth sports director announcement, and 1 YMCA sports programmer job description**

	IMPORTANCE	TIME/FREQUENCY	TOTAL	STUDENT SELF-APPRAISAL OF CURRENT SKILL LEVEL WITH TASK
	Please rate each task statement on a 0–7 scale that reflects, in your opinion, how important that task statement is to the overall job. Use the scale below as a guide to help you rate. (TIP: Review the job descriptions and content outlines and consider: how many times is the specific task mentioned? Is it one of the first things listed in the job description/announcement?) 0 = of no importance 1 2 = moderately important 3 4 = very important 5 6 7 = of greatest importance	Please rate each task statement on the 0–7 scale shown below. Looking at the whole job over approximately a one-year period, how would you allocate the task statements in terms of the time/frequency with which each is done? 0 1 = very rarely 2 3 = sometimes 4 5 = often 6 7 = very often	(Multiply the importance rating by the time/frequency rating to determine the total rating for each task.)	1 = Unable to perform this task; need significant development with this task before starting career 2 = Can perform this task; need more experience to move beyond novice level 3 = Can easily perform task successfully; no additional practice needed
Recruit and hire staff	7	5	35	1
Provide technical resources and coaching to staff	5	4	20	2
Prepare and monitor program budgets	4	5	20	2
Establish and monitor goals and objectives	4	5	20	2
Oversee flyers and marketing materials prepared by other program	4	5	20	3
Develop and monitor athletic programming website content	6	5	30	1
Encourage and demonstrate safe work habits through use of established safety program guidelines	4	4	16	2
Maintain CPR and AED certification and ensure that all staff within supervision does the same	4	4	16	2
Track and evaluate promotion sales	6	6	36	1
Implement, monitor, and evaluate rental programs	7	7	49	2
Supervise programs	3	3	9	1
Arrange and secure program space	5	5	25	2
Plan and implement programs on a seasonal basis	6	6	36	3
Evaluate programs	4	6	24	3

Figure 2.3. Sample Task Statement Form (Adapted from Mulvaney, McKinney, & Grodsky, 2008)

Adding to an assessment of your existing experiences (i.e., the individual analysis), the task analysis can assist you in identifying those areas of responsibility that are vital to a successful career within your specific area of interest, but may be absent from your current professional portfolio. From examining job descriptions and announcements within your specific area of interest to rating the specific tasks associated with these positions, the task analysis can enable you to be more strategic in your internship selection process by prioritizing your development needs. Despite the importance of the individual and task analyses, their value can be negated if the park and recreation agency's working environment is not consistent with the student's expectations. Issues such as the agency's management philosophy, resources available to the intern, and the job placement rate of graduating interns can significantly impact the quality of the student's experience.

The Agency Analysis

The third area to examine when completing an individual assessment is the agency analysis. The agency analysis is an assessment of the internship-related elements associated with the agency. When considering agency sites, you should evaluate an agency in three areas: the agency's culture, its resources available to interns, and the placement rate of interns. Each of these areas will now be discussed in the following sections.

Agency culture. The overall environment in which the agency operates can be a critical factor in determining the quality of the internship experience. For one thing, if an interns to thrive they must be welcomed and supported by the agency and its staff. Furthermore, you must find a working environment that is consistent with your own preferences and management style(s).

It is important to note that the agency's culture can influence the structural nature of the agency itself. For example, agencies operating in dynamic, uncertain environments where there are frequent changes in market conditions (i.e., demographic changes in constituency, increasing service needs, etc.) need structural features (i.e., flexible roles, open communications that cut across hierarchical levels, coordination by committees, etc.) that will allow them to adapt rapidly to the changing environmental conditions (Wexley & Latham, 2002). In contrast, agencies operating within relatively stable environments can function well using a more traditional, bureaucratic structure. These bureaucratic structures require agencies to establish more clearly defined roles and responsibilities among staff that include a one-way, top-to-the-bottom chain of command and the delegation of sufficient authority for each manager to carry out his/her responsibilities.

As the intern, it is your responsibility to determine what type of agency culture you would most prefer. In determining your desired working environment, researchers have suggested considering the following factors (Mathis & Jackson, 2007):

- The supervisor–intern relationship is likely going to be different from the student–instructor relationship, and you need to prepare yourself for this change. In preparing for this change, you should ask yourself, "What are the qualities you are looking for in a supervisor? What management styles do you prefer?"

- Problems are often clearly defined at school, while work during the internship will likely contain more logistical (and political) aspects associated within the problem solving process. With that in mind, it is important for you to identify agencies that perform tasks and responsibilities that are consistent with your own interests. Obtaining and reviewing philosophy, vision, mission, and goal statements from agencies can also provide insight into the overall working environment.

- In academic settings, feedback is often frequent and quantitative, but this will not be the case at most internship sites. Thus, you need to consider the types of feedback you desire and identify agencies that embrace these feedback strategies. A review of the agency's performance appraisal process, employee/intern recognition programs, and incentive programs can assist you in gauging their feedback style.

Resources available to interns. It is necessary to identify whether the agency has the budget, time, and expertise to assist you. As each internship experience is unique, you need to prioritize your resource needs. You should ask yourself, "Do I need a paid internship?" "Do I need housing?" "What time of the year will I complete the internship?" "Based upon my professional development needs, what skill sets do the agency and/or supervisor need to assist me with my development in these areas?"

Placement rate of interns. Arguably one of the most important outcomes of the internship experience is its role in helping get you that first full-time job. Whether it is a job with the internship site or another park and recreation agency, the internship experience is a key component in the job placement process. As a result, you should review the job placement rate of an agency's interns to determine the agency's success rate. More specifically, you should review the placement rate of previous interns, the types of jobs secured, and the time lapse between completing the internship and obtaining full-time employment by the interns.

"ASKING ABOUT PLACEMENT RATES IS CRITICAL. As a recreation professional who has supervised more than 50 interns over the years, the student who asks this question oftentimes really distances him/herself from the other (intern) applicants. They should ask this question. It is an important one. Students need to be thinking with a backward timeline. Start from where they want to be and develop a plan and timeline for getting there. Usually the student who asks about where previous interns have ended up is thinking in this way. As a future professional, you need to be thinking about how the possible internship agency can help them reach their future career goals. The student needs to find an agency with a proven track record of former interns who have gone on to jobs and careers that are aligned with the student's own goals. They must think beyond the internship. The internship is a step, not a finish line."

Summary

One of the first steps in planning for the internship is the individual assessment. The individual assessment involves three steps: self-analysis, task analysis, and agency analysis. Various methods—including personal reflection, surveys/forms, interviews, and reviews of previous coursework and employment experiences—are employed to collect the information. The self-analysis focuses on identifying individual weaknesses or areas of improvement while considering personal factors and their relationship to the internship experience. The task(s) analysis moves beyond an individual's previous experiences and seeks to determine the content needed within the professional setting to successfully perform the job. Agency analysis is an assessment of the pertinent internship-related elements associated with the agency. Taken collectively, the self, task, and agency analyses should provide you with a holistic assessment of your professional development needs.

Chapter 2 Essentials

- The individual assessment is an important component of the career planning process and allows you to research and secure internship opportunities with agencies that are more closely aligned with your professional and career development needs.

- The information obtained from the individual assessment assists you in determining areas in need of improvement, identifies what you must learn/

develop in order to become a competent professional, and provides insight into your preferred working environment (i.e., agency culture, resources available for interns, and placement rate).

- The individual assessment contains three elements: self-analysis, task analysis, and agency analysis.

- The self-analysis involves the assessment of your performance in courses, a reflection of your past and current experiences, and the identification of personal factors affecting your internship plans.

- The task analysis serves as a supplement to the self-analysis by moving beyond the identification of existing performance deficiencies to the exposure of those areas that are currently missing from your list of experiences but are essential components of the job within your given career path.

- The agency analysis is an assessment of the internship-related elements associated with the agency.

Discussion Questions

1. Why is it important to understand the placement rate of previous interns, the types of jobs these interns secured, and the time lapse between completing the internship and securing full-time employment? How would you obtain this information?

2. Develop a plan for retrieving relevant job descriptions related to your career interests. Specifically, where would you go to obtain these job descriptions? What types of certification standards might you also review? Where would you obtain this information? Make sure to include strategies and timelines for locating and organizing this task analysis information.

3. Review the four situational constraints and social support opportunities related to the self-analysis (see "Personal Factors" section). Prepare a one to two paragraph response that describes how you will manage these constraints and opportunities.

Reality Bites?

Sarah is a senior student at a Midwestern university and is completing her final (spring) semester of on-campus coursework for her undergraduate degree. This summer she hopes to complete her internship with a commercial-based recreation agency. Four weeks into her spring semester, she begins searching for internship agencies that are aligned with her interests. She also meets with her advisor and shares her interests. She states, "I am really interested in going somewhere warm. Winters are rough, and I want to work on or near a coastal area, particularly in a resort setting."

Sarah begins searching for agencies that meet her criteria and finds a resort on the east coast. Excited, Sarah shares the information with her advisor and close friends. When asked about her lodging needs, Sarah indicates the agency has a list of nearby rental properties for interns. Sarah submits her application materials and is contacted a few weeks later for a phone interview. The interview goes well, and two weeks later, Sarah is offered and accepts an internship with the resort.

A day after accepting the internship, Sarah contacts her family to share the great news. Sarah informs her family about the process and how the experience will be a lot of fun for her as she engages in recreation programming for resort visitors. Sarah asks her parents about using the family car to help with her move and travel needs during the internship. Sarah's parents indicate the timing of the move will not work with their schedules. Furthermore, her parents need the vehicle during the summer and will be unable to let Sarah borrow it for the entire summer. Sarah does have a car, but it is older and her mechanic expresses concerns over taking the car on long trips.

In addition to the vehicle concerns, Sarah investigates housing in the resort area and discovers her monthly rent will exceed her internship stipend by more than $300 per month (this does not include food, cell phone bill, or utilities). Sarah thinks her family might be able to help with some of these expenses, but is not 100% sure.

1. What are Sarah's options? If you were Sarah, what would you do? Why?

2. Who, if anyone, is at fault for this situation? Could this situation been avoided? If so, how?

3. How can you safeguard yourself against this experience happening to you (with your internship)?

References

Cohen, D. J. (1990). What motivates trainees? *Training and Development Journal,* 91–93.

Mathis, R. L., & Jackson, J. H. (2007). *Human resource management* (12th ed.). Mason, OH: Thomas Learning.

Mulvaney, M. A., McKinney, W. R., & Grodsky, R. (2008). The development of a pay for performance system for public park and recreation agencies: A case study. *Journal of Park and Recreation Administration, 26*(4), 126–156.

Noe, R. A. (2007). *Employee training and development* (3rd ed.). New York, NY: McGraw-Hill.

Wexley, K. N., & Latham, G. P. (2002). *Developing and training human resources in organizations* (3rd ed.). Upper Saddle River, NJ: Prentice Hall.

Formalizing the Plan

The Purpose Statement, Goals, and Objectives

Overview

The information obtained from the individual assessment should serve as the driving force behind your future career direction. The individual assessment represents your personality and perceived purpose and is the foundation for your internship search (and future career path). The individual assessment is a constant reminder of your values and should provide you with a clear, representative statement of where you are and where you want to go in the future.

The individual assessment should guide the construction of the student's internship and early career goals and objectives. The goals and objectives provide a more specific and detailed framework for the student's career plan. That is, these goals and objectives clarify what the student needs to know and do to secure an internship and future career interests (i.e., full-time employment, position(s) type, upward mobility, etc.). This chapter will discuss the process of developing career goals and objectives for the student that will allow him/her to establish a formalized action-oriented plan and direction that is reflective of his/her individual needs and interests. A conceptualization of goals and objectives, including a description of the process associated with developing career goals and objectives, will be presented. In addition, a series of examples and exercises will also be provided throughout the chapter to assist the student in developing his/her own career goals and objectives.

Understanding Purpose Statements, Goals, and Objectives

Despite its importance, the individual assessment wouldn't carry much weight without the development of a list of goals and objectives. An individual's career takes shape and direction through the development of goals. Appropriately developed goals also allow you the opportunity to effectively evaluate your career and the relationship between your desired career activities and your current career experiences.

When initiating the development of goals, Hurd, Mulvaney, Rossman, and McKinney (2008) advocate for a conceptual understanding of goals and their role in the planning process. Specifically, this conceptual understanding and subsequent goal development process occurs in three stages:

1. First, the individual must develop a statement of purpose. This statement of purpose provides a rationale for your career plan and its role in your future development. This purpose should provide a clear link between your professional philosophy/interests and the information obtained from your individual assessment. Simply put, the purpose should articulate what you are doing and why you are interested in doing it.

2. A series of goals that support the purpose statement should be developed. Guided by the purpose statement, goals break down the information obtained from your individual assessment into distinct subareas. Goals are aims that you consistently and continuously strive for, and they define the scope of areas of primary importance to your professional career. Typically, six to 10 goals are developed to adequately address the information obtained from the individual assessment.

3. Once goals are developed, a number of objectives are created that measure the attainment of each goal. Objectives are specific, measurable, and include a timeline for completion. Typically, at least three objectives are developed for each goal.

Developing a Purpose Statement, Goals, and Objectives

The purpose statement outlines the individual's career philosophy, interests, and direction. The information obtained from the individual assessment should be directly aligned with the purpose statement. Guided by the purpose statement and influenced by the individual assessment data, the goals should provide direction to the individual's career plan. Finally, the objectives provide the detail from which the career plan can be put into action and measured.

To illustrate the relationship between the three concepts, consider the example purpose statement below:

Purpose Statement: To work in a reputable, professional setting that allows me to provide a wide range of excellent recreation-related programs and services that "make a difference" in the lives of others.

As you can see from the example, the purpose statement centers on an interest in getting a job where the individual can use recreation programs and services to "make a difference" in the lives of others. Guided by this purpose and the information obtained during the individual assessment, the individual would create a series of goals that support the purpose. To clarify this relationship, let us return to our previous purpose statement example:

Purpose Statement: To work in a reputable, professional setting that allows me to provide a wide range of excellent recreation-related programs and services that "make a difference" in the lives of others.

- Goal #1: Obtain an undergraduate degree in recreation, sport, and tourism.*

- Goal #2: Successfully plan for recreation programs and special events.*

- Goal #3: Acquire and develop the necessary competencies to obtain full-time employment within a public recreation agency.*

* Please note, that while the example only provides three goals, it is likely the individual would create several more goals to support their purpose.

Following are examples of commonly developed goals for the internship seeker and early career professional:

- Gain exposure and insight into the administrative planning tasks of recreation, sport, and tourism industries.

- Engage in the operational planning and management of recreation, sport, and tourism industries.

- Become proficient in policy formulation tasks associated with recreation, sport, and tourism industries.

- Ensure acquisition and maintenance of contemporary knowledge, skills, and abilities within recreation, sport, and tourism industries.

- Enhance my ability to appropriately assess recreation programs and special events.

- Obtain a graduate degree in recreation, sport, and tourism.

- Effectively implement recreation programs and special events.

- Acquire skills and abilities in the budgeting and financial practices of recreation, sport, and tourism industries.

- Successfully engage in the operations and maintenance management aspect of recreation, sport, and tourism industries.

- Enhance my ability to successfully evaluate recreation programs and special events.

- Provide myself with a working environment fostering personal and professional growth.

- Effectively manage personnel within recreation, sport, and tourism industries.

- Demonstrate performance of a high standard in customer service and marketing tasks within recreation, sport, and tourism industries.

- Complete advanced, director-level training consistent with the scope of recreation, sport, and tourism industries.

- Successfully engage in the facility operations associated with recreation, sport, and tourism industries.

Now the purpose statement is taking form and is beginning to develop a sense of direction. In particular, each goal is grounded in the overall career purpose and is based upon the data obtained from the individual assessment that has identified specific development needs for the individual (Noe, 2007). Typically, six to 10 goals are developed during the internship and early career planning stage(s). However, the goals still lack a clear plan of action for the individual to pursue. Rather, they provide a broad overview of a desired outcome with minimal detail. To provide a more detailed plan requires the development of objectives.

Objectives serve as the realistic, measurable, operational statements attached to each of your professional goals (Wexley & Latham, 2002). The attainment of identified objectives describes the degree of goal achievement. Furthermore, the success with goals determines your degree of achievement toward your overall professional plan. Objectives typically include the following: an objective statement, an action statement, and a timeline. The objective statement provides a description of the tasks to be completed. The action statement states how the task(s) are to be completed. The timeline indicates the length of time required to complete the objective.

Returning to our example one more time will illustrate the value of objective statements (see Table 3.1).

Table 3.1

Sample Objective Statements

Goal #1: Obtain an undergraduate degree in recreation, sport, and tourism.

Objective	Action	Timeline
Discuss academic requirements and deadlines with advisor.	Schedule meeting with academic advisor to discuss general education, program, and elective requirements needed for graduation.	Plan to be completed by end first semester of admittance into the academic program.
Develop a timeline for completing all academic coursework required for an undergraduate degree.	Create a list of all remaining coursework, course schedules, and prerequisites for each course. Based upon feedback from advisor and personal factors, plot course schedule for each academic semester until degree completion.	Plan to be completed by end first semester of admittance into the academic program.
Complete all coursework required for degree recreation, sport, and tourism.	Subscribing to the timeline and developed schedule (see objective above), be an active participant in the courses and successfully complete all courses with a 3.0 (out of 4.0) average or above.	Ongoing and should be completed on or before the date established in the timeline (see objective above).

Table 3.1 (cont.)

Engage in activities outside of coursework requirements that will assist in my professional and personal development.	Schedule a meeting with academic advisor to discuss my interests and identify opportunities for extracurricular involvement.	Plan to be completed by end first semester of admittance into the academic program.
Obtain contact/reference information from appropriate mentors, advisors, and/or faculty.	Schedule a meeting with appropriate mentors, advisors, and/or faculty to discuss the possibility of him/her serving as a reference for you. Bring updated résumé and other relevant materials to the meetings.	Plan to be completed prior to the final semester on campus.

Goal #2: Successfully plan for recreation programs and special events.

Objective	Action	Timeline
Discuss interest in recreation program and special event planning with internship (site) supervisor.	Schedule meeting with internship (site) supervisor to discuss program and special event planning possibilities during your internship.	Plan to be completed by end of first week of internship.
Create a list of program and special event planning tasks that are of interest to you and your career.	Review job descriptions and certifications to create a list of desired program and special event planning tasks (i.e., goal/objective development, program content, format, schedule, management plan for delivery, risk management plan, pricing strategies, etc.).	Plan to be completed prior to meeting with internship (site) supervisor (i.e., by end of first week of internship).
Develop a schedule for engaging in identified program and special event planning tasks and responsibilities.	Based upon the results of the internship (site) supervisor meeting, create a schedule of completion for each program and special event planning task to be completed during your internship.	Plan to be completed by end of second week of internship.
Engage in scheduled program and special event planning tasks.	Following your developed schedule, perform each program and special event planning task.	Plan to be completed by end of internship experience.

Table 3.1 (cont.)

Obtain feedback on performance of program and special event planning tasks.	Schedule a meeting with internship (site) supervisor and discuss performance level within each of the program and special event planning areas.	Plan to be completed no later than one week following the internship.
Create a development plan to improve your ability to plan recreation and special event programming.	Based upon the feedback obtained from your internship (site) supervisor and your personal reflection, create a list of improvement areas. The list should include (a) the specific behavior/task, (b) the criteria or identified measure/level of improvement, and (c) a time frame.	Plan to be completed no later than two weeks following the internship.

Goal #3: To acquire and develop the necessary competencies to obtain full-time employment within a public recreation agency.

Objective	Action	Timeline
Identify the competencies of an entry-level recreation employee in a public recreation agency.	Review research on entry-level competencies of public recreation employees; discuss competency needs with current professionals; meet with advisor to discuss competencies.	Plan to be completed by midterm of fall semester.
Identify internship opportunities with public park and recreation agencies.	Review internship advertisements, announcements, and contact agencies to express interest in internship opportunity; establish a short list of six to 10 agencies that provide opportunities to develop entry-level competencies of public recreation employees.	Plan to be completed by week 12 of fall semester.
Secure internship with public park and recreation agency.	Prepare and submit application materials to six to 10 public park and recreation agencies; engage in selection process; accept internship position at appropriate agency.	Plan to be completed by week 6 of spring semester.

Table 3.1 (cont.)

Complete internship with public park and recreation agency.	Discuss career goals and interests with agency supervisor; display enthusiasm; take initiative to complete challenging projects; seek out opportunities to develop entry-level competencies of public recreation employees; network with professionals to learn of potential job opportunities; complete required academic assignments/projects.	Plan to be completed by end of summer semester.

Now It's Your Turn

1. The purpose of this assignment is to develop and articulate your purpose statement, internship/career goals, and objectives.

2. Review the data obtained from the individual assessment. Create a list of priorities for development.

3. Write a purpose statement for your career. Consider your professional interests and philosophies.

4. Develop a list of six to 10 goals that support your purpose statement and seek to address the priorities identified from your individual assessment.

5. Create at least three objectives for each goal. Be sure to include an objective statement, action plan, and timeline for each objective.

6. Share your purpose statement, goals, and objectives with at least one other student. Discuss your strategies for creating your statements with the other student. Discuss your reactions to the process. Was this process helpful? Why or why not? Was it time consuming? What role did the individual assessment play in the process?

Summary

An individual's purpose statement, goals, and objectives help make sense of all of the individual assessment data and provide a clear direction for your internship experience and future career. The purpose statement provides the individual with a written representation of their career interests. The goals seek to capture the elements of the purpose by providing a broad sense of direction. Finally, the objectives provide the specific detail and steps needed to achieve the desired goals.

The development of goals and objectives represents a key stage in the internship and career planning process. They provide the foundation from which all future activities are created. Without them or with poorly developed goals, future internship and career activities (i.e., searching for internship agencies, securing an internship site, obtaining employment, etc.) will be on unstable ground and more susceptible to unanticipated issues or problems.

Chapter 3 Essentials

- Organizing an action plan that is based upon your individual assessment requires three elements: a purpose statement, goals, and objectives.

- The purpose statement outlines the individual's career philosophy, interests, and direction.

- Goals support the individual's purpose statement and provide a broadened direction to the internship and career plan.

- Typically, six to 10 goals are developed for an individual's internship and early career plan.

- Objectives serve as the realistic, measurable, operational statements attached to each of your professional goals.

- At least three objectives are developed for each goal statement.

- The development of goals and objectives is of critical importance to the internship and career planning process. They serve as the foundation for all future internship and career activities.

Discussion Questions

1. Why is the statement of purpose the essential first step in developing your goals and objectives?

2. Prepare a one- to two-sentence personal statement that reflects where you would like to be/what you would like to be doing immediately upon graduation (or within a few years thereafter). Remember, this statement should articulate what you hope to be doing and why you are interested in doing it.

3. Think about it. Have you ever had a weekend go by in which you did not accomplish a single thing that you intended to? How can setting goals help your internship be the most meaningful experience possible?

Fun, Diversifying the Résumé, or Looking to the Future?

Kyle has worked the past three summers at a day camp for his local park district. Starting as a camp counselor, Kyle worked his way up to camp director during his previous summer with the park district. During this experience, Kyle has developed a solid network of public park and recreation professionals within his park district and in the surrounding communities.

At this time, Kyle thinks his long-term goal (about three years in the future) is to return to his hometown and obtain full-time employment as a recreation supervisor for his park district or neighboring districts. Kyle feels he has laid the foundation for achieving this goal through his work with the day camp and his contacts within the district.

As Kyle begins to consider possible internship sites, he is unsure if he should include his park district on the list. Kyle believes he might obtain a richer, more challenging experience with another agency as he already has considerable experience with his local park district. From meeting new professionals to working with new recreation programs, Kyle thinks interning with a new agency will help him branch out and enhance his professional development. However, Kyle also realizes some internships have the potential of leading to full-time employment and wonders if interning with his local park district could help him achieve his long-term goal.

Kyle also wonders if he should use the internship to explore another sector within the recreation field. Kyle believes the internship could address this need by providing short-term, temporary insight into another sector within the field. Kyle's current experiences (and future long-term goal) are in the public sector, but he is interested in learning more about the business and operations within professional sport. A new minor league team has relocated to an area where he has extended family (i.e., lodging), and he is considering applying for an internship with their organization. Kyle also has an interest in traveling and has added a few agencies to his list due to their geographical location.

1. What are the advantages of Kyle interning with his local park district? Concerns?

2. If you were Kyle, is there any additional information that would be helpful in making this decision?

3. If you were Kyle's friend and he came to you for advice, what would you tell him?

4. What role should Kyle's goals play in this situation and future internship decision?

References

Hurd, A. R., Mulvaney, M. A., Rossman, R., & McKinney, W. R. (2008). *Official study guide for the certified park and recreation professional examination* (3rd ed.). Ashburn, VA: National Recreation and Park Association.

Noe, R. A. (2007). *Employee training and development* (3rd ed.). New York, NY: McGraw-Hill Higher Education.

Wexley, K. N., & Latham, G. P. (2002). *Developing and training human resources in organizations* (3rd ed.). Upper Saddle River, NJ: Prentice Hall.

INTERNSHIP SELECTION

Chapter 4

Initiating the Search Process

Overview

At this point, you have collected and analyzed a variety of information about yourself, your professional interests and experiences, desired career path(s), and your academic endeavors. Guided by this information, you have developed a set of professional goals and objectives that is strategically aligned with your career plan. The next step in the internship process is to utilize this information in the identification of recreation-, sport-, or tourism-based agencies that are most conducive to reaching your professional goals.

In setting the stage for your internship search, this chapter will begin with a review of the goals associated with the internship search process. In particular, the goals of the student in the internship search process and the goals of the agency will be discussed. Tips for starting the internship search process will also be provided. Next, the chapter will describe the most commonly used methods and sources by agencies to advertise internship opportunities. The chapter will conclude with a discussion on finalizing your list of potential internship agencies.

Goals of the Internship Recruiting Process

Prior to initiating the internship search process it is helpful to understand the context in which the process occurs. In particular, it is important for you to be aware of the process from the agency's perspective and how its approach to internship recruitment can impact your search strategies. The following section reviews this relationship by providing an overview of agencies' strategies associated with internship recruitment and the role of the student in this process.

Recruiting is the process of developing a pool of qualified applicants who are interested in working for an agency and from which the agency might reasonably select the best individual or individuals to hire (Fisher, Schoenfeldt, &

Shaw, 2006). Both the student (i.e., applicant) and the agency are active agents in this process. That is, just as the agency is looking for qualified internship applicants, the student should also be looking at a variety of potential internship opportunities. Thus, both the agency and the student have recruiting goals (Judge & Bretz, 1992). Simply put, the overarching goal between the agency and student is to find an environment where both sets of goals are consistent.

Student Goals in the Internship Recruitment

The internship recruitment process is a two-way process. Just as the agency is seeking qualified interns who can positively contribute to the agency's mission, you are also reviewing and evaluating several agencies to identify the agency that is most closely aligned with your needs. In finding this fit, you will likely create a pool of interesting and attractive internship opportunities to consider.

These internship opportunities are often analyzed in relationship to your personal and professional goals. Although each student is unique and possesses multiple goals, some common work-related factors influencing the student–agency fit include the availability of financial income/stipend, benefits (i.e., housing, meals, transportation, etc.), and challenging work assignments. In addition, students can also have a number of personal and idiosyncratic factors. For example, some students may want to work close to their hometown, close to where they went to school, in a big city, in a small city, in a nature-based setting, near the ocean, or in a warm climate (DeNisi & Griffin, 2001).

Agency Goals in the Internship Recruitment

At its core, the agency's goal during the internship recruitment process is to create a pool of qualified applicants. Guided by this goal, agencies are also typically concerned with two additional factors: size of applicant pool and the realistic internship preview. A brief overview of each is provided in the following paragraphs.

Size of applicant pool. Most agencies are interested in effectively and efficiently establishing a pool of qualified internship applicants. An important element in the establishment of an effective and efficient internship recruitment process is to have an applicant pool that is of optimal size. For example, if an agency has two internship openings and ends up attracting more than 500 applicants for the two openings, the agency will encounter a hiring situation that is both ineffective and inefficient. In particular, large amounts of time and resources will be required to review and process the 500 applicants, which can become problematic for the agency. In contrast, the agency must have a goal of attracting a talent pool that is greater than the number of available internship positions. Simply put, the agency presumably wants to have some discretion over whom it hires (DeNisi & Griffin, 2001). Returning to our previous example, imagine if the agency had two internship openings but only received two applicants. In this situation the agency cannot be completely confident that they have hired the two best individuals for their two internship positions. Thus, the goal for the agency during the internship recruitment process is to generate an applicant pool that is of optimal size.

Realistic internship (job) preview (RJP). A final goal in the recruitment process for the agency is to provide the student with a realistic internship (job) preview (RJP). A RJP informs internship applicants about all aspects of the internship experience, including both its desirable and undesirable facets (Bohlander & Snell, 2004). A RJP distinguishes itself from a typical internship or job preview by presenting both the positive and negative aspects of the experience (a typical job/internship preview presents only the positive). Oftentimes, the RJP will include the agency providing a tour of the working area and a discussion of the scope, good and bad, of the internship. The RJP is premised on research that has found that applicants who are given realistic information regarding the position are more likely to be successful on the job because there will be fewer unpleasant surprises (Bohlander & Snell, 2004).

> **"I INTERVIEWED WITH THREE ORGANIZATIONS,** and of the three, only one gave me a realistic preview of the internship experience and the scope of my responsibilities. This, of course, was the organization I decided to do my internship with. Having a clearer understanding of the tasks and projects associated with my internship really made me feel comfortable with the organization from the beginning and I really felt that I was able to 'hit the ground running.'"

In summary, students and agencies must understand the needs and goals of each other if the internship experience is to be successful. As the student, it is important that you are cognizant of the agency's goals in the internship recruitment process. In particular, the agency is looking to develop an optimally sized pool of qualified applicants for the internship position. The agency is also likely motivated to ensure internship applicants are provided with a realistic overview of the internship position during the recruitment process.

Tips for Beginning the Internship Search Process

The time has come for you to apply the information collected and developed during the career planning, individual assessment, and goal-setting stages. Guided by this information, you must now identify, investigate, and determine a list of possible agencies for your internship. This process can be time consuming and, at times, stressful for the internship seeker. In an effort to reduce this stress and minimize unnecessary challenges, researchers have identified key factors to consider during the search process (Broscio & Scherer, 2003; Cascio & Aguinis, 2005; Dunham, 2002):

- **Don't panic and stay positive.** An internship search takes time and energy. Many students will spend 6 to 12 months searching for that "perfect" internship. Recognize that it is a process and be prepared to wait. Stay optimistic by finding an outlet, such as exercise or a hobby, to reduce the stress associated with waiting.

- **Don't get discouraged by rejection.** If your top internship agency has no openings, don't dwell on it. It will make it harder to continue the search process. Adopt the attitude that "each no I get means I'm that much closer to a yes."

- **Be honest with yourself.** What are your strengths and weaknesses? What do you do particularly well? What are some areas of concern? Face up to your past performances (i.e., grades, field experiences, etc.), decide your area of interest, figure out where you want to live, and don't delay the search itself for long.

- **The internship is the next step into the "real world."** Be prepared to accept that life and expectations in the professional realm will differ from your current, student-centered experiences. Work to understand and embrace these environmental changes.

- **Prepare yourself for the "hunt."** The heart of a good internship hunt is research. Use the Internet, departmental internship databases, faculty, and advisors when drawing up a list of target agencies. If you are fortunate to secure an offer, talk to a range of insiders and outsiders to learn about the politics and practices within the agency. You don't want to wind up in a situation that could negatively impact your future career.

- **Ensure you have a plan.** The plan should include a reflection of yourself, including geographical preferences, personal values, strengths, preferred leadership style, areas in need of improvement, future career ideas/interests, possible constraints, and a timeline with action items associated with each step in the search.

- **Don't be shy or overeager.** Utilize your personal contacts such as peers, faculty, former supervisors, family, etc. Many internship contacts are initiated through the student's network. You also want to avoid the temptation to accept the first opportunity that comes along. Unless it's absolutely right for you, the chances of making a mistake are quite high.

- **Don't forget about the personal factors.** Make sure you are considering all elements of your life, including those personal factors, when engaging in the job search. A recommended approach is to share your thoughts and plan with your friends and family to avoid any unexpected issues or problems in the process.

- **Don't lie.** Experts are unanimous on this point. Don't lie and don't stretch a point, either on résumés or in interviews. Be willing to address weaknesses as well as strengths.

- **Don't be unprofessional.** If sending an e-mail résumé to an agency, don't send it without writing a message in the body of the e-mail, don't say anything quirky in the e-mail subject line, and don't send it multiple times. Bottom line, practice professionalism at all times.

- **Don't jump the gun on compensation.** Always let the potential agency bring this subject up first, but once it surfaces, thoroughly explore all aspects of your future compensation (and benefits) (Cascio & Aguinis, 2005; Dunham, 2002).

Avoiding the Pitfalls

1. Review the list of things to avoid during the internship search process.

2. Reflect on your own situation.

   a. Discuss the perceived challenges and/or concerns associated with these common pitfalls. Generate a list of strategies you can utilize to avoid these pitfalls.

   b. Share your list with a peer. Take turns sharing your strategies. Work together to generate a revised, comprehensive list of strategies.

In addition to these tips and prior to beginning this process, it is important to note that the internship choice process is oftentimes highly social, with friends and relatives playing a large role in the active phase of the internship search (Barber, Hollenbeck, Tower, & Phillips, 1994; Cascio & Aguinis, 2005).

> **"MY FAMILY PLAYED A HUGE ROLE** in my internship search process. My intention was to obtain an internship in a different state and my family's intention was to make sure I stayed close to home. My family means the world to me, but I also considered that my internship was only going to be 14 weeks long. In the end, I decided to follow my dream of leaving the state. Although my family wanted me stay in state, they were supportive of my final decision."

Networking is also of vital importance in this process (Maher, 2003). For example, consider a study of almost 200 college students. Data on these students was collected at three different time periods: (1) early in the search process (two to eight months prior to employment), (2) immediately prior to employment, and (3) at three months following the completion of undergraduate coursework for those who remained unemployed. The results indicated that individuals tend to follow a sequential model in the search process. First, individuals search broadly to develop a pool of potential jobs (using informal sources such as friends, relatives, and faculty/advisors), and then they examine jobs within that pool in detail and reopen the search only if the initial pool does not lead to an acceptable job offer (Barber et al., 1994).

Finding the Perfect Fit: Matching Interns and Internships

Is this the right internship for me? How do I know this is the right opportunity for me? These are common questions students encounter while beginning the internship search process. Although it is difficult to know the answers to these questions with 100% certainty, there are factors of "fit" to consider that can provide you with a great deal of insight to these important questions. By increasing your awareness of these fit factors, you can hopefully obtain adequate information upon which to base your internship selection decisions.

In particular, a fit indicates a situation where the agency's mission, goals, and expectations are aligned with the student's goals, leading to a successful match and high levels of student performance. In contrast, "misses" occur when an agency or student inaccurately perceives goal congruency between the student and the agency, leading to poor student performance during the internship (or vice versa). Finally, a "rejection" occurs when the student or agency successfully identifies a lack of agreement between their goals and those of the other party.

Student–Internship Fit

Earlier we discussed the role of career planning and individual assessments in guiding the internship selection process. Taken collectively, these activities enable you to analyze tasks to determine the content needed within the professional setting and assist you in being able to successfully perform the job in the future. By identifying these competencies through the task analysis, you are able to measure your knowledge, skills, abilities, and other factors against the competencies required for the job. Often referred to as the person–internship fit, this review and matching process is an important element to consider during the internship search process, as you want to seek an internship with an agency that will be supportive of you developing these competencies.

Student–Agency Fit

In addition to the competencies associated with the internship, you must also spend considerable time ensuring the agency, as a whole, is aligned with your needs. For example, questions such as "What are the agency's values?" and "What is the workplace culture like within the agency?" should be considered. Specifically, do these values and environments match your approach to the workplace? Research has repeatedly shown that agencies oftentimes pass up potential interns or employees for jobs if they don't embrace the values of the agency even if they have excellent technical skills for the job (Cable & Parsons, 2001).

Discovering Internship Opportunities

Internship recruiting strategies used by recreation, sport, and tourism industries will vary. A recreation programming intern for a public park and recreation agency is not likely to be recruited from the same source as a marketing and sales intern for a professional sports organization. Other factors, such as the current labor market, might also influence which recruitment strategies an agency utilizes. For example, a tight labor market (i.e., low unemployment rates) may require agencies to advertise heavily, utilizing a variety of sources. In contrast, during a time of higher unemployment an agency might choose to invest fewer resources into the internship recruitment process as their applicant pool will likely be higher regardless of the strategies employed.

Despite the various approaches to recruiting interns, a majority of recreation, sport, and tourism agencies will embrace at least one of the following sources: advertisements, unsolicited applications and résumés, professional organizations/associations, or employee referrals. An overview of each of these sources is provided in the following sections.

Advertisements

Arguably the most common method of attracting interns is through advertisements. Internship advertisements can utilize a variety of media platforms, including newspaper, radio, television, billboards/posters, and e-mail. Advertisements have the advantage of reaching a large audience of possible applicants and can be directed toward a particular group of readers (i.e., students with specific academic majors, institutions, geographic location, etc.) (Bohlander & Snell, 2004).

One of the biggest mistakes a student can make is to spend little time reviewing the advertisement's content. In particular, agencies spend considerable time developing and writing the content of the advertisement, ensuring that the major assets and responsibilities associated with the internship position are highlighted. As a result, the student should pay careful attention to the content presented in the advertisement, making sure his/her future application materials (i.e., résumé, cover letter, interview preparation, etc.), when possible, speak to their success/experience with the tasks and responsibilities listed in the advertisement. To illustrate this process, consider the facility management internship advertisement below. As the advertisement states, the intern is expected to "market and advertise programs," "coach, supervise, and/or direct programs," "orient DISC patrons to the various amenities of the facility," and engage in "staff supervision and daily facility operations." Guided by this information, the student should prepare a cover letter and résumé that highlights, when possible, how he/she has successfully engaged in program marketing, program supervision, personnel management, and facility operations. In short, the student's goal should be to use his/her application materials to communicate the fit between his/her experiences and the needs of the agency.

Facility Management Internship – Decatur Indoor Sports Center (DISC)

The Facility Management Intern will design and accomplish a set of goals and objectives over the course of the semester. Interns are expected to work 30–40 hours per week for the entire semester (or hours predetermined by the university or college). Interns will market and advertise programs; coach, supervise, and/or direct programs; and orient DISC patrons to the various amenities of the facility. This position will also assist with staff supervision and daily facility operations. DISC shirts will be provided for uniform use, and khaki pants or shorts (at student's expense) are required. **Application Deadlines: Fall Semester = May 1; Spring Semester = November 1; summer internships are not available.**

Unsolicited Applications and Résumés

Another commonly adopted approach to finding an internship is through unsolicited applications and résumés. As many recreation, sport, and tourism agencies don't formally advertise their internship opportunities, the student is forced to initiate contact with the agency. This can be a stressful experience for students as, up until this point in their academic coursework, students have primarily been recipients of information. However, in this situation the onus for initiating and securing the internship primarily falls on the student. Simply put, the student must independently begin communication with the agency, clearly articulate his/her goals, and express an interest in interning with the agency.

The student's initial contact can take a variety of forms: "cold (phone) calling" the agency, e-mailing the agency, or visiting the agency in person. Each form has distinct advantages and disadvantages, and the student should spend a considerable amount of time reviewing these issues prior to determining a preferred strategy. For example, while initiating contact with the agency through e-mail may appear to be the quickest and most convenient approach (for the student), it is much less personal and can be viewed as "the student being lazy" or "the student placing little importance on the internship" by the agency due to its convenience and lack of personal effort/interaction. However, in situations where the agency is several thousands of miles away and/or the agency's hours of operation are not consistent with the student's availability, e-mail may be the only feasible way to reach the agency.

> **"I DID A LOT OF RESEARCH** over the Internet. When I first began my search, my heart was set on being close to the ocean and I wanted to move south. So I started reviewing internship announcements and made several "cold calls" throughout the southeast. The "cold calls" were stressful! Sometimes it was hard to find the appropriate contact person within the agency and when I did speak to someone, I was so nervous! During my first call, I ended up forgetting to ask about the length of the internship and if they had a CTRS on staff. I was so embarrassed. After that first call, I prepared a script and used it to make my introduction more concise and professional. It also really helped me stay focused while reminding me of the questions I wanted to ask them."

Professional Organizations/Associations

Many professional organizations and associations provide updated lists of job and internship announcements. A majority of these organizations and associations utilize an online job and internship database that is housed within their website. In fact, a study by the Society for Human Resource Management found that almost 90% of organizations and associations relied on the Internet to get the word out about new positions (Gale, 2001).

In some instances, individuals seeking internships or employment are also allowed to post their résumé and other relevant materials directly to the association's site for agencies to review. Potential employers can access the posted materials and check for qualified applicants. Some of the more sophisticated application systems allow potential employers to match job/internship requirements with the experiences and skills of applicants. Future trends in this area include the use of Web-based tools, such as online job fairs in which agencies can "meet" candidates in a virtual environment and chat with them online (Bohlander & Snell, 2004).

Common Associations in Recreation, Sport, and Tourism

American Association for Physical Activity and Recreation (AAPAR)
American Camping Association (ACA)
Association for Experiential Education (AEE)
Academy of Leisure Sciences (ALS)
Army Corps of Engineers (United States)
Association of Outdoor Recreation & Education (AORE)
American Therapeutic Recreation Association (ATRA)
Americans with Disabilities Act Information (ADA)
Bureau of Land Management (U.S. Dept. of Interior)
Canadian Association for Leisure Studies (CALS)
Council on Hotel, Restaurant, and Institutional Education (CHRIE)
International Festivals and Events Association (IFEA)
International Society of Travel & Tourism Educators (ISTTE)
Leisure Studies Association, Britain (LSA)
Park District Risk Management Agency (PDRMA)
National Association of Recreation Resource Planners (NARRP)
National Council for Therapeutic Recreation Certification (NCTRC)
National Intramural Recreational Sports Association (NIRSA)
National Park Service (NPS)
National Recreation & Park Association (NRPA)
National Therapeutic Recreation Society (NTRS)
Occupational Safety & Health Administration (OSHA)
Resort & Commercial Recreation Association (RCRA)
Skate Park Association of the United States of America (SPAUSA)
Travel & Tourism Research Association (TTRA)
United States Fish & Wildlife Service
United States Forest Service
Wilderness Education Association (WEA)
World Leisure & Recreation Association (WLRA)

Employee Referrals

Another popular method of intern recruiting is the use of employee referrals, or recommendations made by current employees. For example, an employee may have a former classmate who worked with the employee (when the employee was a student) on several class projects, and the employee feels the student would make a positive contribution to the agency. Through conversations with the former classmate, the employee learns the student is interested in an internship with an agency similar to the employee's agency. Recognizing the student's potential contribution to the agency, the employee speaks with the agency's staff about the possibility of the student completing an internship with the agency. As a result of the student's past experiences working with the employee and overall networking, the student is encouraged to apply for, and later secures, an internship with the agency.

Employee referrals are typically well received by agencies, as research has found the quality of employee-referred applicants is normally quite high since employees are generally hesitant to recommend someone who might not perform well (Swenson, 1999). However, it is also important to be aware of some of the potential dangers associated with landing an internship as a result of an employee referral. Employee referrals can also create controversy and consternation within the agency as the process can sometimes be perceived negatively by agency staff as promoting inbreeding or violating Equal Employment Opportunity regulations. Since employees and their referrals tend to have similar backgrounds, agencies that rely heavily on employee referrals to fill position openings may intentionally or unintentionally screen out certain individuals or discriminate against protected classes. Beyond the impact these issues may have for the agency, the newly hired intern may be faced with starting the internship in a challenging working environment where agency staff are suspicious, reserved, or even openly critical of a new intern before he/she has even started working for the agency.

Internship Search Strategies

At this point, you should now have an understanding of an agency's goals and their relationship to your goals during the internship search process. You should recognize some common pitfalls to avoid during the internship search process as well as the importance of finding the right fit between your goals and the goals of the agency. Finally, you should be more informed about the most common internship recruiting strategies used by recreation, sport, and tourism industries.

Now is the time to apply this information and begin the identification, matching, and prioritizing of agencies, leading to a "short list" of potential internship sites. In completing this process, researchers have recommended completing the following steps (Smith & Moore, 2010):

1. Identify geographic regions.
    - Where are you willing to live? East Coast? West Coast? Midwest? What size of town?
    - Employers often have a variety of locations throughout the United States as well as international locations.
    - Consider what lifestyle and community culture would best fit you.
2. Identify potential internship agencies.
    - List all potential internship agencies based upon your geographic region.
    - Think outside the box. Include other agencies for your career field that aren't so obvious. This can be accomplished by using job type in a query on job search engine websites.
    - Other sources for employers in your prospective career paths include
      - faculty recommendations and advisor recommendations;
      - alumni panels in your classes, industry roundtables;
      - career fairs, company information sessions, campus interviews;
      - online job listings;
      - Google for top employers in your career path; and
      - archived/academic departmental data of internship agencies used by former students.
    - Keep records of your research, preferably in a table or spreadsheet.

3. Prioritize internship agencies in your desired geographic region.
    - Review your individual assessment, professional, and personal goals.
    - Rank and compare internship agencies by
      - the functions of the position,
      - the agencies' ability to address/meet your professional goals and personal needs,
      - how well you match the position qualifications,
      - the workplace culture, and
      - opportunities for professional development (i.e., support for workshops, conferences, networking outside of agency, etc.).
    - Check local news stories for information about your top agencies.
    - Check the placement rate of previous interns within your top agencies.
    - Use the agency's recruiter's behavior as an indicator of their style and culture, but don't rely totally on the recruitment method(s) as an indicator of workplace culture.
    - Use informational interviewing as a way to learn about how comfortable you are with an agency.

4. Develop a targeted résumé and cover letter for your top five to 10 internship agencies (résumé and cover letter development will be discussed in Chapter 5).

Summary

Guided by your career plan, individual assessment, and goals, you should begin the process of identifying recreation-, sport-, or tourism-based agencies that are most conducive to reaching your professional goals. This can be a time-consuming process as you must identify and prioritize a list of potential internship sites that are not only supportive of your professional goals, but also your personal factors (i.e., location, money, values, etc.). In an effort to assist you with this process, this chapter presented the context of the internship recruitment process from both the student and agency's perspective. Tips for you to avoid during this process as well as commonly used internship recruitment sources were also provided. Finally, strategies to assist you in prioritizing and narrowing your list of potential internship sites were presented.

Once a "short list" of five to 10 potential internship agencies has been created, the student can turn his/her attention to developing and submitting the required application materials. Two of the most commonly requested application materials are the cover letter and résumé. Typically, these two application documents are individualized for each internship position to increase the student's marketability for the position. Furthermore, the cover letter and résumé are oftentimes the applicant's first and only chance to "get their foot in the door" and secure an interview invitation. Thus, their importance in the internship selection process cannot be overstated. Chapter 5 will discuss the elements of each of these documents and provide tips and strategies for improving the cover letter and résumé to increase your chances for landing that important interview.

Chapter 4 Essentials

- Both the student (i.e., applicant) and the agency are active agents in this internship search process. The overarching goal between the agency and student is to find an environment where both sets of goals are consistent.

- Initiating the internship search process can be time consuming and, at times, a stressful experience for the student. However, researchers have identified some key things to avoid during the job search process, such as panicking; shyness; laziness; frustration; lying; and ignoring family, friends, or faculty/advisors.

- Research suggests the internship-choice process is oftentimes highly social, with friends and relatives playing a large role in the active phase of the internship search.

- Although it is difficult to know about the quality of the internship experience with 100% certainty, there are factors of student–internship and student–agency fit to consider that can provide you with a great deal of insight into the internship.

- A majority of the recreation, sport, and tourism agencies utilize advertisements, unsolicited applications and résumés, professional organizations/associations, or employee referrals in recruiting interns to their agency.

- As a result of identifying, matching, and prioritizing agencies, the student should be able to develop a "short list" of five to 10 potential internship sites to pursue.

Discussion Questions

1. The chapter spoke of hiring agencies seeking to obtain an applicant pool of optimal size. Recognizing that some of the most interesting internship opportunities could have very large pools (hence creating a problem in efficiency and effectiveness), what impact might this have on how agencies advertise internship openings? What can you do to be sure you are still aware of these internship opportunities?

2. What internship search strategy is the most comfortable to you? Unsolicited résumés? Cold calling? Online submissions? What disadvantages will you have if you only use this one method to apply for internships?

3. Identify one professional association that appears to be a good fit with your personal statement and goals. List the benefits of membership and the yearly membership fee. Is it worth it to join?

Blame it on ...

Kara is a senior majoring in recreation management. She is an honors student and is an active member of several student organizations on campus. She is highly organized, is well respected by faculty and her peers, and is passionate about helping others. Simply put, Kara is a bright star with a promising future.

Within the recreation management major, Kara has concentrated her coursework within the event planning arena. She is interested in event planning as a career path and has begun searching for possible summer internship sites. Early in the spring semester, Kara identifies a company near her hometown as a possible internship site. The company is a newly formed wedding planning company with one full-time employee who is the CEO and one part-time office assistant. Kara really likes the company, its location, and overall mission. As a result of her strong connection with the company, Kara ends her internship search and decides to focus all of her time and energy on this company alone.

Kara contacts the company and shares a brief background of her interests and offers to submit a cover letter and résumé to the CEO for review. The CEO is eager to "get the company off the ground" and encourages Kara to forward her application materials. Two days later, Kara mails her materials to the CEO.

One month later, the CEO contacts Kara to schedule a phone interview. Eager to make a solid first impression, Kara volunteers to travel to the company for a face-to-face interview. The CEO is supportive of the idea, and the interview is scheduled for the following week.

Kara arrives 10 minutes early to the interview and brings additional copies of her résumé and cover letter. Kara also has prepared a list of questions for the CEO and has a portfolio that includes a sample of previous projects, recommendation letters, honors, and certifications. The interview lasts about two hours and includes a tour of the facility and community as well as a formal interview with the CEO. Overall, the interview goes well, and three weeks later the CEO contacts Kara and offers her the internship. Ecstatic about the opportunity, Kara accepts the position.

A few days later, Kara informs her department of the opportunity. Following protocol, the department's office manager asks Kara about the university's internship site application and agreement forms. In particular, the office manager wants to know if Kara has given the company copies of the forms or if they need to be sent to them for completion. Kara indicates she has not given them the forms yet, but will e-mail them to the CEO. Later that day, Kara e-mails the forms to the CEO and requests that the documents be completed, signed, and returned to the office manager.

Three weeks later, the forms are completed and returned to the office manager. The office manager forwards the forms to the academic coordinator for review. Upon review of the application form, the academic coordinator informs Kara that the site does not meet the minimum qualifications for an approved internship site. As a result, the site will not qualify as an internship site, and Kara must find an alternative site to complete her internship. Dejected and frustrated, Kara does not know what to do. It is now the middle of April and Kara has no leads on a possible internship site that is scheduled to begin on May 15.

1. What events have led to Kara being in this predicament?

2. Looking back, what were some strategies that could have been employed to avoid this situation from occurring? Be specific— identify the strategy, who would be responsible for completing the strategy, and when it should be completed.

3. In your opinion, what is the role of the student in the internship search process? What is the role of the university (i.e., department)? Are these roles clearly defined? Why or why not?

References

Barber, A. E., Hollenbeck, J. R., Tower, S. L., & Phillips, J. M. (1994). The effects of interview focus on effectiveness: A field experiment. *Journal of Applied Psychology, 79,* 886–896.

Bohlander, G., & Snell, S. (2004). *Managing human resources* (13th ed). Mason, OH: Thomson South-Western.

Broscio, M., & Scherer, J. (2003). Managing job transitions: Thirteen questions for a successful search. *Journal of Healthcare Management, 48*(5), 287-292.

Cable, D. M., & Parsons, C. K. (2001). Socialization tactics and person-organization fit. *Personnel Psychology, 54,* 1.

Cascio, W. F., & Aguinis, H. (2005). *Applied psychology in human resource management* (6th ed.). Upper Saddle River, NJ: Pearson Prentice Hall.

DeNisi, A. S., & Griffin, R. W. (2001). *Human resource management.* Boston, MA: Houghton Mifflin.

Dunham, K. J. (2002). The jungle: Focus on recruitment, pay, and getting ahead. *Wall Street Journal,* p. B8.

Fisher, C. D., Schoenfeldt, L. F., & Shaw, J. B. (2006). Human resource management (6th ed.). Boston, MA: Houghton Mifflin.

Gale, S. (2001). Formalized flextime. *Workforce, 2,* 39–42.

Judge, T. A., & Bretz, R. D. (1992). Effects of work values on job choice decisions. *Journal of Applied Psychology, 77,* 261–271.

Maher, K. (2003). Corporations cut middlemen and do their own recruiting. *The Wall Street Journal,* p. B10.

Smith, D., & Moore, L. L. (2010). Job search strategies. Retrieved from http://www.eiu.edu/~careers/search.

Swenson, K. (1999). Maximizing employee referrals. *HR Focus, 76*(1), 9–10.

Chapter 5

Developing The Résumé and Cover Letter

Overview

During your college career, you will invariably pick up a number of skills and characteristics that employers are seeking. Regardless of your credentials, your "fit" with a particular job opening, or your passion for the industry, you simply will not get the job if you are not able to effectively communicate your qualifications to the employer. Despite recent technological changes, the résumé continues to be the primary tool that employers use to evaluate the qualifications of job applicants. A well-written résumé will provide an organized and chronological summary of your qualifications, experiences, interests, and skills. It is a snapshot of who you are, where you have been, and what you can contribute to the hiring organization. It is undoubtedly the first and most essential tool in developing your own personal brand (Shakoor, 2001).

While it is widely understood that the résumé should be succinct and letter perfect, a great deal of confusion exists about the organization and content that students in leisure service fields should include in this document. Should the résumé be one or two pages? Do you include references or simply indicate that they are available? Is a career objective a critical component that lends focus to the résumé or simply an annoyance to prospective employers? Should you list your grade point average or your high school accomplishments?

These are excellent questions to which there are no universally correct answers. Students in leisure industries are frequently frustrated by the conflicting advice from otherwise reliable sources. Professors, guidance counselors, and career service employees are all confident in their opinions, but they often contradict each other. Who is right and what is the reason for the discrepancies? The likely reason for conflicting advice is that each profession has its own set of spoken or unspoken preferences in development of the résumé and cover letter.

What is standard practice for graphic design, engineering, marketing, advertising, or corporate business is not always appropriate for the leisure service industry. While seeking input and counsel from trusted sources is of critical importance, students in the leisure industries need to be aware of the preferences of the employers who are most likely to be screening them for employment. The advice that you receive from those who come from other disciplines is valuable but must be tempered by the reality that our field is somewhat unique.

Despite the fact that differences exist, there is one expectation that is consistent across all professional disciplines—quality. Your résumé and cover letter should be representative of your highest quality work, and should accurately represent you in the most compelling manner; it should make employers feel that they *must* interview you. Application materials with errors in grammar, spelling, or format are quite often disregarded before they are even fully read and considered (Gower, 2005). Agency supervisors are quick to discard materials due to a single grammatical error in the cover letter. Although this is frequently difficult for students to believe, these are the expectations of those who will be reviewing your application. Remember, there are no shortages of applicants in many sectors of the leisure industry, and anything short of your best work will seriously reduce your chances of securing an interview. In this chapter, our goal is to assist you in developing a résumé and cover letter that are of the highest caliber and reflect well on your abilities and the institution from which you will obtain your degree. We will begin with a review of the purpose and design of a cover letter and end with suggestions for drafting a résumé that will set you apart from the rest.

The Cover Letter

The cover letter is arguably one of the most important documents a young professional will draft (DeKay, 2006). There is no doubt that the prominence of e-mail and other electronic media has dramatically changed the way cover letters are delivered (see "Sending the Cover Letter as an E-mail") and that the relentless bombardment of our in-boxes has only reinforced the fact that the document needs to be concise. In fact, many college students question the need to draft a cover letter when submitting their résumé electronically. With that said, very few contemporary sources are available that explain the function and key features that an effective cover letter should possess. In the next few sections, you'll find practical suggestions to aid you in constructing a cover letter that will grab the attention of a prospective employer.

A cover letter is aptly named, as it is the document that accompanies, or covers, another application document, traditionally the résumé. Clearly, if the cover letter is not compelling and well written, the odds of the rest of the application materials being reviewed are greatly diminished. For this reason alone, the cover letter is extremely important. The cover letter also provides an opportunity to showcase communication skills while simultaneously promoting your abilities and intangible attributes. Many students make the mistake of using the cover letter to highlight or simply repeat the information that can be found on their résumé. This is a classic blunder. The purpose of the cover letter is to spark the employer's interest in you (above and beyond the other applicants) and to motivate them to review your résumé. Something unique about you must stand out as they review your cover letter.

AN EFFECTIVE COVER LETTER MUST DO MORE than simply recount your recent professional accomplishments. To do this, it must do more than just coldly outline previous experiences. It should leave the employer with the impression that you are highly qualified, enthusiastic, and intelligent. It should establish the fact that you are a young professional who is eager to embark on your career. It should give some insight into why you want to work with this particular agency and highlight the value you would bring to the organization. In addition, a cover letter should establish that you are a person who takes pride in your work and that you pay attention to the smallest details. It must do all of this in no more than one page. Creating a cover letter that does all of this is challenging, but there are some consistent recommendations for you to follow. Read on to learn more!

The Content and Format of a Cover Letter

Traditionally, the cover letter will consist of only three paragraphs, each serving a very distinct purpose. In this text, we will conceptualize these paragraphs as the "opening," the "body," and the "closing." Each paragraph should accomplish certain tasks for the document to have the desired impact on the prospective employer. Once you have identified the content you wish to relay, there are several conservative options for the format of the letter.

How do you identify the content you wish to share? Spend a moment and put yourself in the shoes of the hiring agency. What skills do you think are essential to the job? Identify three, and be sure you include them. What sort of person do you think would be successful in this position and organization? Outgoing? Organized? Strong communicator? Be sure you give employers some insight into what kind of a person you are.

The Opening

The first paragraph of your cover letter, commonly referred to as the opening, should let the employer know why you are contacting them. When possible, indicate the position in which you are interested, and how you learned of the opening. If you have a personal connection with the company (i.e., were encouraged to apply by one of their employees, or had previous volunteer/employment experience with the agency) a brief reference is essential. As with most things in life, first impressions are of crucial importance, and the opening is your opportunity to make a good one with your prospective employer. Regardless of whether you have a name to drop or list the names of publications or job boards where you learned of the opening, you should leave the employer with the impression that you have done your research, are familiar with the requirements of the position, and are confident in your ability to successfully contribute to the organization. Your opening paragraph should be between three and five sentences in length.

How confident are you? The words you choose in a cover letter speak volumes. Avoid using weak phrases, such as "I think" and "I feel," and use more confident phrases like "I am" and "You will find me to be."

ONE OF THE WORST MISTAKES students commit in the opening is to actually introduce themselves. A surprising number of cover letters begin with the sentence, "Hello, my name is Joe Smith, and I am a student at State University." Please avoid making this mistake. You aren't leaving a message in someone's voicemail; you are presenting them with your employment credentials. As you can see in the examples on the page that follow, your name is plainly evident on the cover letter, and beginning a cover letter in this fashion is an amateurish mistake!

The Body

The body is the second paragraph of your cover letter, and is also extremely important. In this paragraph, it is critical that you accomplish three objectives. First, you should clearly demonstrate the fit between your knowledge and skills and the requirements of the position to which you are applying. This should be done without simply reiterating the positions you have held in the past. This is your opportunity to briefly expand on what you have learned, how you learned it, and most importantly, how you will add value to the organization. To do this effectively, it is imperative that you do all you can to secure a copy of the job description. If you don't know what the employer deems essential in the position, you will struggle in determining the content you should include in your letter (Lovelace, 2001). If a job description is not readily available, take the initiative to call the organization and request that it be sent to you, speak to alumni of your program who have worked or interned there, or arrange a brief phone call to discuss the position with the hiring manager. These extra steps communicate your sincere interest in the position and gives you the opportunity to build rapport with the organization before you even submit your application. In short, while it may stretch you out of your comfort zone, it will greatly increase your odds of being contacted for an interview.

Second, the body of your cover letter should sell your intangible qualities. While discussing your fit with the agency, be sure to reveal the attributes that really make you unique. This could include your passion for the field or philosophy of service delivery. It could also be any other professional or personal characteristics you possess (i.e., work ethic, desire to learn, leadership skills, communication skills, interests, or hobbies) that would set you apart from other applicants. Once you have written your cover letter, have trusted friends and family members review your work. If they can't see a glimpse of "who you are" in the letter, chances are the prospective employer won't either. This is particularly important in the leisure industry where many managers tend to "hire the person, and train the employee."

The Real World is Different From College

Writing a cover letter as an academic exercise is different than writing one you intend to use to secure an interview. Several years ago, I was working with one of my best students, Mallory Martin. Mallory is a gregarious person; she is energetic, creative, and fun to be around. When I was grading the cover letter she prepared for my class I was not surprised that she earned 100%. It was formatted properly and free of any grammatical errors. I gave her the A, but called her to my office to discuss. "Mallory," I said, "This is a very solid cover letter and of course you have earned an A." Before she became too pleased, I followed up with " . . . and I hate it!" Mallory was surprised. She had submitted a similar cover letter for at least two other classes at the university, and nobody had ever raised an issue. So what was the problem? I was disappointed that there was nothing in the cover letter that gave me a glimpse into the "energetic, creative, and fun-to-be-around" Mallory. In fact, her cover letter read just like the 60 other cover letters I had just read. The problem was I knew that Mallory was not just like the other 60 students in her class. One of the best students I had ever worked with now sounded and looked just plain ordinary to prospective employers! The bottom line is the work you submit to your school might be enough to earn you the A, but have you done all you can to develop your "brand" in the mind of the hiring agency?

Finally, be sure you are spending a fair amount of time talking about the agency itself. In your cover letter's body, you should demonstrate an understanding of their mission, goals, or programs and explain what it is about the agency that prompted you to apply for the position there. Many students make the mistake of only talking about themselves and what they hope to accomplish or learn in their internship. Chances are the agency already knows that you hope to develop your professional skills. What might be less clear to them is why you think their agency is the ideal setting for this to occur.

Drafting the body of the cover letter is a time-consuming and challenging process. It requires an understanding of the organization and the particulars of the internship opening. It further requires you to take the time to carefully articulate the connection between you and the agency and the benefits you will bring them. It should be concise and easy to read. It also requires that you do all this in about eight to 12 sentences. Clearly, this process will take many attempts and rewrites before you get it just right.

DO YOU HAVE FRIENDS YOU TALK TO on the phone who only talk about themselves? We all do. It does not take long for most of us to completely tune them out. We are still on the phone with them but really have no idea what they are saying. Does this sound familiar? The same thing can be true about the body of your cover letter. Don't discuss only your qualifications and professional goals. Be sure to draft a body that leaves the employer with the impression that you don't just want to begin your professional career, but that you want to begin it with them. Consider the statement from a recreation supervisor at an Illinois Park District: "I review dozens of résumés and cover letters for our internships each term. So many of them only rehash past employment experiences or talk about how amazing an internship will be for them. I want to know 'why here?' and 'why in public recreation?' If a student doesn't impress upon me why he or she wants to work specifically with our organization, I'm probably not going to be calling them in to an interview."

The Closing

The final paragraph of your cover letter should set the stage for an interview. Be sure to thank the employer for the time he or she has invested in reviewing your materials, and let him or her know that you look forward to the opportunity to interview to further discuss your qualifications. Reiterate your interest and commitment to the open position. It is appropriate to provide your phone number and e-mail address as possible avenues to contact you. Some students include a sentence indicating that they will call the employer to discuss the possibility of establishing an interview. This is an acceptable practice (and all students are strongly encouraged to do follow-up phone calls when appropriate), but approach this action with caution. You want to present yourself as someone who takes initiative and who is committed to the position, but you do not want to be seen as intrusive or overly aggressive. The employer should ultimately be responsible for scheduling any interviews. The sentence "I will call you the week of September 19 to discuss my application materials and see if you have any questions for me" is acceptable. A sentence such as "I will contact you the week of September 19 to make arrangements for an interview" is too aggressive. Your closing will likely be three to five sentences in length.

The Format of the Cover Letter

Now that you have an idea for the content that should be included in your cover letter, it is time to review the most appropriate letter formats. The vast majority of literature suggests that a traditional business format is the most acceptable way to format your cover letter (Crosby, 2009). Use of templates and graphics is strongly discouraged. The most widely used business format is "full block style," which will always include the following elements in this order:

- the name, address, and other contact information (i.e., phone number and e-mail address) of the sender;
- the date the letter was written;
- the name and title of the addressee and the name and address of the organization;
- the salutation (i.e., "Dear Mrs. Rubio:");
- the opening, body, and closing;
- the sender's signature; and
- in the case of submission of application materials, you will also want to designate the enclosure of your résumé (i.e., "Encl. Résumé").

In addition to these elements, there are several rules to follow when drafting a full block style letter. First, you will notice that a colon is always used in the salutation, never a comma or a semicolon. Second, in a full block style letter, all the text will be justified to the far left side of the page. You do not indent the beginning of each new paragraph. Third, with the exception of the date (three to four blank lines) and the closing (three to four blank lines), each element is followed by a single blank line. And finally, you will notice that the letter is always evenly centered on the page in a way that balances the white space at the top of the page with the white space at the bottom of the page.

Consider the examples of cover letters on the following page.

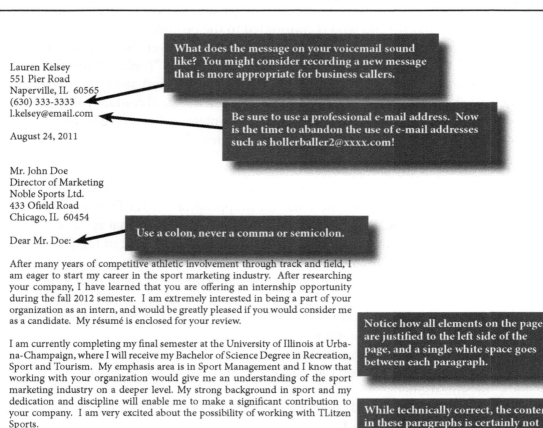

Lauren Kelsey
551 Pier Road
Naperville, IL 60565
(630) 333-3333
l.kelsey@email.com

August 24, 2011

Mr. John Doe
Director of Marketing
Noble Sports Ltd.
433 Ofield Road
Chicago, IL 60454

Dear Mr. Doe:

After many years of competitive athletic involvement through track and field, I am eager to start my career in the sport marketing industry. After researching your company, I have learned that you are offering an internship opportunity during the fall 2012 semester. I am extremely interested in being a part of your organization as an intern, and would be greatly pleased if you would consider me as a candidate. My résumé is enclosed for your review.

I am currently completing my final semester at the University of Illinois at Urbana-Champaign, where I will receive my Bachelor of Science Degree in Recreation, Sport and Tourism. My emphasis area is in Sport Management and I know that working with your organization would give me an understanding of the sport marketing industry on a deeper level. My strong background in sport and my dedication and discipline will enable me to make a significant contribution to your company. I am very excited about the possibility of working with TLitzen Sports.

I would appreciate the opportunity to discuss my qualifications and the possibility of completing an internship with your organization. I will be available for an internship from August to December of 2012, and I am available for an interview at your convenience. Thank you for your time and consideration.

Sincerely,

Lauren Kelsey

Encl: Résumé

What does the message on your voicemail sound like? You might consider recording a new message that is more appropriate for business callers.

Be sure to use a professional e-mail address. Now is the time to abandon the use of e-mail addresses such as hollerballer2@xxxx.com!

Use a colon, never a comma or semicolon.

Notice how all elements on the page are justified to the left side of the page, and a single white space goes between each paragraph.

While technically correct, the content in these paragraphs is certainly not going to be winning over a potential employer anytime soon! What could Lauren have done to really make this cover letter more compelling and interesting?

Leave three to four spaces here for your signature. Be sure to actually sign your cover letter! If you are submitting a digital copy, adding a scanned signature to your cover letter is a nice touch!

Notice that the amount of white space is equal at the top and bottom of the page.

Figure 5.1. Sample Cover Letter in Block Format (most preferred)

August 24, 2011

Ms. Jane Doe
Volunteer and Program Coordinator
Y-ME Illinois
203 North Wabash; Suite 1220
Chicago, IL 60601

> The date and the signature in modified block format are typically indented three inches in modified block format.

Dear Ms. Doe:

In researching fall internships, I learned of several opportunities with the Y-ME National Breast Cancer Society from your listings on the organizational website. I would like to express my interest in the special events internship for the fall of 2012. I am confident that your organization's values and objectives would highly complement my own strengths and enthusiasm. I am very interested in joining the Y-ME Illinois team and have enclosed my résumé for your review.

My previous experience includes a position at the Mattoon Illinois Tourism Department. This position has given me valuable insight into the operation of special events and many of the factors that influence them. My work experience has also given me practice in dealing with people, a vital skill for someone in the special events field to possess. I also have a strong record of leadership and organizational success as evidenced by various positions I have held while in college. I am highly motivated, assertive, and enthusiastic to take on new challenges.

Y-ME Illinois has the qualities that I am looking for in a potential employer: quality training and an overall environment that fosters success. I look forward to exchanging ideas with you concerning an internship at Y-ME Illinois and the positive contributions I would offer as a member of your team. You may reach me at (217) 333-3333 or via e-mail at greuber@email.com to arrange an interview. Thank you for your time and consideration in this matter.

Sincerely,

> Notice that Erin has done a much better job expressing enthusiasm about the position and why she is interested in that specific organization. The content here, however, could still be strengthened to make a more compelling case to fit with the position.

Erin Greuber
508 East John Street
Champaign, IL 61820

Encl: Résumé

Figure 5.2. Sample Cover Letter in Modified Block Format

August 24, 2012

Mr. John Doe
Director of Recreation
Riverside Park District
1919 Realnice Road
Pleasantville, MO 62533

Dear Mr. Clip:

While reviewing the Job Opportunities Bulletin Board at the recent NRPA exposition, I learned that the Riverside Park District is searching for a qualified student intern for the Spring 2012 semester. I have read the job description and qualifications and am confident that I am uniquely qualified for the position. I have enclosed my résumé for your review.

During my college career, I have had the pleasure of working with many community-based agencies on various fundraising projects. These experiences have given me the ability to create, develop, and sell ideas and products. I have also learned how to listen to constituents and how to effectively manage and control group efforts. Most recently, I was involved with a fundraising project for Art Start; a not-for-profit organization dedicated to promoting fine arts in underprivileged communities. As project manager, I am pleased to report that we were able to raise more than $50,000 for the DeWitt County Art Smart program.

I am a confident, capable, and teachable student. I know that I would be an excellent addition to your existing fundraising staff, and I am certain that I could contribute much to your existing programs. I am available for an internship from January to May of 2013. I would very much like to meet with you to discuss further the possibility of joining the Riverside Park District and remain available for an interview at your convenience. Thank you for your time and efforts on my behalf.

Sincerely,

Jason J. Smith
1405 South Side Way
Palos Hills, IL 62454
(708) 555-5555

Enclosure: Résumé

> Jason has done an excellent job communicating what he could bring to the table as well as projecting a positive image of himself. Notice the addition of a MEASUREABLE accomplishment (i.e., raising $50,000).

Figure 5.3. Additional Sample Cover Letter

Hopefully the samples on the last few pages will assist you as you begin to develop your own cover letter. While the samples provided here are certainly solid examples of quality work, be sure that your cover letter is representative of your own work; use your own writing style and vocabulary! The creative process always goes better when you are just being yourself. Some additional tips and final reminders about the cover letter:

- The cover letter should look crisp and professional.
- Is this representative of your highest caliber of work? If you have a sentence that you know isn't quite right, keep working on it until you have perfected it.
- Components of your cover letter should be unique to each position for which you are applying. Mass-produced cover letters are easy to detect and show employers that you did not invest much time and attention in researching and applying for their position. Also, if you have a copy of the job description, you can use keywords from that job description to make your cover letter stand out as it is reviewed. This might be particularly important if you are submitting a scannable cover letter and résumé.
- The name and the address of the writer is always provided. Inclusion of your phone number and e-mail address is strongly suggested.
- The date the letter was drafted is clearly visible.
- You always use the employer's full name, title, agency name, and mailing address.
- A colon (not a comma or semicolon) is used after the formal name in the salutation (i.e., Dear Dr. McDonald:, Dear Ms. Smith:, Dear Dean Pitt:, etc.)
- Always be sure to sign your cover letter. Blue ink is preferred for your signature.
- The term *Enclosure* or *Encl* is used to let the reader know that you have attached additional pages (your résumé) for their review. If they are missing (and these documents frequently travel from desk to desk), they know to contact you for a copy.
- Each of the three paragraphs has at least three full sentences. It takes a minimum of three sentences to construct a true paragraph.
- The cover letter must be free from grammatical errors.

You See What You Expect to See

Once you feel that you have developed a quality cover letter, print it and set it aside for several hours. Take some time to get other schoolwork done, watch some television, or get some exercise. Let your mind take a break. After a few hours have passed, go back to your cover letter and carefully review it. Chances are you will find sentences that could be worded better or even spelling or grammatical errors. Read it through several times, carefully inspecting it for any errors. Go back and make sure that you are following the recommendations in this chapter.

It is critical to take some time away from the cover letter before you review it. When you are actively involved in such a project, you begin to read what you *think* you have written instead of what is actually on the page. Sentences that you have rewritten numerous times may appear to make sense even to you even though they really do not. Words that look like they are spelled correctly may not be. Spell check is a valuable tool, but it cannot tell when a word is improperly used (i.e., there/their). When you can take a fresh look at your work, you almost always find room for improvement.

Once you are comfortable that your cover letter is perfect, give a copy to a competent and capable friend. Notice I said a capable friend, not necessarily your best friend. Ask him or her to carefully read the letter, looking for any errors in grammar, spelling, or sentence structure. Make sure he or she knows that you want honesty. Sometimes friends don't like to let you know that your writing is poor. If this is the case, it is better to hear this from your friend than to make a poor impression on a potential employer.

And finally, once you and your friend agree that your cover letter is perfect, it is time to give a copy to your university internship coordinator, a trusted professor, or career service professional. This will be your final set of eyes to be sure that no mistakes have been made, and he or she can frequently provide additional information about the site to which you are applying. The more people who review and refine your work, the more confident you can be that your materials are ready to go!

Find the Errors

The following cover letter appears solid enough at first glance, but any organization who actually receives a document like this will discard it outright. Review the cover letter and see if you can identify the many (13 minimum) errors.

Bryant Apperson
111 E. Chalmers
Champaign, IL 61820

Ms. Katherine Smith
Division of Intercollegiate Athletics
University of Illinois at Urbana-Champaign
1700 South Fourth Street
Champaign, IL 61820

Dear Ms. Pride,

My name is Bryant Apperson. I recently read about your internship program in a newspaper add in the News Gazette and I am excited to learn about the opportunities I could experience. I would like to apply for the spring 20012 internship and have enclosed my résumé for your review.

I am currently in my senior year of undergraduate studies at the University of Illinois and will meet the requirements for my Bachelor of Science degree in Leisure Studies shorty. As my résumé clearly illustrates, I have the educational and professional experience necessary to make a significant contribution to your organization. I have had previous work experience in ticket sales with the Kane County Cougars, and have worked in marketing with the Peoria Chiefs.

I would very much like to arrange to interview for the spring internship with the DIA. I will call you the week of September 19 to establish a time for our meeting.

Sincerely,

Bryant Apperson

Cover Letter Exercise Key

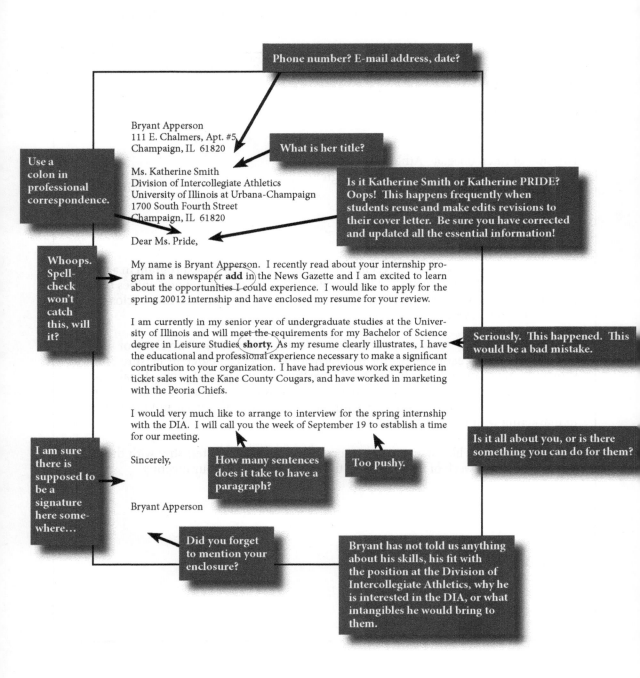

Phone number? E-mail address, date?

Bryant Apperson
111 E. Chalmers, Apt. #5,
Champaign, IL 61820

What is her title?

Use a colon in professional correspondence.

Ms. Katherine Smith
Division of Intercollegiate Athletics
University of Illinois at Urbana-Champaign
1700 South Fourth Street
Champaign, IL 61820

Is it Katherine Smith or Katherine PRIDE? Oops! This happens frequently when students reuse and make edits revisions to their cover letter. Be sure you have corrected and updated all the essential information!

Dear Ms. Pride,

Whoops. Spell-check won't catch this, will it?

My name is Bryant Apperson. I recently read about your internship program in a newspaper **add** in the News Gazette and I am excited to learn about the opportunities I could experience. I would like to apply for the spring 20012 internship and have enclosed my resume for your review.

I am currently in my senior year of undergraduate studies at the University of Illinois and will meet the requirements for my Bachelor of Science degree in Leisure Studies **shorty**. As my resume clearly illustrates, I have the educational and professional experience necessary to make a significant contribution to your organization. I have had previous work experience in ticket sales with the Kane County Cougars, and have worked in marketing with the Peoria Chiefs.

Seriously. This happened. This would be a bad mistake.

I would very much like to arrange to interview for the spring internship with the DIA. I will call you the week of September 19 to establish a time for our meeting.

Is it all about you, or is there something you can do for them?

I am sure there is supposed to be a signature here somewhere...

Sincerely,

How many sentences does it take to have a paragraph?

Too pushy.

Bryant Apperson

Did you forget to mention your enclosure?

Bryant has not told us anything about his skills, his fit with the position at the Division of Intercollegiate Athletics, why he is interested in the DIA, or what intangibles he would bring to them.

Sending the Cover Letter as an E-mail

As mentioned at the start of the chapter, the days of submitting hard copies of résumés and cover letters are numbered. Increasingly, employers prefer to have application materials sent electronically (Honaman, 2009). So here are some recommendations for you to consider:

- When sending an e-mail to a professional, abandon any bad e-mail habits you might have formed over the years. This is professional correspondence. Capitalize appropriate words and use proper punctuation. When in doubt, write your e-mail in a word processing application, check it for errors, and then cut and paste it into your e-mail.
- Subject lines are important. Failure to include a subject line for your e-mail will likely result in the message being directed to the spam folder. The subject line should reference the position to which you are applying.
- If the hiring agency has asked for a cover letter and résumé, send both documents as individual attachments. Write only a few brief sentences in the e-mail and direct them to the documents. Consider doing a trial run first. Send the e-mail to yourself, and then open it on a few different computers. Take a look at how everything appears, and be sure the formatting in your documents has not been compromised.
- If the hiring agency only requests a résumé, use the e-mail to which you are attaching it as a replacement for the cover letter. Many experts recommend copying and pasting your cover letter directly into your e-mail. This might be a good start, but personal experience tells us that professionals dislike lengthy e-mails. Use the same format you would use for a traditional cover letter, but really look for ways to shorten the document. Include only the essentials.

The Résumé

Once you have carefully constructed a cover letter that sets you apart as a unique candidate, you must have a résumé that portrays your skills and qualifications in a way that assists employers in seeing the fit with their position (Ross & Young, 2005). Depending on the expert you consult or the text you review, you will hear many different opinions about what should and should not be included in your résumé. Despite many differences of opinion, there is strong agreement regarding the inclusion of the following categories in the following order:

1. name and contact information
2. education
3. work experience

4. volunteer experience, and
5. honors and activities.

Areas receiving mixed support include

1. job objective,
2. skill summary,
3. executive summary, and
4. references.

We will begin our discussion by considering the categories that have strong support among career service professionals.

Essential Components of a Résumé

Name and contact information. While it might appear obvious to even mention that your name and contact information should be included on your résumé, there are a surprising number of issues that you may want to consider when adding these lines to your résumé. First, your name and contact information should be prominently displayed at the top of the résumé. While the format you select for your résumé may change the size and location, you certainly want your name to stand out on the page. It should be in a larger font size than the rest of the document, and you may consider bolding the text. Second, you might take a moment to consider what name you list on the résumé. Sound confusing? Many students feel compelled to list their full given name at the top of the résumé. After all, doesn't "Robert Heath Gates" sound so much more impressive than "Bob Gates"? Besides, everyone lists their full name at the top of the résumé don't they? Perhaps, but there are a few factors you might consider before you move forward. First, which name is more memorable to you? It is much easier for me to remember "Bob Gates" than "Robert Heath Gates." Also, who sound like a more approachable colleague to you? Do the people who are screening your application materials work in an office of people with names like "Robert Heath Gates" or "Robert H. Gates," or do they work in an office with co-workers named Bob, Beth, Tony, and Jen? The bottom line is you should consider using the name you actually go by on your résumé. While your peers might use their full given name or their middle initial, you will stand out from the crowd and sound like someone the employer can actually see themselves working with.

Think About It

Don't supply contact information that you know you will not be using a few months from now. Your university e-mail or apartment mailing address will soon be inaccessible. Play it safe and supply information that will be relatively stable for the next few months.

Pay attention to the e-mail address and telephone number you list. Employers frequently hold on to applications from desirable candidates for quite some time. We recommend you list an address, phone number, and e-mail address that will be relatively stable over the next 18 months. Consider listing your cell phone number instead of the landline to your apartment. Now is a good time to start a conventional g-mail account. Your educational institution account will be terminated upon graduation, and as previously mentioned, hollerballer3@xxxmail.com is likely not the brand image you are looking to build. If you are unsure about your living arrangements after graduation, see if you can use the home address of your parents or a trusted friend who is unlikely to relocate in the upcoming months.

Education. The simple fact is that you, or those close to you, have paid a considerable amount of money for you to attend school and receive your degree. This section of your résumé provides you with the opportunity to showcase your accomplishment and to begin to benefit from your investment. Listed below are the essential elements for you to share related to your educational achievements:

- the name of your school,
- the name of your degree (i.e., bachelor of science in recreation management)
- your emphasis area (i.e., outdoor leadership) or academic "minors" completed, and
- relevant coursework.

Institution name. Let's begin with the basics. First, it is not necessary to list every institution of higher education you have ever attended. Many students will have taken a few classes at a community college at some point in their college career. As a general rule, if you have completed less than 12 credit hours (or the equivalent of one full semester) at a particular educational institution, it is not necessary to list it on your résumé. If, however, you have exceeded this, or perhaps you have earned an associate's degree or professional certificate, these should be listed independently in the education section. As with all things on your résumé, you should list the institutions in *reverse chronological order*. In other words, the most recent activities go first.

High School Experiences

Students sometimes wonder if they should list their high school education on their résumé. Although some experts support inclusion of high school education on your résumé, (Crosby, 1999) under most circumstances, the answer is a resounding NO! At this stage in your academic career, your résumé should have grown to the point where high school activities have become extraneous. Possible exceptions to this rule are

- you attended a very prestigious academy, with regional, national, or international renown;

- the contact at the prospective agency is also an alumnus of the same high school. Acknowledging this could be excellent for finding commonality and breaking the ice in an early stage of an interview; or

- there is a link between the position to which you are applying and your high school education.

In the absence of these three exceptions (there might be others, when in doubt, ask your school internship coordinator), students are strongly discouraged from using any information related to high school on their résumé!

Degree title. After the name of the educational institution you attended, you should list the name of the degree you are earning and possibly the date you anticipate degree completion and your grade point average. You should use caution and be certain that you get this right. Your peers may be earning a bachelor of arts or bachelor of science degree in another field. Be certain you take the time to be sure you are listing your degree properly!

What Is In a Name?

Failure to list your degree accurately on your résumé can have disastrous implications on your internship or full-time job search. More and more companies are carefully screening applicants as the temptation to embellish the résumé grows in difficult economic times. When organizations contact your educational institution, federal law restricts the information that can be shared without a signed release. Changing the name of your degree, or using only the name of your emphasis or correlate area is not an acceptable practice. A student at a Midwest university recently had a job offer rescinded when the employer was completing the final background check. Apparently, the student had listed the name of his emphasis area (sport management) and when the employer sought to confirm that the student had actually earned this degree, the University only responded "no such degree program exists on this campus." The employer assumed the student had falsified his credentials and made the final offer to another candidate. A silly mistake and one you will want to avoid! Honesty and accuracy are always the best policy.

Grade Point Matters

If your grade point average is favorable, you should strongly consider including it on your résumé. But what is a favorable GPA? Traditional wisdom suggests that averages above a 3.0 on a 4.0 scale (4.0 on a 5.0 scale) are to be included. Many students will not have a cumulative GPA this high, but what about your major GPA, or what if you account for the grades you earned at the local community college? Many students mature or find their academic gifting in the final years of college; consider listing only your last 60 hours if they paint a more favorable picture of your academic abilities.

Emphasis area. Many students, as a part of their required curriculum or not, earn a minor, complete an emphasis, correlate, or certification program along with their undergraduate degree program. Such accomplishments should certainly be listed prominently on the résumé. Remember, any knowledge, skills, or abilities that you possess that distinguish you from the other candidates in the application pool are essential to highlight. A minor in business administration, Spanish, communications, or an emphasis in environmental sciences might be just one additional reason for the employer to arrange the interview. What if your minor bears no relation on your intended profession? Consider including it anyway. It will only take up one line on your document and it tells the employer a little bit about your interests. Who knows, they may share your passion for history or chemistry, and it can be an excellent ice-breaker in the interview setting.

Relevant coursework. Students graduating from parks-, recreation-, sport- or tourism-based degree programs should strongly consider listing some of the relevant coursework completed at your school. For most college graduates, even those who have completed one or more seasonal internships, your college degree remains your biggest selling point. Take the time to be sure you effectively communicate all you have been exposed to and learned as you completed your degree. Although formal programs in parks, recreation, sport and tourism have been around for decades, there is frequently confusion and misinformation among those who are not familiar with these programs of study. When the agency sees that you too have been exposed to courses in marketing, finance, leadership, and administration, along with gaining experience in programming, events, facilities, and service delivery, the value of the degree will be clearer to the person who is screening your résumé!

Work experience. If you have received good advice and been dedicated to developing your professional skills, by the time you are a senior, you should have several work experiences that have exposed you to the profession and enhanced your professional skill set. In this section, it is crucial that you carefully construct each sentence so that it portrays your experience, and more importantly the skills you have developed, so that the fit between you and the job to which you are applying is very clear.

It is not necessary to list every work experience you have had, and in fact it may be advantageous to select only the experiences that most closely relate to the position to which you are applying (if you do this, you should rename this category Related Work Experience). For each experience you had, consider listing the following:

- the name of the organization, including the city and state if desired;

- your title if applicable or advantageous (remember that if you list it for one experience, you must list it for all);

- the dates of employment (seasonal work can be listed as "Summer 2011" or "Summers 2011 and 2012" if you held the same position for multiple years); and

- a list of the skills you learned or demonstrated on the job (Monster.com maintains an excellent list of action phrases/verbs on their website. Please visit: http://adminsecret.monster.com/training/articles/171-action-phrases-and-power-verbs.

Remember to list your work experiences in reverse chronological order. This means list your most recent work experiences first. Ideally, this means your most significant experiences will be listed first and the growth in your professional responsibilities and capabilities will be clear to the prospective agency.

Reverse chronological order still appears to be format employers most prefer in the résumé document (Crosby, 2009).

When possible, don't focus only on what you did, but also on what you learned. For example, you may have been the cashier at a local retail store. Rather than, or in addition to saying, "Responsible for ringing up orders and processing returns" consider "Developed a strong appreciation for listening and providing excellent service to customers." Likewise, when possible, *quantify* your accomplishments. Would a prospective employer prefer to see "Responsible for recruiting sponsors for the Mother-Son Date Night Program" or "Collected more than $10,000 in cash and in-kind donations for the Mother-Son Date Night Program"? I know who I would hire!

Take Your Time and Get it Right

Most employers carefully construct a job description for internship and full-time positions. These job descriptions are created after a careful analysis is done of the desired and necessary characteristics and competencies necessary to do the job (Torrington & Hall, 1987). The job description helps the organization recruit qualified applicants and frequently serves as the basis for evaluating the fit of each candidate with the position. When it is possible, make an effort to use the same language in your résumé that the employer has used in the job description. Using the same jargon or technical phrases will make your résumé stand out and increase the odds that you will be seen as a good fit. If you don't have a copy of the job description, call or write to request it. While customizing each résumé in this way is time consuming, it will make a big difference in the number of phone calls you receive for interviews!

Volunteer experience. Although many college students have not had the opportunity to obtain significant amounts of relevant paid work experience (after all, we have to pay the bills), most have had the opportunity to be involved in numerous volunteer experiences. This experience is important because it also gives the employer an idea of what kind of person you are, what you are passionate about, and the values you hold. It may showcase involvement in the community, with a special cause, or demonstrate a sustained interest in the field. Such experiences may be just what it takes to help your résumé stand out from your peers with fewer or more traditional experiences (Slowe & Pastorius, 2010).

Consider This

If you only have one work or volunteer experience, consider combining these two categories. It might be advantageous to develop a professional experience category.

Honors and activities. The honors and activities section of your résumé is yet another way for you to distinguish yourself from other applicants. This section of your résumé gives you the opportunity to list clubs or organizations with which you have been affiliated. Membership in professional organizations such as the National Recreation and Park Association (NRPA) and the International Festivals and Events Association (IFEA) demonstrate commitment to the field. Likewise, you should list academic or professional recognitions you might have earned (Dean's List, James Scholar, employee of the month, etc.), or unique experiences you have had such as studying abroad or attending professional conferences. If you have been dedicated to learning and growing apart from completion of your required courses, this is your opportunity to benefit from all your hard work.

To List or Not to List?

Students are frequently advised not to list experiences with Greek organizations (i.e., fraternities and sororities) or religious groups. The fear is that the applicant will be discriminated against by those who do not support the values and beliefs represented by such organizations. After all, if you are in a fraternity, you are just there to party, right? And if you are actively involved in your church, then you won't be as dedicated to your work, or worse yet, you may even begin proselytizing on the job. So what is a job applicant to do? Our advice is as follows:

• Carefully consider each line that goes on your résumé. If there is not a clear advantage to listing it, you are likely better off removing it. This is true in ever section of your résumé.

• If the activity is something that is extremely important to you, or from which you have benefited personally or professionally include it. If someone would marginalize you for who you are and what you are committed to, they likely aren't the sort of person you would want to work with anyway!

Other Components to Consider Including

While the aforementioned categories, name and contact information, education, work experience, volunteer experience, and honors and activities are more universally accepted as "résumé essentials," there are other categories over which experts strongly disagree. In this section, we will discuss (a) job/career objectives, (b) skill summary, and (c) references.

The job or career objective. The purpose of the objective is to provide the employer with a general idea of the type of internship you are seeking. For example, are you seeking an entry-level internship or are you looking for something more advanced? Are you looking for an opportunity to increase your experience in sales, programming, or facility management? These are discussion points that could be included in the job or career objective. It should be no longer than two sentences, and most experts agree that one well-constructed sentence is greatly preferred (Gower, 2005). Those who advocate for inclusion of the objective indicate that it provides the employer with a better idea of what you are hoping to gain through the experience.

While objectives have been a staple in the traditional résumé, there are several potential downfalls to address. First, if space is at a premium on your résumé, the job or career objective is probably the only category that you could eliminate from your résumé altogether with little to no impact. Although this information may be useful, it could easily be relocated and addressed in your cover letter. In fact, a good cover letter might make the inclusion of this category on your résumé redundant. Additionally, students often make the mistake of making their career objective too specific. This might inadvertently result in removal or exclusion from the search process.

Career Objective Blunders

Consider the following career objective from a previous student's résumé:

"To obtain an internship in the marketing department of a professional sport team with the intention of learning more about selling season tickets, group sales, and grassroots marketing."

While this career objective sounds quite impressive (the use of marketing terms demonstrates knowledge of the field), it may ultimately work against the best interest of the student. Why? It is very specific. First, it mentions one particular department that the student would like to intern with. This is not necessarily a problem if you are truly only interested in an internship within that single department. Many students, however, are more concerned with obtaining the internship with the organization, and are willing to work in many departments to gain a well-rounded internship experience or to better meet the needs of the organization. For example, if the student who drafted this career objective would also have been agreeable to working in public relations or facilities, then this career objective will work against them. If an internship is not open in Marketing, the potential employer is likely to discard the application rather than make the effort to contact the student to see if they are interested in exploring other departments. A better career objective might read something like this:

"To obtain an internship in a professional sport organization with the intention of gaining progressive experience, with responsibilities that would allow me to directly contribute to organizational goals."

This career objective lets the employer know that you are looking for an internship in professional sport, and more importantly that you are looking for an internship with a higher level of responsibility. At this stage in your academic career, you are likely looking to gain proficiency in many management related duties—not time as the team mascot! It is ambiguous enough to allow the employer to envision you working in a number of different departments, and therefore increasing your odds of being called in for an interview.

In an informal study of 275 site supervisors, Gower (2010) found that the overriding sentiment among those who responded was that job or career objectives should be excluded. Being overly vague, not contributing anything new, and being poorly written were the top criticisms of job and career objectives. This response, from a professional who wishes to remain anonymous, says it all:

I don't spend much time on these [reviewing résumés] at all, so don't make me read something that isn't important. Most of the time this section is just an ambiguous jumble of fancy-sounding words that don't mean anything to me. When students include them, I just ignore them.

Skill summary. Skill summaries, frequently referred to as *executive summaries* or *summaries of qualifications* concisely convey the competencies and characteristics you can offer the prospective employer. In this section, you should identify four or five of your strongest attributes, or any skills you possess that best demonstrate your fit for the open position. Try to move beyond simple statements like "proficient with Microsoft Office applications," and think about the skills you possess that those who are 10 to 15 years older than you may not yet have. Highly desirable skills in many parks, recreation, tourism, and sport agencies right now include foreign language ability, communication and leadership skills, sales experience, and expertise in social media and other Internet applications. Skill summaries can include both human (i.e., leadership, persuasion) and technical (i.e., SWOT analysis, RecWare Online) skills.

Skill summaries for entry-level candidates are typically placed near the end of the résumé after education, work, and honors and activities. If, however, you do not have strong work or volunteer experience sections, you may consider placing your skill summary section at the top (where the objective would usually go) or directly after your education section. Try it a few different ways and ask friends or professors to give you their thoughts on which makes you look most qualified for the position.

References. Many students are under the impression that including references on a résumé is not acceptable. In today's fiercely competitive job market, and in the small and closely knit leisure service industry, the value of positive references should not be minimized. While some résumé professionals have recommended excluding references in the past, these trends are changing, particularly in the government and nonprofit sectors (Gower, 2010). When you consider the high level of direct interaction that entry-level staff in leisure service industries have with clientele, it should come as no surprise that more than 80% of managers in government or nonprofit organizations indicated that they prefer references be included in the résumé (Gower, 2010). Fifty-three percent of those in commercial recreation, sport, or tourism sectors indicated the desire to have references listed on the résumé.

Regardless of whether you intend to include references on your résumé, or provide them on a separate page, what are some things you must consider? First and foremost, you need to be sure that you have consulted with your potential references to determine their willingness to perform this important function for you. This can be done in a face-to-face meeting, over the phone, or via e-mail, but it is a critical step. Additionally, you might consider providing your references with a copy of your cover letter and résumé, as well as any job descriptions to which you will be responding. This will greatly assist them in providing targeted information relevant to the open position.

When selecting your references, think about the information for which potential employers are looking. Select individuals who will be able to give a holistic overview of your capabilities, accomplishments, and personality. Those who have had direct supervisory responsibility for you are preferred. It is recommended that you provide three references to the hiring agency.

Determining Your References

As already mentioned, you should consider the needs and wants of the hiring agency when selecting your references. If you are applying for graduate studies, the majority of your references should likely be those who can attest to your academic ability; most likely your college instructors. Similarly, when applying for professional positions, your references should be able to give insight into your ability to perform in a workplace environment. It is sometimes difficult for recent college graduates to secure three references who have had sufficient opportunity to observe their full range of capabilities. In these cases, you are encouraged to find professors, mentors, or other responsible adults who can attest to both your ability and personality type. The bottom line is you must have 100% confidence that those you select to serve as your references will support you and represent you in a positive light. If there is any doubt in your mind (i.e., strained relationship in the past, conflict between friends or coworkers) you should move on to find another individual who can serve on your behalf.

Given all we have shared so far, you might wonder why anyone would recommend not including references on the résumé. There are some who suggest that references are useless because it is clear that the candidate will take care and select only individuals they know will provide positive feedback. While this is true, reference checks do reveal or reinforce areas of strength and weakness, and are increasingly being checked as a way to prevent résumé fraud (Hannan & Shaw, 2010/2011).

Helpful Hints and Guidelines

Once you have developed the content of your résumé, it is time to begin working on format, composition, and delivery. We have put together a list of helpful hints and guidelines for you to use when putting the finishing touches on your résumé. Once you have completed your résumé, be sure it conforms to the following guidelines:

1. In the business world, appearance does matter. It should go without saying that your résumé should be drafted on a computer using a standard word processing application that most employers will be able to work with. Consider saving your file in an older version (i.e., Word 97-2003) to ensure that most will be able to access your file and to minimize changes in your résumé format.

2. To avoid formatting errors (i.e., spacing and font changes), consider saving your résumé as both a .doc and a .pdf file. Most organizations have Adobe Acrobat on their office machines, and this eliminates any chance that your résumé might arrive in the employer's in-box looking like a kindergartener put it together.

3. If your résumé will be submitted as a hard copy, be sure it is printed on a laser printer. Photocopies are acceptable as long as they are done at a professional copy shop. They must be very high-quality reproductions. Your résumé should be printed on the same paper as your cover letter. Remember, standard résumé paper is 20 lb with at least 25% cotton content. The only colors that you should use are white, off-white, or light gray. Résumé paper is available at most office supply stores.

4. If your résumé is two pages long, you should add your full name to the upper right-hand corner of the second page. If you are going to use a two-page résumé, make sure you have enough content to fill at least half of the second page (references are always a nice filler). If you cannot fill at least half of the second page, go back to the first page and look for ways to condense or expand the materials there.

5. Hard copies of the résumé and cover letter should never be stapled together. You should always bind them with a paperclip in the upper left-hand corner.

6. If you are mailing a hard copy of a résumé and cover letter, do not fold them. Send them in a full-size envelope, and put the mailing address as well as your return address on a mailing label. Do not handwrite the address on an envelope.

7. Never print or copy résumés on the front and back of one page. The back side of the page is likely to be overlooked.

8. The content of your résumé should be organized so it is visually pleasing and easy to read. Narrative format résumés are highly discouraged (i.e., full-sentence descriptions, use of first person, etc). Short, descriptive bullet points are greatly preferred. Remember to use those action phrases and action verbs!

9. Make sure your résumé is free of errors and is completely accurate. As with your cover letter, you should carefully proofread your résumé several times. You should also have at least one or two other people read your résumé to be sure it is understandable and free from errors. Your résumé should also be truthful. It is true that everyone is trying to make their résumés as appealing as possible (by all means, spin, spin, spin!) to potential employers, but the content of your résumé should be accurate. In today's day and age of résumé auditing and open information, you never know when a white lie on a résumé may cost you a job. If you don't think this can happen (and trust me, it does), check out the following link detailing the specifics of Mr. George O'Leary http://sportsillustrated.cnn.com/football/college/news/2001/12/14/oleary_notredame/

10. When you hold your résumé back at arm's length, it should appear to be centered on the page. In other words, all the margins and white space should be equal on all sides.

11. When you hold your résumé back at arm's length, what words or categories stand out to you? If it all looks the same and blends together, consider revising your format to make the most impressive or significant categories stand out on the page. Nothing dramatic here; play around using bold and italics and you should get a good result. Many employers spend as little as 30 seconds reviewing the résumé. In this short amount of time, they are not actually reading your document. They are scanning it and making a snap judgment about your fit with the position. Be sure you are giving them some distinguishing items (i.e., job titles, names of prominent organizations with which you have been associated, etc.) that will increase your odds of making it to the next round!

12. Whatever format you elect to use for your résumé, make sure that you use it consistently. Pay attention to the margins, indentations, and use of bold and italic text, and commas and periods. The pattern should repeat throughout the entire résumé. Attention to detail is critical.

13. When describing skills and duties you have in current positions, be sure to use the present tense. When describing skills and duties you had in previous positions you should use the past tense. When possible, you should avoid using pronouns and first person (i.e., instead of "I was responsible for tracking inventory," you should say, "Responsible for tracking inventory").

14. Pay attention to your answering machine and e-mail. For probably the first time in your life, you are going to have serious-minded professionals attempting to contact you by phone and e-mail. Make sure that the message

A Note from the Author

A few years ago, I called one of my students to discuss the content of this résumé. I was greeted by a 45-second answering machine message that consisted of music and lyrics by 50 Cent (some foul language included), some home-grown rapping, and a lot of laughing. While I am sure the message was fun to record (I admit it, I laughed), it is not the sort of image you want to project to potential employers. Your message should be short, clear, and professional.

You also want to be sure to check your e-mail inbox regularly. If you have multiple accounts (education and personal), be sure you are accessing all of them regularly. While students are typically better with electronic correspondence than professionals, certain times of year (summer, fall, and spring break) students are sometimes tempted to disengage. Unfortunately, these also happen to be prime periods for employers to contact students to make internship offers!

on your answering machine is clear, brief, and legible. Be sure that you respond to e-mails in a timely fashion.

15. What font are you using? Most of your peers will be building their résumé using Microsoft Word. The default font in this program is either Times New Roman, or Calibri, depending on what edition you have. While changing the font may seem like a trivial suggestion, it can have a big impact. Imagine staring at a large pile of résumés and going through them one by one. When you come across anything that is different (different paper, different font, unique format, etc.) you stop and pay a bit more attention. Without boring you with the detail of typography, serif fonts like Cambria, Garamond, Georgia, Lucida or Book Antiqua, are easier to read than serif-sans fonts like Arial, Helvetica or Verdana. Whatever font you use, you should use it for both the cover letter and résumé, and use of more than one font on any one document is strongly discouraged.

16. Font size is important. Many students are tempted to reduce their font size so they can squeeze more onto a page. You should never use a font size smaller than 10 point. Consider using slightly larger font sizes for the prominent categories on your résumé. This will help them stand out more.

17. There are rules about margins. I've seen a number of résumés that look crammed onto the page. Your margins should be no closer than .7" top, bottom, right, and left. Remember: Manage your white space to add to the visual appeal of your document.

18. Avoid using a "résumé wizard" or any pre-installed résumé template in your word-processing application. There are only two or three that are frequently used, and the end result is a résumé that blends in rather than stands out. Take your time and create a custom document. The flexibility and individuality it affords is well worth your investment. Pay attention to details.

19. Follow instructions carefully. If the employer asks for a hard copy of your résumé, take the time to print and mail one properly (see items 3-6 above). If asked for an electronic copy, send one as promptly as possible. If he or she does not specify that a cover letter is required, include one. If he or she says "no calls please," do not call!

20. Follow-up is critical. In today's economy, employers are receiving an extraordinarily high number of applications for each opening. Faith that an employer will review your application, much less get back to you to arrange an interview, is misplaced at best. Unless specifically directed not to, you should contact the hiring agency five to seven business days after you submit your application materials. You can simply indicate that you were calling/ writing, "…to be sure you had received my application, and to see if you had any questions for me?" Students are amazed at how frequently their application materials cannot be found. This might also be a good time to ask the employer when the interviewing process will begin. You will likely be applying to many organizations in the process of searching for your internship. You should keep detailed notes as to where you have applied, who your contact person was, the date you submitted your application, and the dates you should expect to hear back about an interview/offer.

At the end of this chapter are examples of résumés that have excellent formats and content. These examples are intended to be resources for you so you can see what should be included on a résumé and how it should be presented. You will notice that the ones that are especially pleasing to look at carefully use bold text, italics, bullet points, and even lines to enhance their aesthetic appeal. Avoid going overboard by adding too many lines or using different fonts. You want your résumé to be easy on the eye and quick to read. Inserting too many lines or changing font size and style too frequently slows the reading process and will frustrate the hiring manager. Feel free to use these résumés as a guideline, but experiment with ways to make your résumé uniquely yours. Remember, there is no single ideal résumé format. Look for creative but conservative ways to make your résumé stand out from the rest.

Summary

The cover letter and résumé are essential documents as you apply for internship opportunities. It is imperative that you invest a great deal of time in preparing these documents. When preparing your cover letter, be sure it is tailored   for each organization to which you are applying. You should indicate your fit with the position, why the organization is of particular interest to you, and highlight your intangible qualities. Build and promote your unique brand! Of equal importance is proofreading. Go back and review your work (numerous times) before you submit your materials. When preparing the résumé, be sure that you use a simple, but professional, format. Refer back to our tips on categories to include (or not) in this chapter frequently. Most importantly, never stop looking for ways to make your résumé stand out, within reason. Technology is greatly changing what people include in their application materials (links to blogs, Twitter accounts, or video résumés) and how they submit them. This chapter provides a good introduction to the fundamentals or cover letter and résumé design, but a serious job seeker will scour the internet looking for the next innovative, yet professional, way to present these materials to prospective employers!

Chapter 5 Essentials

- Cover letters should be brief but comprehensive enough to demonstrate you have spent time researching the organization and preparing the letter.

- Use your resources wisely. Contact faculty members, former students, or family friends who might be able to give you unique insight into the nature of the internship position. Demonstrating knowledge of upcoming events, past accomplishments, or current service offerings will let employers know you are serious about the position.

- Now is the time for your highest caliber work. Good enough is not good enough, especially in this sluggish economy. Review your work carefully and remember that spellcheck does not catch every common mistake.

- Be consistent in the format of both documents; pay attention to spacing, use of bold or italic fonts, and the white space surrounding your content. Demonstrate an exceptional attention to detail.
- Keep the résumé concise. Don't make employers weed through lines of text to find your most important accomplishments. Present the most important accomplishments first, and consider using bold or italic fonts to make the important matters stand out even more.

- Keep your eyes open! There are a number of emerging technologies that you may be able to use to your advantage when preparing these documents.

Discussion Questions

1. Think about the professional work experiences you have had in the past few years. What have you done? What have you learned? How can you communicate this using terms and phrases that will capture the attention of prospective employers?

2. It is sometimes difficult to begin writing the cover letter. In thinking about the type of internship you would like to obtain, what three skills or characteristics do you think are most important to have? How can you demonstrate your aptitude in these areas to prospective employers?

3. What is a "favorable" GPA? What different ways can you calculate your GPA that most favorably represent your level of ability?

4. Why are references so important, particularly for jobs in service sector positions?

Patience Is a Virtue

Scott is planning for a summer internship with major league baseball. Scott has a contact within one of the teams and is confident about his chances to secure an internship with this organization. In addition, he also has friends in the area to provide him with lodging during his internship.

Despite the contacts, Scott learns in the middle of the spring semester that the possible internship with the professional sports team has dissolved. His contact has left the organization, and the team has filled all of their summer internship openings. However, Scott's friends still remain in the metropolitan area, and he decides to explore other internship opportunities within the city.

Scott attempts to re-craft his cover letter and résumé and forwards it to several agencies within the city. Unfortunately, three weeks have passed since he sent his application materials out, and he has not received any responses from the agencies. Distraught, Scott has contacted his academic advisor for assistance.

Scott meets with his advisor and explains the situation and his interest in an internship near his friends' residence in the city. Scott's advisor provides him with a list of five agencies to consider. These agencies have alumni and well-established connections with Scott's department and might be able to help. Scott's advisor shares the contact information with him and suggests he get started making connections as soon as possible.

Scott contacts the five agencies and learns three of them still have openings. Later that day, Scott puts together his application materials and forwards them to the agencies.

Two days later, Scott's advisor receives a phone call from one of the agencies who had received Scott's application materials. The agency contact asks Scott's advisor, "Did you see his cover letter and résumé? I really want to help out, but I don't think I can bring Scott in for an interview with the quality of his résumé and cover letter. They are poorly written with several errors throughout both documents. I will e-mail you his cover letter and résumé for you to see for yourself. Do you know what happened here?"

- How could this situation been avoided? What strategies (and at what stages) could have Scott employed to avoid this problem?

- If you were Scott's academic advisor, would you share the feedback with him? What would be the advantages and/or disadvantages with sharing this feedback?

- Think about your environment. What resources (i.e., campus resources, faculty, friends, etc.) are available for you to utilize that can help you with the development of your application materials?

References

Crosby, O. (1999). Résumés, applications, and cover letters. *Occupational Outlook Quarterly, 43*(2), 13–17.

Crosby, O. (2009) Résumés, applications, and cover letters. *Occupational Outlook Quarterly, 53*(2), 18–29.

DeKay, S. (2006). Expressing emotion in electronic job cover letters. *Business Communication Quarterly, 69*(4), 435–439.

Gower, R. (2005). [Practitioner preferences for résumé and cover letter design]. Unpublished raw data.

Gower, R. (2010). [Practitioner preferences in résumés]. Unpublished raw data.

Hannan, J., & Shaw, N. (Dec 2010/Jan 2011). Lies, lies, lies—fraudsters: How to identify and deal with résumé fraud? *Human Resources Magazine, 15*(5), 4–6.

Honoman, C. (2009, May/June). Managing the electronic job search. *Healthcare Executive, 24*(3), 68–70.

Lovelace, H. (2001) Writing résumés and cover letters that work. Retrieved from http://www.informationweek.com/whitepaper/Business_and_Careers/wp902771?articleID=902771

Ross, C., & Young, S. (2005). Résumé preferences: Is it really "business as usual?" *Journal of Career Development, 32*(2), 153–164.

Shakoor, T. (2001). Developing a résumé and cover letter that work. *Black Collegian, 32*(1), 16–22.

Slowe, P., & Pastorius, T. (2010). A bit of philanthropy with your résumé? Retrieved from http://web.ebscohost.com/ehost/delivery?sid=7182f89a-1613-4498-9f12-9155958cbfd2%40sessionmgr111&vid=4&hid=123

Torrington, D., MacKay, L., & Hall, L. (1985). The changing nature of personnel management. *Employee Relations, 7*(5), 10–16.

Young, V. (2002). Seeking a faculty position. *Chemical & Engineering News, 80*(47), 60–63.

Sample Resumes

(Personal information has been changed for privacy purposes)

Lauren Anderson

551 Open Circle • Naperville, Illinois 60565 • Cell: 630-333-1000 • Home: 630-333-4000
E-mail: anderson@uiuc.edu

Education	*University of Illinois at Urbana-Champaign • December 2008* Bachelor of Science in Recreation, Sport and Tourism Emphasis in Sport Management
Experience	*Camp Counselor* **Illinois Sports Fitness Camp**: Urbana, Illinois Programmed and instructed daily activities for youth ages 6 to 14 to help facilitate each individual's enjoyment for physical fitness. Worked effectively and efficiently with participants, staff, and parents. **Summer 2004**
	Camp Counselor **Hinsdale Central Track & Field Camp:** Hinsdale, Illinois Supervised and taught children ages 6 to 14 the fundamental skills needed to compete in track and field. Assisted coaches with various skills and improved interpersonal skills with parents and children. **Summer 2001, Summer 2002**
	Volunteer Coach **Chicago and Suburban Area Track Club**: Hinsdale, Illinois Coached and mentored young adults ages 12 to 18 to help motivate and improve their performances. Assisted coaches during practices and track meets while improving leadership skills. **Summer 2002**
Activities and Honors	*Chicago and Suburban Area Track Club* • Two time All-American in the Heptathlon • All-American in the Long Jump and the 100 Meter Hurdles *College* • Scholarship athlete on the University of Illinois Women's Track & Field team • Beginning Freshman year, competed in Indoor and Outdoor Big Ten Championship Track & Field meets for University of Illinois • 2003 earned All Big Ten in the Heptathlon • 2003 and 2005 George Huff Award Winner for accomplishing varsity award status while maintaining 2 consecutive semesters with a 3.0 GPA and above • 2004 – 2005 Women's Track & Field Varsity I Award • Member of 2005 Outdoor Women's Big Ten Conference Champion Team • 2005 Big Ten Conference Scholar-Athlete Award
References	Available upon request

Keren E. Lockwise

103 E. Anthony Drive. Champaign, IL 61820. 847-333-1000. klockwise@uiuc.edu

Career Objective

To obtain an internship in the field of Sport Management with a long-term goal of becoming experienced in the area of sport marketing and public relations.

Education

University of Illinois at Urbana-Champaign
Bachelor of Science in Recreation, Sport and Tourism: Sports Management (expected August, 2008)
College of Applied Health Sciences
GPA: 3.70/4.00
Related coursework:
- Administration
- Facility Management
- Human Resource Management
- Marketing
- Advertising

Work Experience

The Chicago Blackhawks, Public Relations/Communications Intern   **Summer 2007**
- Researched and updated 50 player and prospect profiles for the 2004-05 Media Guide
- Administered and organized donation requests
- Responded to fan mail
- Gathered and preserved media coverage
- Maintained records of funding recipients
- Executed clerical duties

University of Illinois at Urbana-Champaign, Resident Advisor   **August 2004 - Present**
- Founded and currently supervise a student leadership programming organization
- Coordinate and advise student leader and volunteer groups, approximately 15 members
- Prepare and present weekly meetings
- Enforce University Housing policies
- Program floor and hall-wide educational, academic, social, and multicultural activities and events
- Excel in teamwork and leadership skills

University of Illinois Athletics, Concessions Supervisor   **May 2003 - Present**
- Oversee concession stand operations
- Maintain product inventory
- Responsible for reconciliation of cash revenues

Trevian Girls Softball Association, Softball Coach   **Summer 2002 - 2004**
- Organized seasonal practice, game, and tournament schedules
- Administered team and individual practices
- Scouted opposing teams
- Supervised off-season batting practices
- Coordinated team budget

Keren E. Lockwise, 2

Related Experience

Volunteer Work
- Volunteer Board Coordinator for University Residence Halls (2004-2005)
- Relay for Life team captain and coordinator (April 2005)
- Coordinated fundraising for Medical Miracle Makers, tallying over $400 (December 2004)
- Raised over $200 for the University of Illinois Library Fund (November 2004)
- Volunteer at the Dave Duerson Foundation annual golf outing (May 2004)
- Volunteer video recorder for a Lou Gehrig's Disease Fundraiser, raising over $7,000 (April 2004)
- Job shadowed Mark Giangreco, ABC's Sports Director/News Anchor (March 2004)
- Registration Volunteer for University of Illinois Football Family Fest (March 2004)
- Adopt-A-Family coordinator (December 2003)
- Organized and promoted campaign to raise money to support The American Red Cross (April 2003)
- Discovery cart volunteer for outpatient children at Children's Memorial Hospital (Summer 2003)
- Constructed homes for underprivileged Mexican Families (May 2002)

Skills Summary

- Team motivation
- Planning and conducting formal meetings
- Microsoft Word, Excel, PowerPoint and Access
- Budgeting
- Program planning
- Goldmine 6.0 Corporate Edition

Honors and Activities

University of Illinois Honors Student - James Scholar program (2003; 2004)
University of Illinois Dean's List (Spring 2003, Fall 2003)
Member of the National Dean's List
Certified Illinois Ethics Employee
Member, American Marketing Association
Nominated for National Colligate Scholar
Resident Advisor of The Year (2003-2004)
Resident Advising Staff of the year (2002-2003)
Nominated/Runner-up for Resident Advisor of the Year (2002-2003)
Leadership Conferences:
- Illinois Insight Leadership Conference (February 2003)
- Illinois Imprint Leadership Conference (February 2004)
Illinois General Assembly Community Service Scholarship (2002-2003; 2003-2004)
Intramural Team Captain: Flag Football, Basketball, and Softball (2003-2005)
University of Illinois Varsity Softball Team (2001-2002)

References

Jane Doe	John Smith	Michael Carter
Director of Community Relations	Investment Broker	Resident Director, Hopkins Hall
Chicago Blackhawks	Chicago Board of Trade	University Housing
Chicago, Illinois 60612	Northfield, Illinois 60093	Champaign, IL 61822
312-555-1234	312-555-5678	217-555-0123
jdoe@chicagoblackhawks.com	jsmith@hotmail.com	mcarter@uiuc.edu

Christine M. Grant

27720 S. Kedzie Avenue, Momence, IL 60449
W: (773) 333-1000 C: (708) 333-4000
cmgrant@yahoo.com

Qualifications	*Innovative leader and motivator possessing solid business and work ethics. Works well independently or as a member of a team. Experienced in marketing, promotions, and community relations. Strong written, verbal and interpersonal communication skills.*
Education	**University of Illinois at Urbana-Champaign** College of Applied Health Sciences Bachelor of Science in Recreation, Sport and Tourism, Expected August 2005 Specialization in Sport Management *Grade Point Average: 3.52 /4.0*

Work Experience

Summer 2005 to the present   Chicago Rush Arena Football   Chicago, IL
Corporate Sales Intern
- Researching various partnership leads and collecting strategic information on organizations.
- Contacting and communicating with current and potential partners.
- Developing communication and negotiation skills through the creation of partnership proposals.
- Compiling sponsorship fulfillment books.
- Assisting with special events focused on hospitality toward partners.
- Participating in multiple projects with the community relations, marketing and ticket departments.
- Handling and maintaining confidential partnership contracts.

2003-2005   University of Illinois   Champaign, IL
Peabody Area Office Desk Clerk
- Managed clerical duties - answered phones, filed and maintained documents.
- Provided customer service to students.
- Handled and maintained confidential student information.
- Representative of the University - guided tours in resident halls for perspective students.
- Assisted with the hiring and training of new staff.

Summer 2003   New York and Company   Champaign, IL
Sales Associate
- Handled cash and maintained register sales.
- Provided sales assistance to customers and promoted credit card enrollment.
- Maintained displays and signage in accordance with company standards.
- Monitored merchandise for loss prevention.

Summer 2003   Champaign Park District   Champaign, IL
Student Intern
- Helped market and promote special events for the park district.
- Compiled Taste of Champaign summary for media and event sponsors.
- Led promotions/pre-event marketing for the 22nd annual Mini-Triathlon.
- Contacted and communicated with sponsors for various events.

Christine M. Grant, 2

Work Experience
(continued)

Fall 2002   Walt Disney World Corporation   Lake Buena Vista, FL
College Program Intern – Magic Kingdom
- Developed customer service skills and utilized interpersonal skills.
- Given exposure to a highly diverse workforce.
- Gained an understanding of Disney business philosophies and operations.

2000-2002   Rainbow Farms Enterprises   Monee, IL
Office Assistant
- Assistant to Marketing Director - assisted with marketing kits and promotions.
- Responsible for both accounts receivable and accounts payable.
- Interacted with customers on a regular basis and provided sales support.
- General clerical duties- answering phones, filing and sales data entry.

Activities

Student Alumni Ambassadors
- Volunteered at various events on campus for students and faculty sponsored by the Alumni Association and the University of Illinois.
- Escorted visiting alumni throughout campus.
- Promoted activities of organization and guided Alumni relations.

Student Workshop 2005
- Workshop provided by University of Illinois Recreation Sports and Tourism Department and Alumni.
- Discussed current trends in the leisure field.

Champaign Park District Nite Lite Egg Pursuit
- Planned and implemented 2004 Nite Lite Egg Pursuit for adult Champaign residents.
- Obtained donations from community businesses for prizes.
- Conducted event surveys and wrote event summary.

Student Alumni Association
- Responsible for public image of University through programming and activities.
- Responsible for promoting planned activities and programs to students and community.
- Worked on the public relations and outreach committee for Homecoming.

Awards/Scholarships

- Dean's List- Fall 2004, Spring 2005
- Illuminators Memorial Scholarship Award, 2004-2005.
- Peabody Area Office Inaugural "Desk Clerk of the Month" for October 2004.
- Champaign Park District "Volunteer of the Month" for November 2003.
- First United Bank Four-Year Leadership Scholarship, 2001-2005.

References

Mike Jones	Susan King	Joe Phillips
Vice President Sales	Director of Marketing	Store Manager
Chicago Rush Football	Champaign Park District	New York and Company
4915 Allison Dr.	706 Kenwood Ave.	2000 N. Neil St.
Chicago, IL 60631	Champaign, IL 61822	Champaign, IL 61820
312-555-4321	217-555-0000	217-555-6421

Chapter 6

Navigating the
Interview Process

Overview

The prospect of being interviewed for an internship position is frequently reported as one of the highest sources of stress for undergraduate students. While you may have interviewed for part-time or seasonal employment in the past, the process may seem very different when you realize that you are now seeking to secure a position from which to launch your professional career. Feelings of self-doubt, inadequacy, and anxiety are normal, but as you will soon discover, interviewing does not need to be such a taxing experience. This chapter will explore the types of interviews you are likely to encounter and outline strategies for how you might approach them. Perhaps most important, this chapter should help you realize that interviews are a process in which you are an equal partner. Not only are interviews an opportunity for employers to assess your skills and qualifications, they are also an opportunity for you to assess the organization, your potential coworkers, and ultimately for you to determine whether the position is a fit for your aspirations.

Before you begin, you should know that preparing for an interview is a time-consuming process that will require a great deal of self-knowledge and a solid understanding of the prospective agency. And as you are putting in the long hours to prepare for the interview, one of the most important facts for you to remember is that out of all the applications the organization received, you were one of the few to be selected for an interview. Feel good about that. They are impressed with some aspect of your background and see a potential fit for the position, or they would not invest their time and resources in bringing you in to interview. They see something they like; it is now up to you to stand out from the competition and to secure an internship offer. While you should become very familiar with the organization, its programs, its staff, and its facilities, it is equally important for you to know what tangible and intangible attributes you offer and how you could contribute to their mission. If you have not done so already, go back and read Chapter 3, Completing the Individual Assessment.

It is important to remember that an interview goes two ways. Too often, students think of an interview as something that is *done to them*. To the contrary, an interview is a process in which you should be an active participant. You should be evaluating the staff you meet, the quality of the facilities, and the overall work environment to determine if you are truly interested in accepting a position there. You should develop a strategy for how you will elicit this information in the interview and prepare questions that will help you make an informed decision. You should actively reflect on your personal and professional goals to determine the likelihood of this opportunity helping you to achieve them. Entering into the interview with this mindset is of utmost importance. Research has shown that managers prefer candidates who are active participants in an interview; so by all means, ask questions and make observations (Marks & O'Connor, 2006). This is much more appealing than the candidate who sits meekly and provides concise and generic answers to questions as they are asked.

And finally, remember that these people don't know you. They don't know that you used to eat paste in grade school or that you struggled to pass macroeconomics in college. You have the unique opportunity to reinvent yourself. The only thing that they will know about you is what you choose to reveal. There is a certain amount of role-playing in any interview. This is your opportunity to play the part of the promising young professional we are convinced you will become. Be confident in your abilities, honest in your responses, and aware of the job responsibilities, and you will impress the interviewers.

The Interview Experience

While going into the interview with the right mindset is very important, having a more comprehensive understanding of the interview process will help you feel more confident in your performance. A basic understanding of the types of interviews you might encounter and the questions you will likely be asked will greatly assist you as you prepare.

There are a number of different approaches to interviewing, and the diversity of the leisure service industry makes it challenging to predict which approach your prospective employer might adopt. Nevertheless, there are three common interview formats that students in this field should prepare for: the structured interview, the unstructured interview, and the behavioral interview. A basic understanding of these interview formats will help you frame realistic expectations for what you might encounter, better prepare for the interview, and ultimately deliver a stronger performance.

The Structured Interview

As the name implies, a structured interview is a very formal and sometimes impersonal experience. Organizations who utilize structured interviews ask each job candidate the same questions in the same order (Kvale & Brinkman, 2009). There are two reasons why organizations may elect to use a structured interview. First, structured interviews ensure that each candidate is given equal treatment and that no unfair advantage is given to one candidate above another. Managers are frequently drawn to hire individuals with similar personalities, and structured interviews are one way that organizations can minimize discriminatory bias in the hiring process (Mathis & Jackson, 2007). Structured interviews also allow the organization to more effectively compare the responses of the job candidates to determine who has given the most comprehensive answer and who would most likely be a good fit for the position.

Since each candidate is given the same questions in the same order, it is common for students to report feeling very uncomfortable in structured interviews. Students frequently use descriptors such as "cold," "mechanical," and "impersonal" to describe their experience in this type of an interview. As a result, students often leave the interview feeling as if they were not able to make a connection with the interviewers or that they were unable to convey the significance of their individual accomplishments in relation to the job requirements. In short, they feel as if the interview did not go well. Rather than being dejected about your performance, you should recognize that such interviews are employed specifically to eliminate such intervening biases. Having concise and personalized responses developed in advance for questions you are likely to be asked is essential if you are to set yourself apart from the rest of the candidate pool.

The Unstructured Interview

Unlike organizations that perform structured interviews, organizations that use unstructured interviews have significant latitude in the manner in which they will conduct the interview. There may or may not be definite questions to be asked, and the interviewers are free to change their questions to follow up on points of interest and to ask questions that allow them to gain a better understanding of your unique personality and skill set. Employers in the service industry tend to favor unstructured interviews as they allow for a more natural conversation to emerge, afford an opportunity to gauge your ability to interact with others (including future clientele), and provide more latitude in collecting more personalized information about each candidate. However, such interviews can be time consuming and may make it more difficult for employers to reliably compare the quality of the candidates' responses.

Student experiences in unstructured interviews are frequently more positive as they often leave the interview having been asked personalized questions that gave them the opportunity to connect and build rapport with the interviewers. In fact, some students have reported leaving the interview feeling as if they weren't really "interviewed" at all.

Regardless of whether you find yourself in a structured or unstructured interview format, it is imperative to remember that the interview begins the moment you walk through the door of the hiring agency. By their nature, unstructured interviews create a natural and welcoming environment, and students frequently let down their guard and don't realize that the interviewer is actually paying careful attention to what appears to be just a "casual exchange between colleagues." They are looking for any indication of what type of a team member you will be by examining how you speak about your previous employers, co-workers, or university professors. All of this seemingly nondirective dialogue gives them a very good sense of how you will represent the organization to its constituents. Remember to always be loyal to those who are not present and be positive in your responses.

> **"I REMEMBER LOOKING AT THE CLOCK** on the wall and realizing I had already been there for half an hour. I kept waiting for the interview to begin, but we kept talking about sports, my university, my teachers, and my aspirations for the future. Never once did they ask me about 'my biggest weaknesses, or 'why am I more qualified than the other candidates' or any of the other questions I'd prepared for. They walked me around the facility, introduced me to the staff, and sent me home. It really felt like a casual exchange between colleagues, and not like an interview."

The Behavioral Interview

Behavioral interviews are becoming more common in the leisure service industry as employers are looking for more reliable ways to predict the quality of your job performance should they hire you. Like the unstructured interview, a behavioral interview will allow you to give very personalized responses to interviewer questions. In this interview format, the interviewers will either give you a scenario and ask you to provide them with a solution, or they will ask you to reflect on a previous work experience and to relate how you handled it or what you learned from the experience (Latham, Saari, Pursell, & Campion, 1980). Employers are hoping that they will be able to predict your future performance with them based upon your handling of previous work situations.

Is Honesty Always the Best Policy?

Many students fail to recognize that their responses might be perceived as having a negative tone by the interviewer. Consider the following scenario:

Interviewer: Can you tell me why you are not reapplying for an internship with the organization you worked with last summer?

Student Response #1: *Well, the organizational structure there just wasn't a good fit for me. I had two supervisors and would frequently be given conflicting assignments. They couldn't seem to agree on what they wanted me to do, and I found that very frustrating. And also, it is such a large business that I wasn't sure that people would notice my efforts, and I really want to be in an organization where I can contribute effectively.*

While that response may seem honest and not overtly negative, compare it to this more favorable response:

Student Response #2: *"I really learned a great deal from my experiences last summer. I picked up some good professional experience and learned quite a bit about the type of environment in which I am most productive. I'd like to have the opportunity to learn from different managers and explore different business models. I am looking for new challenges, and from what I have seen so far, really feel as if your organization could provide these for me."*

In the second response, the student was able to give an honest response without casting a negative light on his/her previous employer. The student also conveyed his/her desire to learn, grow, and excel as a professional and emphasized his/her fit with the potential internship site. Everyone finds elements of his/her job dissatisfying. The key is to emphasize what you are looking for or could provide without dwelling on the negative details. The network of professionals in the recreation, sport, and tourism industries is quite small. You never know how someone might be connected to your previous employer, and gossip can quickly spread through the grapevine if you are not careful.

Behavioral interviews are often challenging for students and young professionals. This interview format requires the interviewee to reflect on previous experiences and to draw on that knowledge to demonstrate his/her ability to perform necessary job functions. As a college student, your professional experience is likely limited to two or three part-time or seasonal jobs, and you may struggle to make connections with the provided situations. Employers know this, and for entry-level positions behavioral interview questions are likely to be very straightforward. Possible examples include the following:

- "Tell me about the most successful project you have worked on. What did you do to make it successful?"

- "Give me an example of how you have dealt with conflict in the workplace in the past."

- "Tell me about an experience you had with an unhappy customer and how you handled the situation."

- "Tell me about a situation where you tried very hard and utterly failed. What did you learn?"

> **"IT WAS THE MOST HORRIFIC EXPERIENCE** of my life. When they asked me the question I could not think of a single thing to say, but that didn't stop me from talking. I just kept talking and talking and didn't even know what I was talking about! I wish I would have just told them I'd never been in that type of a situation before and moved on to the next question...UGH!"

It is very important in this type of an interview to take your time and give thoughtful responses. Students often dread the awkward silence that can come after a question is posed in an interview. Remember that it is preferable to pause for a few moments to collect your thoughts than to begin rambling about the first topic that comes to mind only to realize a few moments later that you cannot make the connection. If you are asked a behavioral question to which you cannot immediately think of a good response, it is perfectly acceptable to ask if you can come back to the question after you have had more time to think about it. Remember, in a behavioral interview they are looking for how you are likely to respond to a situation. Responding by calmly asking for more time or to move on to another question for the time being is more desirable than frantically stammering over your words trying to draft a coherent reply.

Stages of the Interview

Despite the fact that most interviews will follow one of the three formats listed above, every interview experience is different. Some interviews are one-on-one conversations, others involve large groups of people, and some interviews for internships even happen over the phone. While it is impossible to fully know what to expect going into an interview, most interviews will go through the same stages from beginning to end.

Rapport Building

The first stage of the interview is often called "rapport building." In this stage of the interview, the employers will generally attempt to make small talk to help you feel more at ease. This may be done as you are walking together to the room where the interview will take place or may occur as you sit around the table before the interview begins. Typical topics of conversation include school, sports, traffic, and even the weather. Even in structured interviews, there is usually a brief moment of time where the interviewers will seek to find a common thread or build a rapport with you. As was mentioned previously, remember that the interview begins the moment you walk in the door and that first impressions are critical. Be sure to project a positive, outgoing, loyal, and confident self-image. The rapport building stage is an important part of the interview. Some studies have suggested that employers have made their mind up about the candidate in the first two minutes of the interview (Swider, Barrick, Harris, & Stoverink, 2011). The employer will generally use this stage to slowly transition into the second stage of the interview—exploration.

Exploration

During this stage of the interview, the employer will begin asking you questions related to the internship position. The questions they ask will likely be geared toward your educational and professional preparation and experience and your professional goals and aspirations. This is the stage of the interview students fear the most. If you have done your homework on the organization and have prepared answers to potential interview questions (see the next section), you should have no difficulty with this portion of the interview. Most interviews for internships last 20 to 30 minutes; the exploration stage usually accounts for most of this time. Remember to keep your answers clear and concise, never speaking for more than one minute at a time.

Closing

The final stage of the interview is the closing. During this portion of the interview, the employer will seek to answer any questions you might have about the organization or the internship. You are strongly encouraged to make a list of questions prior to arriving for your interview. Often the answers to your questions may have been addressed during the exploration stage of the interview. You are encouraged to ask the employer questions, but it is better to ask no questions than to ask questions that are contrived or forced. One of the most important questions you can ask is about next steps in the employment process and when you can expect to hear back from them. It is imperative to have a firm understanding of their timeline for hiring so you can make educated decisions about scheduling other interviews and accepting internship offers. Be sure to thank them for taking the time to interview you and emphasize your renewed interest in working with them. It is generally not a good idea to ask about compensation at this stage of the interview.

Making Informed Decisions

As a student who is seeking to secure an internship for college credit, you are likely applying for and interviewing with a number of potential internship sites. One of the most important pieces of information for you to collect during the interview is the timeline for hiring decisions to be made. Consider the following scenario:

Damien has always wanted to be involved in the administration of professional sport. He has spent the last two summers gaining valuable experience and building a solid résumé. He has had what he considers to be three successful interviews: one with the St. Louis Cardinals, one with the Memphis Redbirds, and one with the Kane County Cougars. He is immediately drawn to the Cardinals internship as they are a MLB team, and the potential for advancement in the organization seems good. The Memphis Redbirds are one of the most successful Triple-A teams, have an amazing stadium, and are affiliated with the Cardinals. The Cougars are a successful Class A team with a recently renovated stadium. He has heard wonderful things about the internship opportunities at all three organizations from his internship coordinator and previous interns, but is convinced that the St. Louis Cardinals would best fit his interests and aspirations. Today he received a call from the Memphis Redbirds and has been offered an internship in Events and Promotions. They need a firm commitment from him in the next three to five business days. While Damien is thrilled to have the offer, he can't help but think about the internship with the Cardinals. Damien wonders what he should do? He would hate to accept the internship and later be offered a position with the Cardinals that he can't take. Conversely, it seems foolish to pass up an excellent internship opportunity when he has no idea if or when he will get an offer from the Cardinals.

If Damien knew that the Cardinals would not conclude their interview and selection process for another two weeks, he would know that he is going to have to make a very tough decision about his internship placement. Having all the information you need is necessary to make sound and ethical decisions about your internship placement.

Learning Opportunity

Ask your school's internship coordinator what you should do if you find yourself in a similar situation.

1. Should you accept the position with the Redbirds for the time being, hoping that the Cardinals will contact you later?

2. Should you ask the Redbirds for a few more days/weeks to make your decision?

3. Should you call your contact at the Cardinals and let them know about the offer from Memphis and ask them to expedite their response to you?

Preparing for the Interview

Researching the Organization

Prior to applying for an internship with an organization, you probably spent at least a little time researching the organization to determine if they are the type of organization with which you would like to intern. While this research was likely very general (what type of company are they, where are they located, what type of position are they offering, do they pay interns, etc.), the research you should conduct prior to the interview should be much more detailed. There are a minimum of three things you should research prior to the interview: *the departments and programs, the staff,* and *the physical location of the organization.*

Departments and programs. While we are certainly not advocating memorizing the departmental organizational chart, you should familiarize yourself with the different departments and their primary functions within the organization. Being familiar with the different departments and their functions will allow you to ask intelligent questions and contribute to the flow of the interview.

This information is usually available on the organizational website. When you know what the organization does, you are better able to demonstrate your potential fit with their operations and better equipped to communicate what you hope to learn while you are interning.

Which Candidate Would You Hire?

Interviewer: If you were to be selected to intern with us, what is something you would really like to do or learn more about?

Candidate #1: *I've always been interested in youth programming. I have had some experience running summer camps with previous employers and really enjoy creating fun and educational experiences for children. I know that I would like to be involved with your youth recreation programs.*

or

Candidate #2: *That is a great question. I've had the opportunity to review your program guide, and I am really interested in the Teen Dance and Band Night programs you offer. I have always been very interested in youth programming, and have enjoyed working with this population in my previous positions. I understand that these two programs are run with the cooperation of the Mayor's Office and would be really interested to see how two governmental units cooperate to build better communities. To me, that is what this profession is all about. So, I know I would like to have the opportunity to work with Dan Johnson in your youth programming efforts, but I am also interested in exploring other opportunities you may have for me.*

Both candidates gave solid answers, and both indicated that they had previous experience working with youth programming. However, Candidate #2 did several things that Candidate #1 did not do:

- provided specific programs in which he was particularly interested in working with and why he was interested in working with them;

- gave some insight on his professional philosophy by indicating that he understood the profession was about building healthy communities;

- demonstrated a more complete understanding of the programming efforts and supporting external constituents; and

- dropped the name of the staff member responsible for the programs, thereby demonstrating their strong interest in the organization and a higher level of preparedness.

The staff. I also recommend that students use the organizational website to find information about the staff. While this is not always practical or possible (some organizations are simply too big, and some do not make this information public), it can have a dramatic impact on the interview process. Many organizations maintain a list of staff that includes a picture, their job title, and sometimes even a brief biography. I remember a time when I was a member of a search committee and the candidate came into the room and knew the names and faces of everyone in the room. She was also able to make casual conversation about our professional or educational achievements. When a name was mentioned, she was able to say, "Oh, he is the public relations director, right?" It was apparent that she had done her homework. As a result, she came to the interview relaxed and confident. All the members of the search committee were impressed, and she was offered the job that day.

Physical location. Familiarizing yourself with the physical location of the organization is extremely important. It is absolutely unacceptable to arrive late for an interview. Most students are comfortable using websites such as MapQuest to find driving directions, but there is much more to it than that. Many leisure services organizations are located in congested urban areas and traffic and parking may be an issue. If you are not very familiar with the neighborhood in which the organization is located, when possible, you are strongly encouraged to make a practice trip in advance of the interview. When this is not practical, you are advised to ask for detailed directions when scheduling the interview.

Aside from the Internet, there are two other acceptable ways to get the logistical information you need about the physical location of the interview. You can either ask at the time you are offered the interview, or you can call a few days prior to the interview date (often called a confirmation call). It is perfectly acceptable to call to confirm the specifics of the interview (date, time, location) and simultaneously gather information about transportation and parking details. While students usually make mistakes regarding interview times, practitioners have made them also. We have had students who have traveled long distances only to be told that the person they were to interview with was "in a meeting," "home sick," or was not aware that they had a meeting scheduled. This is very frustrating to say the least.

"**I WAS ABSOLUTELY ECSTATIC** to be interviewing with an organization in downtown Chicago. As a central Illinois native, I'd always known that I wanted to move to the city to begin my career. I'd been downtown several times, but wasn't overly familiar with the area that the organization was located in. Still, I was careful to print driving directions from the Internet and bring them with me in the car. Unfortunately, that summer [Interstate] 294 was under major reconstruction efforts. I sat in traffic for what seemed like hours and didn't know how to get off the interstate or another route to take me to the organization even if I could. I called to let them know that I was running behind due to traffic. When I arrived 45 minutes late for the interview I was told I would need to reschedule. I called back several times, but they never ended up rescheduling with me."

Prepare and Practice

Practicing for an interview is a very valuable exercise. Many colleges and universities offer mock interview experiences through their career service center. Even though these interviews are not the same as the authentic experience, most students still report feeling nervous before and during the mock interview exercise. Students are encouraged to continue practicing and refining interview skills through the use of mock interviews. If you prefer to practice at home with friends, simply provide them with a copy of the job description and your résumé and ask them to develop some likely interview questions. Videotaping your interview gives you a unique third-party perspective. Students are usually amazed at all the nervous gestures (i.e., rocking in their chair, tapping their fingers, not making direct eye contact, using phrases such as "um," "yeah," or "like" in every sentence) that they exhibit when they review their experience. Taking a video allows you to go back and scrutinize your performance, draft better responses, and refine verbal and nonverbal communication.

While there is no complete list of questions that you might be asked during your interview, most employers will seek similar information and use similar questions to obtain it. Answering the questions and writing your responses in Figure 6.1 should help you think through some of these issues in advance of your internship. Take a moment to write your responses to the questions, and keep them on hand to review them prior to each interview. You should not attempt to memorize your responses, but instead should just answer questions naturally during the interview. Trying to regurgitate memorized responses will seem inauthentic and mechanical. Not to mention the fact that you would likely forget most of what you wanted to say and thereby add stress to your experience. The purpose of this exercise is not to provide you with scripted responses, but instead to raise your awareness to the types of questions you are likely to encounter and to give you a starting point for your response in the interview.

- What are your long-term goals, and how do you see this internship facilitating the attainment of those goals?

- How did you decide to join the (recreation, sport, or tourism) profession?

- Why did you choose your college major?

- What things have you learned in school that will help you as a student intern?

- What are your greatest strengths and weaknesses?

- How would one of your professors or references describe you?

- How do you deal with stressful situations? Can you give me an example?

- What aspects of our organization appealed to you when you were applying for internships?

- Describe a major mistake/problem you have encountered and what you learned from it?

- What do you know about our organization?

- What characteristics or skills do you have that make you a better candidate than other students I have interviewed?

- What qualities do you think a good intern should demonstrate?

- What does success mean to you?

- What type of management/leadership style do you feel most comfortable working with?

- Tell me what you are doing to stay abreast of industry trends.

- Money or happiness?

- What experience have you had working in groups or as part of a team?

- What motivates you?

- What job/experience have you had that was the most rewarding to you? Why?

- What software applications have you used?

- What concerns do you have about your internship?

- What are your organizational skills like? Can you give me examples?

- Do you prefer to work in groups or alone?

- Tell me about yourself.

- Where do you see yourself in five years? (hint, do not say "doing your job")

- Do you have any ideas on programs or projects you would really like to be involved with?

- What extracurricular activities were you involved in?

- Are you willing to work longer hours and nights and weekends?

- What are you looking for in a supervisor?

- Do you have experience working with people from diverse backgrounds?

- What are your salary expectations?

Figure 6.1. Sample Interview Questions

Developing answers to these questions and reviewing them prior to the interview will help you relax, as you know you are ready to answer virtually any question they might ask. Did you forget to include something in one of your responses? Relax. You are likely the only one who realizes it.

Helpful Hints for Interviewing

"Of all the things you wear, your expression is the most important."
—Janet Lane

"Fashion can be bought. Style one must possess."
—Edna Woolman Chase

As mentioned in previous sections, the importance of first impressions cannot be overstated. Along with making a good first impression, there are many others helpful hints to consider.

- Pay attention to your grooming and attire. It is imperative that you are neat, clean, and appropriately dressed for an interview. For men, this means wearing a suit and tie, for women a suit jacket and slacks or a skirt. You should select clothing that is traditional in color and fit. Bright colors or attire that might be overly revealing should be avoided.

  You should dress professionally, even when you know that the interviewers are likely to be dressed very casually. In leisure service organizations, employees often go to work in very informal attire, and students worry about feeling overdressed. Remember, those who work there already have a job. By dressing professionally, you are sending them the message that you are taking this interview seriously and are sincere in your interest in gaining an internship with them. It is always better to overdress for an interview than to underdress.

- Avoid things that might distract from the interview. The first thing that comes to mind is odor. Nobody wants to be the "stinky intern." Believe it or not, I have heard employers complain about a candidate/intern's breath, body odor, and even their choice in antiperspirant. Perfume and cologne are also to be avoided on an interview. Cleanliness is enough. If you are a smoker, you should not smoke in the clothes you will be wearing to the interview; nonsmokers often find the odor very offensive. Avoid spicy or heavily scented food prior to (even the day before) the interview. I am fully aware that many of these suggestions sound a bit ridiculous, but experience has proven that employers do notice and care about these things.

- Pay attention to your nonverbal communication. Sit up straight and don't fidget or squirm. Find a comfortable position and hold it for several minutes before repositioning. As already indicated, mock interviews should highlight any bad habits you have which you might not be aware of.

    Be sure to make good eye contact at all times. This sends a signal that you are confident and listening to what the interviewer is saying. Glancing down to take notes from time to time is acceptable. Lean in as the interviewer is making an important point about the position. This demonstrates that you are genuinely interested in what they are saying.

- Demonstrate a firm handshake. It has been and still is a universal truth in interviewing. It is one of the elements of the first impression that you cannot take back. Remember, firm does not mean overbearing. If you have sweaty palms, try to discretely wipe them off in the seconds before the handshake will occur.

- Be sure to project your voice well.

- Answer all questions completely, but make sure to avoid lengthy replies. Your answer should usually take less than 1 minute, less if you are completing a phone interview.

- Be early. Make every effort to arrive 10 to 15 minutes early for your interview. Use the extra time to review materials you have put together, stop by the restroom, and check your appearance. You should check in with the secretary just a few minutes before the interview is scheduled.

- Be human. It is perfectly normal to be nervous or to struggle to find an answer to a question. If you find yourself in an awkward moment, smile, take a long pause (it may seem like forever, but it will only be a few moments) and move forward. If you don't have a good answer to give, it is fine to admit that, but profess your willingness to learn.

Common Courtesies

There are two common courtesies that you should always display in the interview process. We have already discussed the first and most important courtesy you should display—timeliness. You should never arrive late to an interview. This is a waste of the interviewer's time, not to mention the fact that it is almost guaranteed to exclude you from further consideration. Second, you should always show up for scheduled interviews. After scheduling the interview, you may change your mind about the organization for a variety of different reasons: you may have received a better offer, decided it is too far away, learned that they do not pay interns, and so forth. If this is the case, you should make every effort to cancel the interview no less than 48 business hours (leaving a message over the weekend about a Monday interview does not count!) in advance. When cancelling an interview, you should thank them for the invitation and give them a brief, but nondescriptive reason for why you will be unable to attend (i.e., I have secured an offer with another organization that I am planning to accept). You should never "no-show" an interview. It reflects poorly on you and your educational institution. If you cannot cancel in this time frame, you should plan to attend the interview and use it as a good learning experience and as a networking opportunity.

Thank-you Letter

Once you have completed the interview, you should always send a handwritten thank-you note. These notes do not need to be formal or lengthy; generally, four to five sentences are sufficient. Your thank-you letter should

- thank them for taking the time to interview you,

- specify something about the interview/organization that particularly interested you, and

- remind them that you are looking forward to hearing from them about the position.

Although it is common business practice for these thank-you letters to be handwritten, it is better to send a typed note than one with illegible writing or misspelled words. Remember to make sure that your name is clearly legible on the note. See Figure 6.2 for a sample thank-you letter.

Dear Ms. Edwards:

I would like to thank you for the opportunity to interview with the Mayor's Office of Special Events. I left the interview with a renewed interest in securing a fall internship. I found your description of the Thanksgiving Day Parade to be very motivating, and I am confident that my previous experiences with McCormick's Place have equipped me to take on such an exciting challenge. Thank you again for meeting with me, and I look forward to hearing back from you in the near future!

Quinn Holderfield
Central Illinois University
holderfield@ciu.edu

Figure 6.2. Sample Thank-you Letter

Summary

Going into the interview with the correct mindset is essential. There are two important things for you to remember. First, remember that you were selected, likely out of a fairly large pool, to be brought into the organization for this interview. While some organizations may interview every intern that applies, most do not. Something about your credentials impressed them, and that alone should improve your confidence. Second, remember that an interview is a screening process that goes both ways. While you are interviewing, pay attention to the workspace (i.e., the physical accommodations and the overall climate). Is it an atmosphere in which you would feel comfortable? Keep your short- and long-term professional goals in mind. Will this agency really be able to help you achieve them? Keep in mind that there is no perfect internship and that compromise will be necessary. Think about your immediate short- and long-term goals, and be certain that the agency can help you achieve them. While there are a number of interview types that you might experience, there is one thing that will help you excel regardless of which format you encounter—preparation. You should spend several hours researching the organization, its staff, its current service offerings, and the competition, and looking for any recent headlines in local news before you arrive on site. Don't forget to be sure you confirm the date, time, and location a few days before the interview actually takes place. And finally, the best piece of advice we can give you as we close out the chapter—relax. Once you have done your preparation, don't anguish over the interview anymore. Most professionals in the service industry are "people people" and will be very welcoming and accommodating in the interview. We all remember our early interview experiences, and you are not expected to be a smoothly oiled machine. You are expected to be eager and to demonstrate a basic understanding of what you are getting yourself into. So, relax! If you follow the advice in this chapter, chances are you will do a great job on the interview.

Chapter 6 Essentials

- There are three basic interview types that you are likely to encounter: the structured, unstructured, and behavioral interview. Be familiar with all three, and understand why organizations may select one format over another.

- You can never overprepare for an interview. Be prepared to tell them, in some detail, why you are interested in their position above and beyond any other positions for which you are applying. Even if the agency is your second, third, or fourth preference, there should be something unique about their operations that you can highlight as a reason why you would like to intern with them. Be sure to know whom the key players are and some of their basic service offerings, and scour the Internet for recent headlines about the agency.

- Don't forget that you are interviewing them as much as they are interviewing you. We have frequently heard that the student's "first choice" became much less appealing after the interview was completed. Always think about your goals, the agency culture, and the "little things" (i.e., the commute, parking, dress code, etc.) that might become more bothersome a few weeks into the experience.

- Go overboard on etiquette. Send thank-you notes to everyone who takes an active role in your interview process. Send these as soon as possible after the completion of the interview. Be sure to mention something specific about the interview as well as something that you took away from the experience, so that your face and name will be more readily remembered.

- Relax. You are going to do just fine. Do your homework and be yourself. That should be good enough for anyone, and if it isn't, maybe you don't really want to work there anyway.

Stories from the Field

We recently asked site preceptors to share some of the worst mistakes they had seen candidates make during an interview. Here are some things you will definitely want to avoid:

1. **Taking a call/sending a text message on the cell phone during the interview.** As unbelievable as it may seem, this turned up a number of times in our conversations with the preceptors. Be sure to turn your cell phone off before you enter the building for your interview. You can update your Facebook status or send a "tweet" when the interview is over.

2. **Lack of professionalism in conversational tone.** This concern was cited by a number of hiring managers as they reported that college students today just don't seem to be able to "talk like adults." Although many interview settings encourage casual and frank dialogue, it does not mean that professional etiquette is to be abandoned. As one preceptor said, "I am your boss, not one of 'your peeps.'"

3. **An apparent lack of interest/knowledge of the position.**
Site preceptors are generally very passionate about what they do and are seeking to hire an intern who can support them in their efforts. They are looking for visible signs of interest and want to hire someone who shares their passion for the profession. Keep a smile on your face at all times. Maintain good eye contact. And most important, reaffirm your interest in learning about what they do. If you don't appear to be interested in them, they certainly won't be interested in you.

4. **Crossing the line between confidence and arrogance.**
While you should be confident in yourself and your abilities, you must be very careful to frame your responses in a way that does not make you appear to be arrogant. No matter how good you are, remember, you are the student, and they have several more years of experience than you. Be optimistic about your abilities, but always express your interest in learning and growing as a professional. Believe it or not, you really don't know it all...yet.

5. **Dressing inappropriately**
We've said it before, but we must stress it again. Professional attire is a must, even for internship positions in recreation, sport, and tourism. One preceptor said, "Your student came to the interview in cutoff shorts, a polo shirt, and flip flops. He seemed like a very nice kid but didn't send me the message that he was serious about getting this job."

6. **Not listening**
While nerves and inexperience may make it difficult to focus on what the interviewer is saying (sometimes you may have no idea what they are talking about), it is crucial that you focus on being an active listener. Interviewers typically guide you with their discussion, hoping you will jump in to elaborate on parts of your past or ask questions/make observations about what they are doing. Failure to do this leads the interviewer to believe you are present, but not really engaged.

7. **Asking the wrong questions**
Asking questions and showing your sincere interest in the position is important, but it is clear that some students are simply asking the wrong questions. At the end of the interview

is not the time to ask about salary/pay, vacation time, or whether there might be an employment opportunity at the conclusion of the interview. Such negotiations are important (and will be talked about in upcoming chapters), but during the interview you should be focusing on what you can do for them. Once you have the offer in hand you can begin to ask these important questions.

8. **Be realistic**
   Remember, you are applying for an internship. You are not applying to be a manager or the CEO of the company. It is good to have dreams and aspirations, but be realistic about the types of projects an agency is going to trust to a soon-to-be college graduate with little professional experience.

Discussion Questions

1. Which type of interview would be the most comfortable for you? Why? What strategies could you employ to make the other two types less intimidating for you?

2. Why do you think behavioral interviews (or at least situational interview questions) are becoming so popular in the service sector? What does this tell you about what they are looking for in a candidate? What can you do to project the right image?

3. What is your biggest fear about the interview? What are some practical steps (list at least three) that you can take right now that would minimize this fear? How long would this take, and is it really worth it to you?

4. What does a "successful" interview mean to you? How will you measure your success?

Have a Drink on Me

Michelle is looking for an internship with a special event planning company. Unfortunately, she has little experience in this industry, but is hoping the internship will really help her obtain some firsthand exposure to the "ins and outs" of the business. Because of her limited experience, Michelle believes the internship selection process is critical for her career development, as it will serve as the foundation for all of her future professional endeavors.

With this in mind, Michelle decided to meet with her academic advisor and faculty with special event planning backgrounds and interests. During these discussions, she learns of an opportunity with a special event planning company in a metropolitan area. The company has everything she is looking for—diverse events, including a combination of city celebrations and exhibitions. The company is well established with over 30 years of experience and several contacts throughout the country. In addition, the internship supervisor for the company, Mark, is an alum of Michelle's university and also serves on the department's alumni advisory board.

Michelle's academic advisor contacts Mark to request information about their internship program. Her academic advisor learns the company has an opening for an intern and puts Michelle in contact with Mark. Excited about the possible opportunity, Michelle forwards her résumé and cover letter to Mark.

Two weeks later, Mark contacts Michelle to discuss the internship opportunity with his company. Mark informs Michelle that he will be on campus in three weeks for the biannual alumni advisory board conference and suggests meeting after the conference (about 4 p.m.). Michelle agrees to meet, and Mark sets the popular campus bar as the meeting location. Mark suggests they can discuss the internship over a few drinks while he reminisces about his "old college days."

1. Is this an interview or just a "meet and greet"? What do you think? How do you know?

2. If you were Michelle, how would you prepare for the meeting? Would you bring application materials (i.e., résumé, cover letter, portfolio, university forms, etc.) to the meeting? What would you wear?

3. Should Michelle (who is over 21 years of age) have an alcoholic drink with Mark? What are the potential consequences (positive or negative) associated with her decision?

4. How could Michelle be better prepared for this meeting? Be specific.

References

Kvale, S., & Brinkman, S. (2009). *Interviews: Learning the craft of qualitative research interviews.* One Thousand Oaks, CA: Sage.

Latham, G., Saari, L., Pursell, E., & Campion, M. (1980). The situational interview. *Journal of Applied Psychology, 65*(4) 422–427.

Marks, M., & O'Connor, A. (2006). The round-robin mock interview: Maximum learning in minimum time. *Business Communication Quarterly, 69*(3), 264–275.

Mathis, R., & Jackson, J. (2000). *Human resource management.* Cincinnati, OH: South-Western College Publishing.

Swider, B., Barrick, M., Harris, B., & Stoverink, A. (2011). Managing and creating an image in the interview: The role of interviewee initial impressions. *Journal of Applied Psychology, 96*(6), 1275–1288.

Chapter 7

Securing the Internship

Overview

At this stage in the internship process, you have narrowed your list of possible internship agencies, prepared and submitted your application materials, and completed the interview process. The next step is the process of securing the internship. This stage in the internship search process can be a stressful one as oftentimes students wait days or even weeks before learning of an internship agency's hiring decision.

Despite its potential for stress, there are strategies you can employ to reduce the anxiety associated with the experience while assisting you in selecting an agency with the greatest potential for personal and professional development. An overview of these strategies will be presented in this chapter, including an overview of the internship selection process, what to expect following the interview, how to manage the internship offer, and how to make the final decision.

As an internship candidate, it is important for you to have a basic familiarity with the steps in the overall internship selection process. By understanding the internship selection process, you can effectively prepare yourself for the upcoming phases and outcomes associated with each of the steps in the process. From preparing yourself for a possible second interview to rehearsing your response to an internship offer, a working knowledge of the steps in the internship selection process can allow you to be better positioned to secure that top internship on your list. Furthermore, this increased awareness and familiarity with the process can help in reducing anxiety and stress levels associated with the overall internship search process. A brief discussion of each step is provided in the following sections.

Step #1: Completion and Screening of Application Forms

One of the first steps in most selection systems requires internship applicants to complete an employment/internship application form. The application asks individuals for various bits of personal information, such as name, educational background, career goals, and experience (DeNisi & Griffin, 2001).

Step #2: (Preliminary) Interview

Depending on the agency, this phase might be combined with the next phase (Internship Testing/Additional Interviews) in the selection process. Generally, the preliminary interview is used to determine whether your skills, abilities, and task preferences match any of the available internship opportunities in the agency. The interview is typically brief (about 30 minutes), exploratory in nature (to screen out unqualified or uninterested applicants), and may contain a combination of internship and goal-related questions (Byars & Rue, 2004).

Step #3: Internship Testing/Additional Interviews

In recent years, some agencies have implemented tests within their selection process. Common test categories include aptitude, psychomotor, proficiency, interest, and personality. Aptitude tests are used to measure an internship applicant's capacity or potential ability to learn and perform tasks (i.e., verbal, writing samples, numerical tests, reasoning tests, etc.) (Byars & Rue, 2004). Psychomotor tests are most commonly adopted within outdoor-based recreation settings and are used to test a person's strength, dexterity, and coordination. Proficiency assessments measure the job-related knowledge possessed by the applicant, while interest tests are designed to determine how a person's interests compare with the interests of successful people in a specific job/internship position (Fisher, Schoenfeldt, & Shaw, 2006). Finally, personality tests are used by agencies to identify an applicant's personality traits.

Table 7.1

The Five Major Dimensions of Personality Inventories/Tests (Barrick & Mount, 1991)

Personality Dimension	Personality Description
1. Extroversion	Sociable, gregarious, assertive, talkative, active
2. Emotional stability	Level of anxiousness, anger, security, contentment
3. Agreeableness	Courteous, flexible, trusting, good-natured, tolerant, cooperative, forgiving
4. Conscientiousness	Dependable, hard working, careful, responsible, organized, persevering, thorough, achievement-oriented
5. Inquisitiveness	Imaginative, cultured, curious, original, artistically sensitive, broad-minded, playful

In addition to selection tests, many agencies will use a second or follow-up interview as an important step in the selection process (Byars & Rue, 2004). Similar to the preliminary interview, the interviewer(s) will ask a series of internship-related questions to determine the suitability of the applicant for the position. See Chapter 6 for an overview of the most common types of interviews.

Step #4: Reference Checking

Although it varies by agency, most reference checking will occur before or after the second interview. Despite the variability in the timing of reference checking, it is a widely utilized step in the selection process. For example, one survey found that almost 60% of agencies in the United States said they regularly checked references for part-time, seasonal, or intern workers (Fisher et al., 2006).

Table 7.2

Facts about Reference Checks

- On average, 2.7 references per candidate are checked, and an HR representative or supervisor checks them.

- Information checked most frequently is past work histories, including former employers, lengths of employment, and previous titles.

- Information most likely to be falsified by applicant: length of employment, former wages, and former titles.

- Eighty-five percent of reference checks are done by telephone.

- Ninety-six percent of applications contain a warning statement that any falsehoods discovered during the hiring process are grounds for dismissal. Nevertheless, many applicants still falsify reference information.

(CCH, Inc., 2004)

One of the primary goals of the reference check is to verify information that you have already provided to the agency, such as academic degree timeline/status, dates of employment, job responsibilities, and previous performance. A secondary goal of the reference check is to discover new information on your history or past performance (i.e., criminal convictions, reasons for leaving previous job, etc.) (Fisher et al., 2006).

Step #5: Conditional Offer and Hiring

The final phase of the selection process occurs when the agency makes you an internship offer. Oftentimes, the offer is initially extended over the phone with a formal contract and/or required paperwork to be completed once the offer has been accepted.

Understanding the Internship Selection Process

1. Review the steps in the internship selection process.

2. Meet with your academic internship advisor and obtain contact information for two internship agencies where students from previous years completed their internship experience.

3. Contact the two internship agencies and obtain information regarding their steps and timelines employed during a typical internship selection process.

4. Reflect on the information obtained from the two agencies. How are the steps adopted by the agencies similar? Are they consistent with the steps described in the text?

What to Expect Following the Interview

By this stage in the internship search process, you have likely submitted the necessary application materials, engaged in a first and maybe even a second interview, as well as completed any selection test required by the agency. You may have even heard from your references that they were contacted for a reference check on your behalf. Now what? More specifically, what can you expect next in this process? In addressing this question, Ivancevich (2007) recommends internship candidates complete two tasks. First, the candidate should submit a thank-you note within one day of the interview. The letter should be concisely written (four to five sentences). Furthermore, the letter should thank the interviewer(s) for the opportunity to interview, identify an aspect of the agency that was appealing, and remind the interviewer(s) that you are looking forward to hearing from them about the internship position (see Chapter 6 for tips on thank-you letters).

In addition to developing the thank-you letter, you should also educate yourself on all of the possible outcomes associated with the interview. The first point to keep in mind is that the process associated with each interview experience is unique. From the format of the interview to the types of questions asked, each interview experience is distinct. For example, some agencies utilize a panel interview method while other agencies might conduct the interview in a one-on-one environment. Some may adopt a structured interview approach while others might subscribe to an unstructured approach. Your interview with one agency may last one to two hours while your interview with another agency lasts 30 minutes (see Chapter 6 for an overview of the interview process). Regardless of the interview format, the outcome of the experience typically falls into one of these categories: a rejection, an on-the-spot offer, or a delayed offer. A description for each of these outcomes is provided in the following paragraphs.

Rejection

Despite having a good feeling about the interview, you can sometimes get a rejection response from the agency. This can be a challenging experience and one of devastation, frustration, confusion, and an overall deep concern for what you did that eliminated you from contention for the internship. A common feeling among those who did not land the internship is "What did I do wrong?"

The answer to this question may never be known for sure, but sometimes the answer is "nothing." Internship opportunities become more competitive with larger applicant pools and skill sets requiring substantial expertise that are more defined. You may have been equal, and even ahead, of many candidates in some areas; however, the agency must make a decision, and an individual will get the internship while some well-qualified people whom the agency liked will not be selected.

Regardless of the reason for the rejection, you must manage the situation and move forward to your next step. In making this challenging transition, Adams and Stinnett (2010) offer the following tips.

Don't take it personally. Don't use the internship interview as a measure of your professional worth. The decision to not hire you was based on the agency's specific criteria and needs that may or may not have anything to do with how you showed up at the interview. That you weren't the perfect match doesn't mean that you're not an outstanding professional with excellent attributes and talents.

Be professional. If you are given the opportunity to speak to the hiring supervisor, be professional. Politely ask for feedback, keeping in mind that it can be difficult to give (and accept) bad news; don't get upset if you don't get a straight response. Don't get defensive or angry if you don't agree with their feedback. Keep the discussion as professional as possible; you never know if you are the backup candidate or if you may apply to their agency in the future.

Learn, reflect, and let go. Despite your frustration, it is important to view this as a developmental experience. Reflect on your experience. Record what you learned about yourself, the experience, and identify areas of improvement. This process can assist you in "letting the experience go" and moving on to prepare for your next internship interview.

On-the-Spot Offer

Although rare, some agencies will make an offer to a student immediately following the interview. You may have completed several other interviews that you have not received feedback on the hiring decision. You may also have some interviews scheduled in the future, but have now received an immediate, on-the-spot offer. Worse things can happen, but you are still faced with a dilemma. If the agency is your first choice, it is likely that you will accept the internship. However, if it is not your first choice you are forced to make a decision with limited insight into other possibilities. Strategies to manage this situation will be discussed in the upcoming sections.

Delayed Offer

The most common approach utilized by agencies is the delayed offer. In contrast to the on-the-spot offer, the delayed offer occurs when the applicants are informed of the hiring decision after a period of time has elapsed. The time between the interview and the offer varies by agency and situation. The agency may have other applicants to interview, they may be dealing with EEOC or similar hiring practices, or the interview committee may be faced with scheduling conflicts (i.e., vacations, busy work schedules, work responsibilities, etc.) among the staff who are serving on the committee. Despite these uncertainties, many agencies will provide you with a tentative timeline, such as "We'll be making a decision by the end of the month."

In summary, an internship offer is an exciting and gratifying experience. Whether on-the-spot or delayed, the internship offer is a culmination of months of self-reflection; goal development; searching internship announcements; discussions with friends, family, and mentors; and networking. You've sent out your résumé(s) and completed several interviews, and now the moment you've been waiting for is here. You have an offer, and it is now time to make a decision. However, the decision can be a difficult one as there are a number of factors you must consider. Issues such as the availability of a stipend, benefits, location, work schedule, work environment, and so forth are things you must consider while managing the internship offer.

Finding Alumni Support: Sharing Internship Experiences

1. Work with your university to obtain a contact list of two to three recent graduates who interned in areas similar to your interests (i.e., outdoor, resort, professional sports, municipal recreation, etc.).

2. Contact the recent graduates and ask them the following questions:

   a. What were your experiences following the internship interview? Did you have a second interview?

   b. Describe your experiences with the internship offer? In particular, was it an on-the-spot offer or delayed? How did you handle the experience? What do you think you did well? What would you do differently?

   c. Did you ever receive an internship rejection? What, if anything, did you learn from the experience?

3. Record their responses to the questions listed in 2a–2c.

4. Share and discuss the responses with three to four members of your class. What were some themes that emerged from everyone's responses?

5. Reflect on the group discussion and identify two to three strategies that you can utilize to become better prepared to handle the possible (rejection, on-the-spot offer, or delayed offer) outcomes associated with the internship selection process.

Managing the Internship Offer

Although everyone is different and what is important to one person may be insignificant to another, there are common elements to consider when evaluating the internship offer. To assist you in successfully managing the internship offer experience, an overview of these elements is presented in the following paragraphs (Smith & Moore, 2010).

Compensation/Stipend

Compensation is only one factor in an ideal internship offer, but it is often thought of as one of the most important. When evaluating a compensation package, be aware of any pay differentials. For example, a stipend that may not seem appropriate for the Northeastern United States could be competitive in the Midwest.

Benefits

If the offered compensation/stipend is a bit lower than you expected, you may want to take a look at the benefits package associated with the internship. Examine the benefits packet carefully, and don't hesitate to ask the agency questions about possible housing, meal plans, relocation costs, opportunities to pick up extra (paid) hours, and so forth.

Location

If commuting is an issue for you, take this into account in your overall evaluation of the offer. Research whether the employer is accessible via bus, subway train, or shuttle.

Work Schedule

Many internships will require working nights and weekends. Be sure to consider and discuss (with the agency) your work schedule. Review your schedule and weigh it with your preferred lifestyle.

Career Development

One of the primary goals of the internship is to assist you in developing the knowledge, skills, and abilities necessary to become a successful professional. Thus, it is important to intern somewhere where your career growth will be supported and encouraged. Some questions you should consider include the following:

- Does the agency have a policy on helping with continuing education costs (conferences, workshops, technical training, writing courses, etc.)?

- Is there the potential for future (employment) opportunities within the agency?

- How often will your performance be reviewed?

- Will you be given challenging opportunities?

Office Culture

Also consider the environment you will be working in. Your supervisor, co-workers, and the overall focus and drive of the agency can greatly impact your happiness, productivity, and success.

Self-Reflection on Goals

Do not get caught up in the excitement of the offer and lose track of your professional goals. Adequate matching of your needs, abilities, preferences, and motivation with an agency's opportunities will not just happen. You must take responsibility for ensuring the opportunities associated with the internship will help you achieve your goals. Consider the internship offer, and ask yourself questions, such as the following:

- How and where will the agency allow me to improve upon my strengths?

- How, where, and who will work with me to address my developmental needs?

- Will the internship opportunity challenge me? In what ways?

- Do the experiences associated with the internship match my current and future career interests (be specific)?

- Does the internship agency's philosophy and working environment match my values and/or personal style (be specific) (Ivancevich, 2007)?

Placement Rate of Interns

Arguably one of the most important issues to consider during the interview process is the placement rates of previous interns. Where are some of the company's previous interns currently working? How long did it take for them to find a full-time job? When possible, you should contact previous interns directly to discuss these questions and obtain feedback on their experiences interning with the offering agency.

> **"SOMEWHERE ALONG THE LINE** of development we discover what we really are, and then we make our real decision for which we are responsible. Make that decision primarily for yourself because you can never really live anyone else's life."
>
> — Eleanor Roosevelt

Making the Decision

You now have an internship offer (or several) to consider. Sooner rather than later, you will have to make a decision about the offer(s), which can have important implications for your professional future. Oftentimes, it is not an easy decision to make as most individuals are able to distinguish "good" from "bad," but it can be much more difficult to decide between good and "better." ". With your list of internship offers, you are likely faced with identifying the "best" opportunity among several "good" ones. Clearly, this can be a stressful experience.

In managing the challenges associated with making this important decision, researchers have outlined the following strategies and techniques:

Tip #1: Managing Multiple Offers or Pending Offers

Oftentimes, students receive more than one internship offer. Or students may receive an offer but are more interested in other internships that are still pending. Students in either of these situations are faced with tough decisions. One method to address this situation is to ask for time to consider the offer(s). Although you risk disappointing the offering agency by not immediately accepting their offer, it is common practice to take a little time before making a decision. Asking for time allows you to reflect on the opportunity, speak with family, friends, advisors, mentors, etc., and determine the overall feasibility of the experience prior to accepting an internship position. When you ask for time to consider the offer, be sure to display appreciation, interest in the position, and sincerity. Some offering agencies may give you a timeframe to respond, such as a week, while other agencies may ask you to give them a timeframe. Typically, the timeframe allowed for considering the offer is between one to two weeks.

Depending on the situation, it might also be acceptable to contact your first-choice internship agency to inform them that you have another offer. Inform them that you remain very interested in their agency. When appropriate, you can also ask the agency about their hiring decision timeline. Hopefully, the information they provide will give you some insight into your status within their hiring process.

Tip #2: Problem or Opportunity?

Clearly, considering the internship offer can be a stressful one. Questions such as "Is this the right internship for me?" or "I have two offers and both seem great; how do I know which one to take?" can be challenging to answer as it is unlikely you will be able to answer them with 100% certainty. Oftentimes, individuals in this situation forget to find the positives. Rather than dwelling on the challenges and potential problems associated with making the decision, you should spend more effort on identifying the possible opportunities tied to this offer. As you consider the offer(s), you should view the decision as an opportunity for growth and development rather than solving a stressful or frustrating problem. For example, suppose you receive an offer from your second-choice internship agency before you have an offer from your top choice. You may turn this stressful situation into an opportunity to practice your negotiating skills by contacting your second-choice agency and requesting additional time to consider the offer. In addition, you could use this experience as an opportunity to further research your second-choice agency to obtain a more detailed perspective of their agency, its operations, and intern experiences.

Tip #3: Regulate your Emotions.

It is important to recognize that your decision will not be free from emotions as selecting an internship that represents a key step in your future career plan can be stressful. Rather, you must ensure your decision is guided by a balance of linear thinking (i.e., rational thinking, attention to concrete data and facts, etc.) and nonlinear thinking (i.e., attention to feelings, emotions, intuitions, etc.) (Thiel et al., 2012).

You will likely encounter a series of positive and negative emotions and attitudes as you navigate through the internship search process. Research has suggested that an overabundance of negative emotions toward the experience can promote increased feelings of anxiety, depression, poor decision making, and even a behavior withdrawal (i.e., "giving up" on the internship, the search, and decision) (Pfister & Bohm, 2008). In contrast, an excessive amount of positive emotions (i.e., overconfidence in yourself) can lead to gross overestimations, oversight, and/or lapse in judgment (Lerner & Keltner, 2001). Thus, the key is to recognize your decision will not be void of emotions, but work to regulate them. Techniques such as relaxation activities/exercises and honest self-appraisals of your goals and weaknesses can help in systematically reducing your emotional reactions within the decision-making process. Spend time reviewing your self-assessment and career goals (see Chapters 2 and 3) to identify areas needing further development and ask yourself "Which internship helps me achieve the greatest number of career goals?" At the same time, avoid making hasty or quick decisions. For example, spend some time reflecting on your opportunities and their relationship to your individual assessment. Then put the information aside and "sleep on it" or engage in a hobby or activity (i.e., running, visiting with friends, go to a movie, etc.) and come back to the internship decision at a later time. By intentionally removing yourself from the issue for a few hours, you are able to revisit it in a much more refreshed state of mind, leading to a more informed decision-making process.

Tip #4: Utilization of Forecasting Techniques

Forecasting can assist you in making informed predictions about potential future outcomes based on your current observations and experiences (Thiel et al., 2012). Forecasting is a strategy that can help an individual solve rather complex problems by identifying multiple solutions to the problem. This strategy allows you to methodically review the situation, identifying all of its elements – the positive and negative ones as well as the certain and uncertain areas to accurately predict the consequences of your (potential) decisions (Thiel et al., 2012).

A few forecasting strategies that you can employ in making your internship offer decision are paired comparisons, futures wheel, and decision matrix analyses.

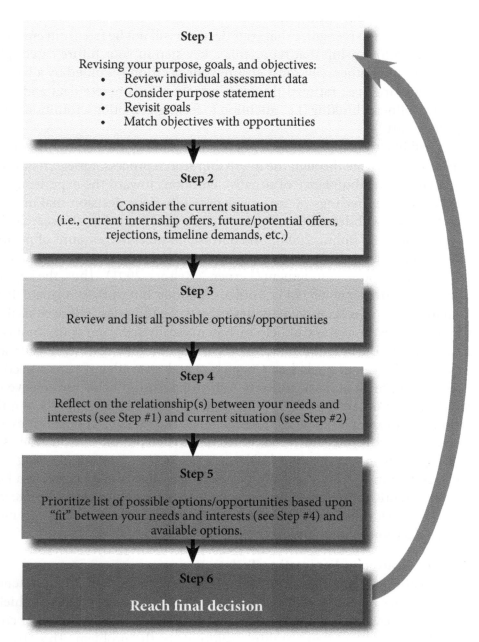

Figure 7.1. Internship Decision-making Model

Paired comparison analysis helps you to work out the importance of multiple internship offers relative to each other. The paired comparison technique can be particularly useful when you lack information that places one (internship) offer significantly higher than other offers. Figure 7.2 illustrates the process of completing a paired comparison analysis.

	Seaside Internship	Sunny Beach Internship	Mountain Camp Internship	Convention Center Internship
Seaside Internship		3	2	3
Sunny Beach Internship	1		2	2
Mountain Camp Internship	2	2		3
Convention Center Internship	1	2	1	
Average Scores	**1.33**	**2.33**	**1.66**	**2.66**

Figure 7.2. Paired Comparison Analyses Steps

1. Utilize a spreadsheet or create a table and list your internship offers in the first column. These offers should also be listed in the first row.
2. Use the grid to compare each offer with each other offer, one by one. For each comparison, decide which of the two offers best meets your professional and personal needs, and then assign a score based on how the agency in the column heading compares to the agency in the row heading. In the table above, a 3-point scale was utilized (1= Does not meet as many professional or personal goals as the other agency; 2 = Meets more professional goals, but not as many personal goals as the other agency or vice versa; 3 = Meets more professional and personal goals compared to the other agency) to compare each offer.
3. Sum each column (i.e., offer) and divide by the total number of values in the column to determine an average score for each offer (see "Average Scores" row in example).

As Figure 7.2 indicates, the Convention Center Internship has the highest score (2.66) compared to the other three internship offers. Thus, the Convention Center Internship would be the top offer to consider (and accept) when compared to the other three internship offers.

Another forecasting tool that can assist you with the decision-making process is the futures wheel. The futures wheel is a way of organizing thinking and questioning about the future; it is a kind of structured brainstorming (Glenn, 1994). Similar to the layout of a concept or mind map, the futures wheel is a diagram outlining the layers of consequence(s) associated with a decision. This technique can be particularly useful when a student is faced with a limited number of internship offers (one to four) as it can be rather time consuming to complete. In completing the futures wheel, the student would start by listing and circling an internship offer in the middle of a piece of paper. The student would then create a list of consequences associated with accepting this internship offer and map them around the internship offer listed on the paper. Next, the student would create a list of consequences associated with each of the consequences listed within the first ring of consequences. This process would be repeated until the student feels the list of consequences have been exhausted.

A third decision-making technique is the decision matrix analysis. The matrix analysis requires the student to compare each internship offer against their personal and career goals. It is particularly useful when you have several strong internship offers to consider and many different factors to take into account with your decision. First, the student would list their offers in a row of a spreadsheet or table. Next, your list of personal needs and professional goals (i.e., the factors) that are important for making the internship decision should be listed in the first column of the spreadsheet or table (see Figure 7.3). Next, using a scale from 1 (*very unimportant*) to 5 (*very important*), assign a relative importance value to each of the factors you created. You can also use these numbers to weight your preferences based on the importance of each factor. The next step is to work your way across your table, scoring each offer on each of the important factors you created. Score each option from 0 (*poor*) to 3 (*very good*). Multiply each of your scores by the values for your relative importance. This will give each factor an overall weight. Finally, add up these scores for each of your offers. The offer with the highest score is the best option.

Consider the example in Figure 7.3. The student identified eight factors to consider when evaluating the four internship offers. In particular, the student has evaluated the four offers based on four professional and four personal goals. Next, the student reviewed each professional and personal goal and rated them on an importance scale (1=*very unimportant goal*, 5=*very important goal*). For example, the student felt professional goal #1 was very important to his/her internship experience. As a result, the student gave professional goal #1 a rating of 5. The student then rated (0=*poor*, 3=*very good*) each internship offer based on its ability to help the student meet each of his/her eight professional and personal goals. The student multiplied the rating by the goal's importance value. For instance, the student issued a "fair" rating for the Seaside Internship's ability to meet professional goal #1. The "fair" rating has a numerical value of "1" (see scale provided in Figure 7.3) and professional goal #1 has an importance weight of "5". Multiplying the two values (1 x 5), the student obtained a weighted score of "5" for the Seaside Internship's ability to meet professional goal #1. Once values and weights had been assigned for each goal and each internship agency, the student summed the total weighted scores for each agency. As shown in Figure 7.3, the Convention Center Internship received the highest score (64) and has been identified as the top choice based on the decision matrix analysis.

	Seaside Internship	Sunny Beach Internship	Mountain Camp Internship	Convention Center Internship
Professional Goal #1 (Importance weight=5)*	Fair(5)**	Poor(0)	Poor (0)	Fair (5)
Professional Goal #2 (Importance weight=5)	Fair (5)	Fair (5)	Fair(5)	Very good (15)
Professional Goal #3 (Importance weight=4)	Poor (0)	Fair (4)	Fair (4)	Fair (4)
Professional Goal #4 (Importance weight=4)	Good (8)	Poor (0)	Poor (0)	Very good (12)
Personal Goal #1 (Importance weight=5)	Fair (5)	Good (10)	Fair (5)	Good (10)
Personal Goal #2 (Importance weight=3)	Fair (3)	Fair (3)	Very good (9)	Good (6)
Personal Goal #3 (Importance weight=3)	Very good (9)	Poor (0)	Fair (3)	Fair (3)
Personal Goal #4 (Importance weight=3)	Very good (9)	Good (6)	Very good (9)	Very good (9)
Total Score **(Sum of weighted scores)**	**44**	**28**	**35**	**64**

Scale: 0=Poor, 1=Fair, 2=Good, 3=Very good
*Each factor has been assigned a value(1=Very unimportant to 5=Very important) based on the student's views of the factor's importance.
**Each score (i.e., 0=Poor to 3=Very good) was multiplied by the factor's importance weight to obtain an overall weighted score for each factor.

Figure 7.3. Using a Decision Matrix Analysis in the Internship Selection Process

Tip #5: Be Patient and Open

Oftentimes, students will assume that there is only one "good" solution to the situation. This process will lead students to reach conclusions without fully considering possible alternatives. In some instances, the internship seeker will decide on an internship agency before concluding the search. This approach will result in the student halfheartedly "going through the motions" for the remainder of the internship search without giving full consideration to the remaining agencies on the list. This can be problematic for the student as he or she previously spent significant amounts of time and energy creating a short list of potential agencies only to ignore the full list of opportunities. One approach to avoid making hasty or predetermined decisions is through the use of a pro/con list. The individual can create a list of potential positives and negatives associated with each offering agency. By creating these lists and reviewing the positive and negative impacts of each agency, the student can embrace a more open, honest, and thorough assessment of not just one, but all offers.

Tip #6: Don't Be Blind to Feedback

By confusing failure with feedback, students fail to learn from previous experiences of those around them (Wallace & Rijamampianina, 2005). Rather, seek out those around you for guidance, support, and feedback during the decision-making process. Speak with professionals, faculty, recent interns, friends, and family. Many of these individuals have gone through this experience and can provide some experience-based advice to help you make your decision.

Communicating the Decision

Taken collectively, the previously mentioned tips can assist you in making your internship decision while avoiding mistakes that could have a negative impact on your future professional development. Once a decision has been made, the next step is to communicate your decision to all parties. You must communicate your decision to accept an offer as well as inform the other agencies that you have turned down their offer or, in the case of those offers that are still unknown or pending, ask for your name to be removed from consideration. The following sections will discuss the strategies associated with communicating the rejection and acceptance processes.

Rejecting the Offer and/or Pending Offers

After careful reflection and consideration, you have decided to accept an internship. You are likely excited and relieved to finally come to a decision. Despite your excitement, you must now share the news with the agencies that you selected for an internship. This can be difficult, as you have likely gotten to know several individuals within the agencies through the application process. However, you must respect their time and efforts and inform them of your decision. Just as you waited and waited for that first choice offer, these agencies are waiting for your decision. Furthermore, you don't want to "burn any bridges" by leaving them in the dark and not sharing your decision with them.

A recommended approach for communicating your decision to reject the agency's offer is to contact them by phone or in person. A phone call portrays professionalism and can show your appreciation for the opportunity. Thank the agency for their time and assistance and inform them that you are turning down the offer. If they ask for reasons, be honest in your response, but be careful not to be negative about your experiences with them (you never know when you may need their help in the future).

Accepting the Offer

Once you have identified your top choice, contact the agency and accept the offer. Speak to the agency over the phone or in person, and inform them of your decision. At this time, you should also remove yourself from consideration in any other internship opportunities (see the paragraph above). By accepting an offer, you are committing to the agency, and it is unprofessional to change your mind and accept another offer down the road.

In addition to informally accepting the offer, you will likely need to complete paperwork to formalize the relationship between you and the agency. Many agencies and universities require students and supervisors to sign internship contracts that state the terms and conditions of experience. You should check with your university and the agency to determine the required paperwork and corresponding deadlines associated with these documents.

Summary

The time during the internship selection process can be one of stress and uncertainty. Particularly following the interview stage(s), you are left to wait for days or even weeks before learning of your future plans. Although this process can be a period of stress, there are strategies to reduce the anxiety associated with the experience. This chapter discussed these strategies while also introducing important factors to consider when managing internship offers. As discussed in this chapter, it is not always an easy decision to make when you must decide between a good and a better internship offer. However, the tips presented in this chapter can be used to assist you in making an informed internship decision while avoiding mistakes that could have a negative impact on your future professional development. Once a decision has been made, the next step is to communicate your decision. You must communicate your decision to accept an offer as well as inform the other agencies that you have turned down their offer or, in the case of those offers that are still unknown or pending, ask for your name to be removed from consideration. This chapter concluded with a summary of the appropriate steps and process associated with communicating these internship decisions.

Chapter 7 Essentials

- The time following the interview can be a stressful one as, oftentimes, students wait days or even weeks before learning of an internship agency's hiring decision. Having a basic familiarity with the steps in the overall internship selection process, you can effectively prepare yourself for the upcoming phases and outcomes associated with each of the steps in the process.

- The candidate should submit a thank-you note within one day of the interview.

- The outcome of the interview experience typically falls into one of these categories: rejection, on-the-spot offer, or a delayed offer.

  - Despite having a good feeling about the interview, you can sometimes get a rejection response from the agency. Regardless of the reason for the rejection, you must manage the situation and move forward to your next step.

  - Although rare, some agencies will make an offer to a student immediately following the interview.

  - The delayed offer is the most common approach utilized by agencies. In contrast to the on-the-spot offer, the delayed offer occurs when the applicants are informed of the hiring decision after a period of time has elapsed. The time between the interview and the offer varies by agency and situation.

- There are some common elements to consider when evaluating the internship offer. These include compensation/stipend, location, work schedule, career development opportunities, office culture, self-reflection of goals, and the placement rate of interns.

- Researchers have outlined several strategies to help students manage the challenges associated with making an internship decision.

- You must communicate your decision to accept an offer as well as inform the other agencies that you have turned down their offer or, in the case of those offers that are still unknown or pending, ask for your name to be removed from consideration.

Discussion Questions

1. It is quite probable that you will apply to several internships and that you will never hear back from them.

   a. What will you do to initiate contact with the agency?

   b. What constitutes "crossing the line" between persistence and obnoxious in seeking to make contact?

2. Assume you have just been given an "on-the-spot" offer from an agency in which you are interested. Unfortunately, you have yet to get a response from your first choice. What are some strategies you can employ to delay making a decision on the spot?

3. If you have accepted an internship, is it acceptable to back out if you get an offer from a better agency? Why or why not?

Should I Stay or Should I Go?

Ellie is a senior student majoring in recreation, sport, and tourism at a regional comprehensive public university in the Midwest. Ellie has focused her studies and work experiences within the area of outdoor recreation. In particular, she has taken courses in outdoor and adventure recreation, environmental interpretation, camp administration, outdoor activities (i.e., rock climbing, canoeing/kayaking, hiking, rafting, camping, etc.), and natural resource management.

In February, Ellie began searching for summer internships with many of these located in the western part of the country. Within a week, Ellie narrowed her list down to her top five sites. Some of her top five sites are geographically close to each other. In fact, her first and third choice internship sites are within the same state and are separated by only 90 miles.

Ellie sends her application materials to her top choice site first and waits a week before sending out the remaining four applications. She hopes this strategy will allow her to know the status of her application with her top choice before learning the fate of her other four options. However, things do not go as planned, and she is contacted by her third-choice site for a phone interview. Ellie completes the interview and feels good about the interview, the agency, and the possibility of working with them.

A few days later, Ellie is offered an internship with her third-choice agency. Ellie asks if she can have a few days to consider the offer and is given a one-week deadline. That afternoon, Ellie is contacted by her first-choice site for a phone interview, which they schedule for later that week. Ellie is excited and agrees to complete the interview. Two days later Ellie completes the interview and remains excited about the agency and its opportunities. The first-choice site indicates a decision will be made within a week.

The one-week deadline comes, and Ellie has not heard anything from her first-choice site. After much reflection, Ellie verbally agrees to accept the internship opportunity with her third-choice site. She feels good about her decision, and the agency is eager to work with her in the very near future. Two days later, Ellie receives a call from her first-choice site and is offered an internship with the agency.

1. If you were Ellie, what would you do?

2. What are some of the immediate and long-term potential consequences associated with accepting or rejecting the offer from her first choice site?

3. Could this situation been avoided? If so, how? Be specific.

References

Adams, L., & Stinnett, W. (2010). *Rejection: Or I thought I was doing a great job.* Retrieved from http://www.gordontraining.com

Arsham, H. (2010). *Leadership decision making.* Retrieved from http://home.ubalt.edu/ntsbarsh

Barrick, M. R., & Mount, M. K. (1991). The big five personality dimensions and job performance: A meta-analysis. *Personnel Psychology, 44*(1), 1-26.

Byars, L. L., & Rue, L. W. (2004). *Human resource management* (7th ed.). New York, NY: McGraw Hill Irwin.

CCH. (2004). *Reference-checking practices.* Riverwoods, IL: CCH Incorporated.

DeNisi, A. S., & Griffin, R. W. (2001). *Human resource management.* Boston, MA: Houghton Mifflin.

Fisher, C. D., Schoenfeldt, L. F., & Shaw, J. B. (2006). *Human resource management* (6th ed.). Boston, MA: Houghton Mifflin.

Glenn, J. C. (1994). *The futures wheel*. Washington, D.C.: AC/UNU Millennium Project.

Ivancevich, J. M. (2007). *Human resource management* (10th ed.). New York, NY: McGraw-Hill Irwin.

Lerner, J. S., & Keltner, D. (2001). Fear, anger, and risk. *Journal of Personality and Social Pyschology, 81*, 146-159.

Pfister, H. R., & Bohm, G. (2008). The multiplicity of emotions: A framework of emotional functions in decision making. *Judgment and Decision Making, 3*, 5-17.

Smith, D. & Moore, L. L. (2010). *Job search strategies*. Retrieved from http://www.eiu.edu/~careers/search.

Thiel, C., Bagdasarov, Z., Harkrider, L., Johnson, J., & Mumford, M. (2012). Leader ethical decision-making in organizations: Strategies for sensemaking. *Journal of Business Ethics, 107*(1), 49-64.

Wallace, E., & Rijamampianina, R. (2005). Strategic decision making with corporate emotional intelligence. *Problems and Perspectives in Management, 3*, 83-91.

MANAGING THE INTERNSHIP EXPERIENCE

Chapter 8

Experiencing the Internship

Overview

"Only by wrestling with the conditions of the problem at hand, seeking and finding his own solution does one learn."

– John Dewey

The internship is an experience that many students eagerly look forward to during the college years. Most likely your instructors, advisors, and family have all told you what an amazing opportunity this is to get out of the classroom, to learn from those who are actively involved in the profession, and to begin your own career. Even the first few pages of this text use words such as memorable, challenging, and rewarding to describe what awaits you. But will your internship really be as glamorous and wonderful as you envision?

The internship is an *opportunity*. The dictionary defines opportunity as "a chance, especially one that offers some kind of advantage." The internship represents a *chance* to gain an advantage. These advantages have been covered in Chapter 1. But if there is a chance to gain this advantage, is there a chance that you will *not* gain this advantage? It is a real possibility. In this chapter we will explain how learning through internships is entirely different from any educational experience you have encountered before. We will also present you with information about what you are likely to confront before, during, and after the internship. This knowledge, along with a few practical suggestions, should go a long way in improving the likelihood that you will have a memorable, challenging, and rewarding internship experience.

Experiential Learning and Internships

In Chapter 1 we discussed the rationale for including an internship experience in a quality undergraduate curriculum. Outside of the pragmatic benefits that accrue to students and agencies alike, educators have long recognized that students learn more effectively when they are placed in real-life settings in which they can test, apply, and better understand knowledge acquired in traditional classroom settings (Beauchamp, 1982; Dewey, 1938; Kolb, 1984). In short, internships are about learning. Students who approach an internship by thinking of it as a work experience are only seeing part of the larger picture. Recognizing that your internship is about learning is the first step toward maximizing your internship experience.

INTERNSHIPS ARE NOT ABOUT WORKING. Internships are about learning. Work is simply the vehicle through which you learn!

Take a moment to reflect on the way that you have learned in traditional classroom settings. An instructor has presented material through lectures. You diligently took notes, read your textbook, and were given the opportunity to reveal your level of mastery of the material through exams, quizzes, or other assignments. This is the model of education that has dominated American schools and the way that you have been taught to learn for the past 15 years. In this model, you are a semipassive recipient of information that you are expected to retain and apply as requested. To have a successful internship, you must abandon this model of learning and embrace another approach. It will not be easy, but there are basic understandings you must embody if you hope to have a successful internship experience.

The Emphasis Is on the Student Not the Teacher

You need to approach this internship recognizing that this is your opportunity to explore your personal and professional interests. You must take an active role in establishing the agenda for your internship. On the first day of a traditional class, you are given a syllabus that clearly explains the goals and intended outcomes of the class, the readings you are required to review, and the assignments you must complete. The instructor is completely in charge of setting the direction for the class. In an internship, you must be an active partner in "writing the syllabus" for your class.

- What are *your* goals?

- What are *your* desired outcomes?

- What assignments would *you* like to complete?

- How will *you* know if the experience has been successful?

It is important to note that this is a process you must negotiate with your site preceptor and your university internship coordinator, but you must be prepared to play an active role in this process. It may be helpful to return to Chapter 3, Completing the Individual Assessment, to reflect once more on your personal and professional goals.

Learning through an internship is also a much more fluid and dynamic experience than learning in a traditional classroom setting. Frequently, once you have begun the internship and have had the opportunity to explore the organization, you become aware of new interests and opportunities. Share these with your site preceptor and your university internship coordinator, and look for an occasion to explore them further. Goals should be set both *prior to* and *during* the internship as your understanding of the professional environment increases. While there are always limitations, a good site preceptor and university internship coordinator should always look for ways to facilitate achievement of realistic goals.

Learning Is Dependent Upon the Learner

It should already be clear that in an internship setting, you must take an active role in initiating the learning process.

Survey Says

A recent survey of agency supervisors uncovered an interesting trend in their dissatisfaction with student interns. While their overall impression of students was very positive, there was one area that was consistently reported as a concern. They were not concerned about a lack of training or professional experience, but instead reported that students failed to demonstrate sufficient initiative. The dictionary defines initiative as the process of "making something start; to cause something, especially an important event or process, to begin." What are you going to do to be seen as an intern that takes initiative and makes things happen?

If you make the mistake of thinking of your internship as a work experience, it would be logical for you to expect to show up, be told what to do, and complete the tasks and go home. Remember, internships are not about working; they are about learning. When you have interests, have questions, or uncover problems, take the initiative to find the answers. Use the full range of resources available to you including your site preceptor, coworkers, and other interns; faculty members at your university; and professional publications or discussion boards. Be careful not to burden any one source too much.

Write your ideas down, and share them with your supervisors. In the past, some interns have created their own full-time position by coming up with a creative idea for improving service delivery.

Think About It

Organizations accept student interns for a number of different reasons. Some enjoy the energy and creativity young professionals bring to their organization. Others feel a sense of responsibility to the profession to train the next generation of leaders. Unfortunately, still others accept interns because they are seen as an inexpensive source of labor. If you suspect that this is true, the importance of taking initiative is all the more important. In these types of internships, the organization will reap the maximum benefit by giving you repetitive tasks that require little investment (i.e., training) on their part. If you drag this out over 12 to 16 weeks, you have the perfect recipe for a disappointing experience. Keep in mind that the organization hired you to fill a particular need, but take initiative to find a balance between their need for production and your need for learning and gaining experience.

The Learner Is the Evaluator

While it is true that you are likely to receive periodic performance appraisals from your site preceptor and your university internship coordinator, the most important evaluator of your experience is you. Only you will really know how much you have grown through the internship. Unfortunately, self-assessment is a skill with which college students frequently struggle. Here are some concrete suggestions for helping you evaluate your performance.

Set deadlines. When establishing your goals and objectives, be sure to set deadlines by which they should be achieved. Share them with the agency and your university to be sure they are realistic. If they are, stick to them.

Reflect on your performance. Make it a regular part of your routine to do the following:

- Review your current goals and monitor your progress toward completing them. Do this weekly. If a week goes by and you have not made progress toward any of your goals, some changes need to be made in the following week.

- Reflect on the day-to-day activities in which you have been involved. Take notes (field journal) on activities in which you have been engaged, problems you have encountered, and what you have learned or done as a result of these experiences. Do this weekly or biweekly. If you find that you are reporting the same thing week in and week out, how much are you really learning? If you don't have something new to share, you need to be sure you have set challenging enough goals for your internship.

- Based on the activities above, you should be able to develop new goals or activities to explore in what remains of your internship. These goals don't always have to be grandiose or focus on gaining certain proficiencies. Think about small opportunities that will help you gain a greater understanding of the profession or that will enable you to build a stronger professional network.

Experiential Learning Summary

Experiential learning is entirely different from what most college students have experienced during their college years. In order for this pedagogy to be effective, you must do several things.

- You must want to learn. Identify areas of interest and communicate this interest with others.

- You must do more than requested. Show initiative and look for opportunities to help the organization and to further enhance your personal or professional skill set.

- You must be honest with yourself. Take the time to reflect on what you are doing and what you are taking away from the experience. Keep going back to your goals and make sure you are getting the experience you want.

In a very real sense, an internship will be what you make it.

Stages of Experience

Just as learning through internships is an entirely different process than learning through traditional settings, the situations and emotions that confront student interns are very unique. Recognizing the tremendous potential of experiential learning, researchers have long been interested in understanding student experiences (Diambra, Cole-Zakrzewski, & Booher, 2004; Inkster & Ross, 1998; Kiser, 2000; Sweitzer & King, 1999). Researchers have found that, as a whole, students do have very similar experiences while interning. Several models have been developed to define stages of development as students progress through their internship. This research has provided valuable insight in understanding student perceptions. It has also greatly improved university supervisors' ability to provide meaningful advice to interns as they encounter problems or report dissatisfaction. Understanding the stages of development is important for students, university supervisors, and site supervisors if the experience is to be maximized (Sweitzer & King, 1999). It is important to note, however, that each student will be unique and that no one model will fully define your experience. But recognizing that students learn from and adapt to challenges that are anticipated (Inkster & Ross, 1998), we will use the Sweitzer and King Model as a framework from which to provide you with practical suggestions to help you navigate your internship experience.

Sweitzer and King (1995, 1999) presented a model in which they described the transitions students frequently report in their internship experiences. In this model, they put forward the following five stages: (a) anticipation, (b) disillusionment, (c) confrontation, (d) competence, and (e) culmination.

Do You See What I See?

Take a moment to look at the descriptors used for the stages of internship experience reported by Sweitzer and King (1995, 1999). Do these look like the memorable, challenging, and rewarding experiences you were hoping for? Anticipation? Disillusionment? Confrontation? Sound like fun to you? Don't get discouraged yet. The final stages—competence and culmination—sound (and are) much more enjoyable. But how you approach and handle the challenges in the first three stages will determine whether you ever make it to the final two. Read on to discover more.

Stage 1: Anticipation (Pre-internship through First Few Weeks of Experience)

In the first stage, anticipation is experienced, as students are still uncertain as to their placement or the specifics of their internship functions and responsibilities. In the weeks prior to the internship, it is very common for college students to question their ability to excel in professional settings. "Who is going to hire me?" "What if they don't like me?" "What if I can't do the work?" These are all common questions and emotions to feel in the weeks leading up to the internship. Couple this with the fact that many placement decisions are made as students are writing final examinations and making arrangements to leave campus, and it is no wonder that anticipation and stress levels are frequently high. Once you arrive on site, this level of anxiety usually remains high for a few weeks until you have a chance to settle in. It may seem as if you will never learn everyone's names or figure out how to use the copy machine. You will learn the names and will be a pro on the copier in no time. Below are other suggestions to help you navigate this first stage of your internship.

Take control. If you are worried about securing placement for your internship, use all your available resources and actively pursue any leads. If you are anxious about receiving more detailed information about your placement and responsibilities, contact the agency directly to request it. If responses are slow to come, consider asking your university internship coordinator for assistance.

Be realistic. There are some things that are honestly outside your ability to control. Focus on the things that you can control. If you are already placed, spend time reviewing the organizational website, studying the staff directory, and making sure you know the surrounding community. Have you developed your goals and objectives? If they are open to it, initiate a dialogue with your site preceptor, share these goals, and attempt to develop a tentative timetable that outlines your major responsibilities and when you will complete them. Having this done before you arrive for the first day of the internship will help reduce miscommunication and will enable you to accomplish more.

Go with the flow. Task accomplishment in the first week of your internship is usually pretty low. Give yourself a break, and recognize that it will take you a while to adjust to your new surroundings. Focus instead on giving a great first impression. Dress for success, and be early to work. Smile, and accept responsibility without hesitation. Although it is uncomfortable to do, introduce yourself to staff members—even those outside of the area in which you may be working.

Keep your eyes open. Remember, this is not the stage where you are expected to be overly productive. Watch what other people are doing, take notes, and ask questions when appropriate.

Stage 2: Disillusionment (First Few Weeks of Internship)

In the second stage, disillusionment, students begin to realize that their expectations of the internship experience do not reflect their current state. According to Sweitzer and King (1999), it is common for students in this stage to allow their task performance to drop and for students to begin to demonstrate negative feelings for their agency and university supervisors. Why does this happen? There are a number of scenarios that could contribute to disillusionment in the early days of the internship. Perhaps the internship is not all you had idealized it would be.

- You are working hard but are not doing the work you were promised during the interview.

- You are completely bored. The jobs you are being given are easy, and you finish them within minutes.

- You are being overworked and haven't been given a single day off (including weekends) in the past two weeks.

- You are slowly realizing that all the wonderful things you were promised in the interview (grassroots marketing, seeking corporate sponsors, grant writing, scoring leagues, and implementing programs) are still just work. In fact, it is work that is sometimes repetitive and boring.

- The site preceptor who seemed so composed and put together in the interview is frankly not as impressive as you thought he/she was.

- You cannot seem to figure out exactly what is expected of you. You aren't getting the information you need to proceed, and you cannot find anyone to answer your questions.

Whatever the root cause, how you cope and deal with your disillusionment will impact the quality of your internship experience. Here are some key strategies for dealing with this challenging stage.

Be an optimist. Although things are less than enjoyable now, with just a little planning, communication, and hard work, things will improve. This is a normal part of the internship experience, and if you hope to move beyond it, attitude is everything. Even if you are disgruntled, keep a smile on your face and eagerly accept projects (even bad ones) that are given to you.

Vent. You need others who you can talk to about your experiences and frustrations. In talking with your peers who are interning elsewhere, you are likely to find that they are having similar problems. Learning that you are not alone does help, and you may even be able to share ideas and strategies for moving forward. Remember, however, that you should never vocalize frustrations with coworkers or other interns in the host organization. Despite being very unprofessional, you never know how or to whom your frustrations will be shared.

Professionalism 101

One of our students had accepted an internship with a large record label in Nashville, Tennessee. This student was ambitious and hard working, and in fact had a very impressive résumé for a soon-to-be college graduate. On the first official day of his internship (the student had actually begun working a few weeks before the start of the semester) the student had a critical lapse of judgment. Over his break, he exchanged IMs with another intern. He began complaining about his supervisor and questioned her intellectual capability. He closed his IM with "...she is an idiot, and I am a Sport Management god!" The other intern printed out the IMs and delivered them to the internship supervisor. There was a brief meeting that ended with the "Sport Management god" being escorted from the building by security. Internship terminated.

The lesson to learn is we all have frustrations in our workplace. How we deal with them and whom we share them with may determine whether we continue to have a workplace.

Identify the *real* problems. Some of the problems you are experiencing stem from the fact that the internship is introducing you to common workplace issues. Office politics, coworkers you don't enjoy, long commutes, and being given work assignments you don't like are, frankly, part of life. If, however, the problems are more significant and are impacting your ability to achieve your learning goals, take some time to write them down. Be as specific and detailed as you can be. Try to independently identify ways you can solve the problem or identify what would need to change for the problem to be minimized. Share these with your university internship coordinator when practical.

The Agency Perspective

It is true that in the first few weeks of the internship, many students report being given trivial, mundane, or even too few responsibilities. Why is it so common for students to feel so underutilized? Let's consider the perspective of the hiring agency for a moment. They have just brought a relatively inexperienced and unknown college student into their organization. This is their full-time job, and you will be with them for just a few short weeks. How wise would it be for them to trust you with major projects when they are unaware of your capabilities? In these first few weeks, your site preceptor may be watching you carefully to see how you perform and respond to certain situations. If you can't excel when given small responsibilities, the chances of you being trusted with more is minimal.

Stage 3: Confrontation (Early to Midpoint of Experience)

As the famous American poet Robert Frost once said, "The only way around is through." The outcome of the internship will largely depend upon how you deal with this stage of your experience. In this stage, you must address your concerns, adjust your expectations, and take steps necessary to ensure your internship goals will be met in the upcoming weeks. Students who do not make the effort to go through the third stage will continue to disengage from the experience, and the internship will end in frustration and unmet expectations.

Unfortunately, and for a variety of different reasons, many students make critical mistakes at this juncture of the internship. Some students are tempted to take the path of least resistance. Instead of seeking to resolve issues, the intern decides to just keep quiet and do what he or she is told. The internship will be over soon enough. Some students may internalize the problems they are experiencing. After all, good interns—ones who know what they are doing—wouldn't be having these issues, right? Still others go to the opposite extreme and project problems on to other people and refuse to accept any responsibility for problems in the workplace. One thing is certain, students who do not navigate the third stage successfully will never move on to the fourth stage, competence. What are some things you must do in this stage?

Communicate. Now that you have identified the problem and some possible solutions to these problems, it is time to communicate them. First, share them with a trusted friend, instructor, or your internship coordinator. Be sure that your frustrations are legitimate and that the solutions you have identified appear reasonable. Once you have done this, schedule a time to discuss them with your site preceptor. This should likely be done in a face-to-face meeting. You should avoid e-mailing or providing a hard copy of your list to your supervisor, as it is likely to be seen as a "list of demands" rather than an attempt to solicit their assistance. When applicable, refer to your internship job description, your timetable, or the goals you established at the onset of the internship to remind your site preceptor of what you hope to accomplish. It is amazing how much impact a 20-minute meeting can have on the rest of your internship. Frequently mismatched or poorly communicated expectations are at the root of internship problems, and a simple meeting is all that is necessary to find agreeable solutions.

Listen. An essential component of quality communication is listening. You should enter this meeting fully prepared to listen to your site preceptor. Perhaps there are performance or attitude issues that need to be addressed? There may have been changes in the internal or external environment that have made it impossible for certain promises to be kept. Advocate for yourself, but be willing to listen and accept legitimate compromises.

Stage 4: Competence (Mid-internship through Completion)

In the fourth stage, students have come to a better understanding of their responsibilities, have communicated interests and expectations with the site supervisor, and have improved their self-esteem and report higher morale. Is the internship perfect? Most likely it is not, but major problems have been addressed, and new understandings about your role in the organization have been gained. While it can be tremendously rewarding to feel a greater sense of belonging and proficiency, research suggests that there are significant challenges that may confront interns at this stage.

It is common for students at this stage to experience significant burnout and to demonstrate signs of exhaustion (Zunz, 1998). Still other students may face the temptation to simply "coast to the finish line." It is imperative that you work diligently in these final weeks. Finish strong, and leave a lasting impression on your coworkers. There are practical suggestions for you to consider in this stage of the internship.

Resist comfort. If you begin feeling too comfortable in your internship assignments something is terribly wrong. Comfort sets in when you are no longer being challenged and pushed outside your comfort zone. Keep looking for things to explore and opportunities to grow.

Seek affirmation. If you are experiencing burnout, it is time to speak with your supervisor (Zunz, 1998). This stage of your internship is a good time to schedule a meeting to assess your performance and to rearrange duties and responsibilities if necessary.

Stage 5: Culmination (Final Weeks of the Internship)

In the fifth and final stage, culmination, students face closure with the clients, coworkers, and supervisors with whom they have worked. Culmination is frequently punctuated with elation that the experience is now complete, contrasted by a profound sadness to be leaving an environment in which so much time and energy was spent. There are many emotional and logistical transitions that accompany this stage:

- completing projects for submission prior to termination of internship,

- making comprehensive notes and sharing critical information about projects that will continue or be completed after your termination date,

- redirecting clients to staff for consistency in service delivery, and

- saying goodbye and establishing communication lines between friends and coworkers.

Summary

Your internship, in a very real sense, will be what you make of it. There are circumstances that will be outside your control, but the extent to which you take control over your learning and goal accomplishment will play a large role in determining how meaningful your internship will be. Cast a vision, communicate, take initiative, and evaluate your performance. Be aware that every internship will have its natural ebbs and flows (Diambra, Cole-Zakrzewski, & Booher, 2004). Think strategically about how you approach these, and you will greatly increase the likelihood of attaining your internship goals. Most important, don't give up. If you are overwhelmed, things will soon improve as you find your fit in the agency. If things are really out of control, speak to your supervisor and university coordinator, and they can give you assistance. If things are not what you anticipated, share your concerns. While at times you will undoubtedly have to compromise by doing tasks that hold little interest to you, never quit pushing to achieve your short-term goals. How you handle yourself when things are slow or stressful speaks volumes to prospective employers about the type of full-time employee you will become.

Chapter 8 Essentials

- Internships are not like any other educational experience you have had. You are responsible for "creating your own syllabus" in this class. While you will have to follow organizational and university operating procedures, you are really the one who should be setting the tone for what you want to learn and achieve.

- Hold yourself accountable. While it might be easier to just go with the flow, regularly go back to your goals and be sure that you can see progress toward achieving them. If a week has gone by and you cannot see any progress in any of your goals, schedule a time with your supervisor to make a plan of action to correct this.

- Keep dreaming. While you are interning you should find new interests to explore. Continue to add to both your short-term and long-term professional goals.

- Hang in there. Internships, by design, will likely not be all sunshine and roses. You will have problems. You should have problems. These problems afford you the opportunity to learn and grow.

- Think ahead. As soon as you begin the internship, you should also begin thinking about the next stage of your professional career—full-time employment. Look to the chapters ahead for some good advice on how to proceed.

Discussion Questions

1. What are some practical things you can do now to help reduce the level of anxiety you might have going into the anticipation stage?

2. In the early days of your internship, it is likely that you will be given some projects that are not overly challenging or are clearly beneath your level of ability. Why do you think you are being assigned these tasks, and what strategies will you employ to attempt to secure more meaningful learning experiences?

3. The confrontation stage sounds very intimidating. If you find yourself in this stage, what are your responsibilities, and how will you handle yourself?

Throw in the Towel?

Jon is an intern at a beachfront resort. The resort includes beachfront property; an aquatic complex (i.e., splash pad, hot tubs, and two pools); miles of trails; a convenience store with a bicycle rental shop; lodging; banquet/meeting rooms; activities center with youth, adult, and senior recreation programming; and an area for adventure-based recreation programming. Jon's professional goals are to obtain employment within the commercial recreation industry, and he is hoping this internship will be a springboard for his career.

During the interview with the resort, Jon is asked about his career interests. Jon shares his desire to strengthen his skill sets in programming, aquatics, special events, marketing, personnel management, and finance. The interviewer indicates student interns are exposed to many of these areas during their internship with the resort. A few weeks later, Jon is offered the internship and completes all the necessary paperwork and is scheduled to begin at the conclusion of the spring semester.

During Jon's first week of the internship, his supervisor (i.e., the one who interviewed Jon) accepts a position with a different agency and leaves the resort. Jon is one of five interns who reported to the departing supervisor and all of them have been assigned to a supervisor from another department within the resort. Jon has been told this is a temporary situation until a replacement for the departing supervisor can be hired. However, when Jon asks about the timeline, the resort director informs him that the hiring process typically takes between two to three months (Jon's internship is 12 weeks in length).

It quickly becomes apparent that the newly assigned internship supervisor is busy juggling responsibilities of two jobs: his current position and that of the departing supervisor. As a result, Jon feels the supervisor is investing a limited amount of time in the internship program as he and the other interns have spent the past two and a half weeks working at the front desk of the pool distributing towels to the guests. Jon has spoken to the other interns about his concern over the quality of the internship and limited opportunities for development. However, the other interns appear content working the front desk where they can socialize with the guests, watch TV, and hang out near the pool all day. Jon has asked them to collectively meet with the supervisor to discuss his concerns, but they are strongly opposed to this idea and want to maintain the current work schedule.

1. As you consider this situation, what should Jon's next step be? What are the potential positives and negatives associated with this next step?

2. Who, if anyone, is at fault for this situation? Could this situation have been avoided? If so, how?

3. How can you safeguard yourself against this experience happening to you (with your internship)?

References

Beauchamp, G. (1982). Curriculum theory: Meaning, development, and use. *Theory Into Practice, 21*(1), 23–29.

Dewey, J. (1938). *Experience and education.* New York: Macmillan.

Diambra, J., Cole-Zakrzewski, K., & Booher, J. (2004). A comparison of internship stage models: Evidence from intern experiences. *Journal of Experiential Education, 27*(2), 191–212.

Inkster, R., & Ross, R. (1998). Monitoring and supervising the internship. *National Society for Experiential Education Quarterly, 23*(4) 10–11, 23–26.

Kiser, P. (2000). *Getting the most from your human service internship: Learning from experience.* Pacific Grove, GA: Brooks/Cole.

Kolb, D. (1984). *Experiential learning: Experience as the source of learning and development.* Upper Saddle River, NJ: Prentice-Hall.

Sweitzer, H. F., & King, M. A. (1995). The internship seminar: A developmental approach. *National Society for Experiential Education Quarterly, 21*(1), 22–25.

Sweitzer, H. R., & King, M. A. (1999). *The successful internship: Transformation and empowerment.* Pacific: Grove, GA: Brooks/Cole.

Zunz, S. J. (1998). Resiliency and burnout: Protective factors for human service managers. *Administration in Social Work, 22*(3), 39–54.

Chapter 9

Networking

Overview

One of the frequently cited benefits of undergraduate internships is the opportunity they provide students to develop their professional network (Surujlul & Singh, 2010). But what is a professional network? How do you develop and maintain it over time? It is imperative that students understand what networking is and what it is not and develop a comprehensive strategy for maximizing this unique opportunity.

What is Networking?

One of the unique opportunities an internship affords a student is the opportunity to develop a professional network. Unfortunately, it is very common for students to have an incomplete understanding of what networking is all about. In the simplest terms, *networking* is an opportunity to connect with others who have similar personal or professional interests. But why do we seek to connect with these individuals? An informal survey of undergraduate students revealed that 86% believed that the purpose of networking while interning was to assist in procurement of full-time employment upon completion of the internship (Gower, 2008). While this would certainly be a welcome outcome, it represents a short-term perspective on networking that is likely to lead to disappointment and frustration. Consider the following exchange with a graduating senior:

Interviewer: "What, then, was your biggest dissatisfaction with the internship?"
Student: "That I wasn't able to really connect with anyone who could make a difference."
Interviewer: "What do you mean?"
Student: "We are always told to 'build our network,' but the only people I interacted with were interns or other entry-level staff...I mean, what can they possibly do for me?

This discussion is telling as it points to a fundamental misunderstanding of what networking is all about. First and foremost, networking is not entirely about connecting with those in positions of power or influence. Networking, in a business sense, is about connecting with others with similar professional interests. Student interns, seasonal workers, frontline employees, and secretarial staff are all excellent additions to your professional network. If you consider networking to be only about interacting with those in positions of power and influence, you should rightly ask yourself why anyone would consider networking with you, the lowly student intern?

This leads us to a second truth about networking, which is that it is not something that is solely engaged in for your own personal benefit. Your primary goal in networking should be to benefit your organization and its constituents. Networking is an activity that should make you a better employee and, as a result, should improve services for your clientele. You may not see it on your job description, but serving as a liaison with related agencies is an essential management function (van der Smissen, Moiseichik, & Hartenberg, 2004). Personal introductions and benefits received from your networking efforts should be seen as a derivative of this process.

Third, networking is something that is best viewed as a long-term investment. The fact of the matter is that directors, managers, and CEOs do consider it a valuable investment of their time to get to know and build relationships with student interns. Is it because of the tremendous wealth of knowledge that you can contribute to their organization or your ability to help them advance in their career? The answer, surprisingly, is yes. Those who truly understand the nature of networking know that you do not connect with people based on what you can gain in the short term, but rather that you build relationships today based on who and where that person may be some day in the future. At the early stages in your career, it is normal to feel as if you "need" more than you can "give." More seasoned professionals understand this and view any investment of their time or tangible assistance they give you as an investment in your future. As the renowned business mogul and inspirational speaker Harvey Mackay once wrote, they are "digging their well before they are thirsty" (Mackay, 1999).

And finally, the most essential truth about networking, which in many ways encompasses the first three, is that it is about relationships, not just trading business cards, connecting on LinkedIn, or receiving personal introductions. Every person in your professional network is a valuable resource for you, and like any resource you must invest time and effort to maintaining it, or it will deteriorate to the point of being useless. On an occasional basis you should reach out to each person in your professional network in either a personal or professional capacity. Consider sharing an interesting article you have recently read, an idea for a successful event your agency just held, or the outcome of a legal case that may impact your contact. You get out of any relationship what you put into it, and the relationships developed in professional networking are no exception.

Why Build Your Network?

Networking is much more than building relationships in the hopes of advancing your professional career. Experts suggest that there are at least four demonstrated benefits to devoting serious time and energy to networking.

Continuous Learning

Professional networking is one of the best opportunities to learn about your profession (Ramsey, 2004). Ideas for successful events, fund-raisers, and marketing campaigns can all be gleaned from your professional network. As a recent college graduate, networking in this way allows you to benefit from the successes and failures of other professionals. As you become more experienced, networking with younger professionals allows you to benefit from their ideas and creativity. Regardless of the quality of the institution from which you are earning your degree, we can all benefit from the collective wisdom of those in our professional network.

Strategic Advantage

In a professional climate where resources are increasingly becoming scarce, strategic partnerships and contractual labor agreements are permanent fixtures in most leisure service organizations. Developing a professional network may reveal opportunities for organizations, even those who might otherwise be competing for clientele, to pool resources and develop mutually beneficial business arrangements (Jacobs, 2009; Tjosvold & Weicker, 1993). To do this effectively, you must look to expand your professional network to include representatives in allied professions. Think back to your introductory level classes—the leisure service system is extremely broad, and all elements are tied to another.

Become Indispensable

While it is true that no one employee is irreplaceable, developing a strong professional network certainly works to your advantage. There may be other people that possess the same knowledge, skills, and abilities that you have, but do they know the same people? Can they draw on the knowledge and experience of the people in your network? Do they have the personal relationships that give your organization the strategic advantage in a challenging economic climate? If the answer is no, you may not be indispensable, but your employer will recognize and value the contributions you bring that others cannot. The personal relationships you will develop make you extremely valuable to your employer.

Knowledge of Opportunities

As you are in the process of developing relationships, those in your network will come to know your interests and aptitudes. When they become aware of opportunities, you will become aware of opportunities. This is the benefit that most students hope to achieve from networking, but in fact is one of the last ones to be realized. It will take some time to establish trust and confidence with your associates (Hoffman, 2007). Along the way there will be numerous opportunities to assist others, and that will increase their likelihood to reciprocate for you.

Where to Network

Now that you understand what networking really is and what you can realistically hope to gain through it, a natural question should be "How do I get started?" Naturally, one of the best places to begin networking is in your place of business. This is why internships are frequently seen as a student's first real opportunity to build a professional network. As already mentioned, everyone you meet, regardless of his/her current position in the organization, could potentially represent a networking opportunity. Additionally, vendors, suppliers, community leaders, and customers are all potential contacts.

Outside of the internship, there are a number of other opportunities for young college graduates. Professional conferences are a great way to meet like-minded people. Whether in educational sessions, exhibit halls, or in the pub after hours, attending professional conferences is a good first start to building your network. Each year you attend, the impact on your efforts will be magnified (Abram, 2008). Staying in touch with your college professors is also a good practice. They will introduce you to the next generation of college students, rely on you to provide advice grounded in your professional experience, and, in turn, introduce you to other former students with which you may have many commonalities.

Social media sites such as LinkedIn, Facebook, and Twitter all have "groups" dedicated to specific professions. At the time of this writing, on LinkedIn alone there are more than 1,800 such groups dedicated to tourism and hospitality, 2,300 dedicated to sport professions, and 530 dedicated to recreation. Joining such groups exposes you to new ideas, trends, and issues related to your profession, and allows you to locate others with whom it might be worth building a stronger professional relationship. These groups frequently have national, regional, and even local get-togethers that provide a more personal approach to relationship building.

How to Network

There are a number of excellent textbooks that provide detailed instructions on best practices in building your professional network. We won't try to capture everything that has been written, but here are a few of the best suggestions to consider.

Become a Detail Person

After you have been introduced to someone take a few moments to write some notes about your interaction. Write down his or her name, who introduced you or how you met, and any other pertinent information (i.e., a big project he or she is working on, a common challenge that you share, etc.). Enter this information in your contact list on your phone or computer. As your relationship matures, you will uncover more information that should also be added (e.g., the name of his or her spouse, children, birthdays, anniversaries, favorite sport teams, or favorite television programs). These details will help you find common ground and build rapport.

Learn to Follow Up

Based on the detailed notes you have taken, follow up with your new contact after important events. For example, if you know the deadline for his or her big project is days away, send an encouraging e-mail. Send a note on his or her anniversary. Commiserate over the loss of a favorite sport team or contestant on *Dancing with the Stars.* In short, take a genuine interest in his or her life. We can all sense when someone is taking advantage of us. By genuinely taking an interest in their lives and taking just a few moments to follow up with your contacts, you will demonstrate that you are different from the rest.

Be Proactive, Not Reactive

If you have taken the advice provided in the chapter to this point, this won't be a problem for you. In short, don't wait until you need something to check in with one of your contacts. Sure, you might have to do that from time to time when unexpected events take place, but you are encouraged to build rapport (and hopefully earn a few favors) with the members of your professional network as far in advance as possible. When something unexpected comes up, you won't have to wonder if your contact will be willing to come through for you. You know they will because you have already come through for him or her.

Think Strategically

Obviously, you can't build the close personal and professional network we are describing in this chapter with hundreds of people. While you should develop a very extensive contact list, you will need to think strategically about whom you will really invest your time and energy in building relationships with. This group of people should be relatively small, perhaps 20 to 30 in the early stages of your career. Along with the other members of this "inner circle," think strategically about anyone else you might be interested in bringing into the group in time.

Summary

As you prepare to go out on this internship, spend some time thinking about how you will keep track of the people you will soon be meeting. Facebook is probably not the best tool for you to use. Consider joining LinkedIn, or explore the contacts and calendar software on your personal computer or smart phone and familiarize yourself with the functions they offer. Someday, there will probably be an app for your iPhone or Android. However you do it, take the time to record notes about who you meet and what is important to them. Then, take the time to follow up and check in with them from time to time. Remember, networking is about building relationships.

Chapter 9 Essentials

- Networking is about connecting with others with similar interests.

- Don't always look "up" in the organization. Carefully cultivate relationships with peers (and subordinates).

- Don't be selfish. Use your connections to benefit your current employer or other contacts. Invest in others now and they will be prepared to help you when you need it most.

- Get organized, and make this a daily routine. However you do it, keep your contact information up to date. Make it a regular practice to think about what you could do to help one of your connections.

Discussion Questions

1. Identify three people with whom you have worked with in previous experiences. What do you know about them, and what could you do to help make them a valuable asset to your contact list?

2. What conferences (regional, state, or national) might you attend to help you advance your education and build your professional network?

3. Do a little exploring on LinkedIn or Facebook. How many professional "groups" exist that you might benefit from joining?

What Happens at Conference...Doesn't Stay at Conference

Shane is an intern at a public recreation agency. During the internship Shane learns that his agency is funding his attendance at the upcoming state conference. Shane is excited as the three-day conference will allow him time to network with other professionals, obtain insight on upcoming job opportunities, and attend sessions on the latest trends and issues in the field. This will be his first time attending the conference, and he looks forward to the experience.

Prior to attending the conference, Shane maps out his schedule for the three-day event. Shane has identified several education sessions to attend and plans to get involved with the daily professional development workshops (i.e., job hunting, résumé development, mentoring, etc.). Shane also plans on attending the evening social events to network with professionals throughout the state.

During his first day of the conference, things are going well. The sessions are insightful with dynamic speakers, and the career development activities have allowed Shane to meet several other student interns and professionals. However, when the evening socials begin, Shane encounters a problem. To his surprise, some of the professionals attending the social event become inebriated and begin to display behavior that Shane would consider unprofessional. One of these professionals is his internship site supervisor.

As the evening social progresses, Shane's supervisor encourages him to ride with him (and other professionals) to the local sports bar/restaurant. Shane has not been drinking and drives the group to the restaurant/sports bar, which is about 15 miles from Shane's hotel. While at the restaurant, Shane's supervisor and other professionals express interest in attending an "adult-social night club" (i.e., ladies/gentlemen's club) that is across the street from the restaurant. Shane expects his supervisor (and other professionals) will use their agency's per diem money to attend the club. Shane initially expresses hesitation about attending the club, but his supervisor begins to get angry at his decision. In fact, Shane's supervisor has threatened him with a poor evaluation and reference should he decide to not go with the group.

1. If you were Shane, what would you do? What role, if any, do values play in the decision-making process?

2. What are the potential consequences of the situation?

References

Abram, S. (2008). Scaffolding the new social literacies. *MultiMedia & Internet@ Schools, 15*(2), 21–23.

Gower, R. (2008). *Internships in recreation, sport, and tourism: Exploring student perceptions* (Doctoral dissertation). Retrieved from http://vufind.carli.illinois.edu/vf-uiu/Record/uiu_5779097/Holdings.

Hoffman, T. (2007). If you're networking for a job, it's already too late. *Computerworld, 41*(44), 54.

Jacobs, G. (2009). Online professional networking. *Contract Management, 49*(8), 10–14.

Mackay, H. (1999). *Dig your well before you're thirsty.* New York, NY: Doubleday.

Ramsey, D. (2004). What's new in networking? *Supervision, 64*(4), 6–8.

Surujlul, J., & Singh, C. (2010) Internships as a mechanism for professional preparation of sport management personnel: An empirical study of students' perceptions. *South African Journal for Research in Sport, Physical Education, and Recreation, 32*(2), 117–130.

Tjosvold, D., & Weicker, D. (1993). Cooperative and competitive networking by entrepreneurs: A critical incident study. *Journal of Small Business Management, 31*(1), 11–21.

van der Smissen, B., Moiseichik, M., & Hartenberg, V. (Eds.). (2004). *Management of park and recreation agencies.* Ashburn, VA: National Park and Recreation Association.

Chapter 10

Thinking Strategically about Your Career and the Internship

Overview

For many students, the path to a career in parks and recreation follows an interesting series of twists and turns. Although a few students identify with a career in recreation, sport, and tourism at a very early stage in their lives, many discover the field by previous experiences, through relationships, or by simple luck. For example, some students develop an interest for the field as a result of part-time seasonal employment with an agency and encouragement from current professionals. Other students might develop an initial interest in the field due to their previous participation in recreation programs or services. For other students, the recreation, sport, and tourism major might have been "discovered" while moving from academic major to academic major in search of that one major that is most closely aligned with their personal and career interests.

Regardless of the path, each student has likely experienced a unique series of events that brought him/her to the field of recreation, sport, and tourism. Some of these events were determined by the student, some by external sources (i.e., recreation agency, mentor, advisor, etc.), some by circumstance, and some by luck or chance. But regardless of the exact set of events or their consequence, each makes up the student's initial career path that has shaped not only the life of the student but will also impact the recreation experiences of thousands of others they will serve in their future career.

"**As an incoming freshman,** I was like most first-year college students, I had no clue what major I wanted to pursue. It was not until my sophomore year, after enrolling in an intro recreation class and learning about the numerous career opportunities in parks and recreation, that I found where I belonged."

When examining the career development of an aspiring recreation professional, academic and work experiences are obviously important elements of this process. However, an equally important element in the development of the student that is oftentimes absent from the process is the set of activities and experiences that constitutes career planning and management. As you are actively engaged in your internship and the latter stages of your undergraduate academic experience, the need for careful career planning is of growing importance. In addressing this essential function in your career, this chapter begins by exploring the concepts of career planning and management in detail. You will then be introduced to student-centered career planning and the strategies associated with these career planning efforts. After discussing career management and student-centered career planning, the chapter will turn to reviewing the relationship between career choice and personality. Finally, you will be exposed to potential career challenges young professionals encounter and strategies for coping with these early career challenges.

Career Planning

At this stage in your life, you have spent several years and invested personal resources in your academic program to foster your professional development. You have an important stake in your career, as you are the one who most directly experiences the benefits and rewards of a successful career. Conversely, you are also the one who incurs the most cost and frustration associated with career pitfalls and shortcomings. Furthermore, your perceptions and experiences associated with your career successes and failures are likely to have a significant impact on your self-esteem and overall self-worth (Noe, 2007).

Clearly you have a vested interest in your career, but how can you better position yourself to avoid those frustrating career pitfalls and failures? One widely recognized strategy is to regularly review and monitor your career to identify the reasons behind successes and failures. This will allow you to more clearly understand why you were or were not hired, promoted, given a raise, and so forth and will provide you with a good assessment of your future promotion prospects and possibilities. Furthermore, by accepting the responsibility of managing your career you will be better prepared to deal with unanticipated career setbacks, such as failing to secure that top-choice internship, job loss, or demotion.

Despite its importance, many students and professionals are surprisingly uninformed and uninvolved in their own careers. For example, consider the new professional or intern who goes to work but pays little attention to their role in the agency beyond the scope of their specific responsibilities. As a result of this approach, the new professional has little understanding as to how they came to be in a particular position, what their next position is likely to be, and how they might better prepare to handle that position when they are placed in it (DeNisi & Griffin, 2001). Simply put, they have no career plan. In contrast, by engaging in career planning, professionals or interns invest themselves in their agency and profession at a level deeper than is required by their job description, enabling them to have a clearer understanding of their career goals and future direction.

The Importance of Career Planning

Career planning requires a careful review of your interests and abilities. In general, most career planning systems involve the steps shown in Figure 10.1.

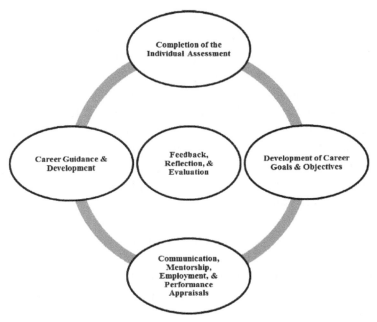

Figure 10.1. Steps in Career Planning

The first step in the career planning process is the individual assessment. The individual assessment is a review of your previous performance, experiences, and personal factors; an analysis of the tasks associated with the jobs of interest; and an examination of agencies' culture, resources, and placement rate. The process and recommended strategies for completing the individual assessment were discussed in Chapter 2. Guided by the information obtained from the individual assessment, a list of career goals and objectives are created (see Chapter 3 for a discussion of goal and objective development).

In addition to the individual assessment and the development of career goals and objectives, the presence of ongoing feedback, reflection, and evaluation are vital components to your career plan. Feedback can be formal or informal. Almost all agencies utilize a performance appraisal system to measure the intern or employee's performance during a specified period of time. The information obtained from the performance appraisal reviews provide you with insight into your performance effectiveness and can be used to identify areas in need of development or improvement.

Did You Know?

Career counselors predict "Generation Y" employees will make five different career changes over their professional lifespan—not five different jobs, five different careers!

A much more informal feedback mechanism is communication. For example, an agency may know the paths that are most likely to be followed from one position to another and may be able to gauge the probability or likelihood that a specific individual will follow this path at a prescribed pace. But if this information is not communicated to the individual intern or employee, then it will be of little to no value to anyone (DeNisi & Griffin, 2001). It is also important to note that while effective managers oftentimes make a concerted effort to coach and mentor student interns, student interns must also take initiative to seek this information out.

The final component of an effective career planning system is career counseling. Ongoing and present throughout the entire career planning process, career counseling involves the interaction between you and a career counselor. In this instance, the career counselor could be a variety of people, including a faculty member, an advisor, a professional supervisor, or an HR manager. Regardless of the individual, the counseling session typically involves some form of open and informal dialogue with the goal of making sure your assessment and the counselor's assessment are consistent with one another.

Individual-centered Career Planning

The working world has shifted from long-term employment environments to strategic, competitive, global environments that are quick to respond to changing conditions. For the professional, this shift has caused a change in career mindsets from that of job security (the belief that an individual will retain employment with the same agency until retirement) to a focus on employment security (having the kinds of skills that employers in the labor market are willing to pay for) (Cascio & Aguinis, 2005).

In thinking about these changing trends and their relationship to your career planning, it is important to be aware of the potentially temporary relationships between the employee and the agency. Consider the comment made by one professional who was the victim of three budget and staff reductions in four years: "A job is just an opportunity to learn new skills that you can then peddle elsewhere in the marketplace" (Daniels & Vinzant, 2000). Clearly this employee has a rather cynical view on today's workplace; however, the fact is that the responsibility for your career planning and development in today's workplace rests on your shoulders.

Despite the professional's important role in career planning, few individuals are prepared or willing to handle this activity (Cascio, 2006). This is not surprising as few college programs specifically address the challenges of managing one's own career. In response to this lack of preparation and to assist you with managing your career, the following guidelines are provided (Bolles, 2005):

1. To successfully plan for your career, you need to establish macro, long-range goals and objectives. You need to think in terms of where you ultimately want to be, recognizing, of course, that your career goals will likely change over time (see Chapter 3 for a discussion on goals and objectives).

2. Consider each internship and/or employment opportunity in relationship to your long-range career goals. When reviewing internship and job opportunities, you should ask yourself, "How well does this position help me achieve my career goals and objectives?" For example, if you aspire to secure a recreation director position in seven to 10 years, how does your current (or potential) job/internship help you develop the skill sets (i.e., leadership, communication, public speaking skills, personnel management, budgeting, etc.) required for a directorship position (Barrett & Beeson, 2004)?

3. Be prepared to accept short-term trade-offs for long-term benefits. Whether it is a lateral move or a lower paying job, you may need to consider temporary employment opportunities to assist you in reaching your long-term career goals. For example, it may be necessary for you to accept part-time employment if these experiences are helpful in developing your knowledge, skills, and abilities. These opportunities may also be needed to establish career contacts and develop your professional network that can assist you in "getting your foot in the door." The transition to the ideal position may need to happen a few years down the road.

4. Be cautious in your job selection. You should carefully consider whether to accept highly specialized internships or jobs that might restrict or impede your visibility and career development (Cascio, 2006). You do not want to limit your options early in your career by pursuing isolated internship or job opportunities that enable you to only develop a very narrow or specific skill set that will limit your marketability in the labor market. A task analysis of desired jobs and certification programs (i.e., Certified Park and Recreation Professional) can help you limit the probability of securing a highly specialized internship or job (see Chapter 3 for a discussion of the task analysis).

"**FRESH OUT OF COLLEGE** and I had a tough decision to make. The parks and recreation agency where I completed my internship did not have a full-time job available but really wanted to hire me. So they offered me a part-time job with the hope of it becoming full-time in the future. At the same time, I also had a full-time job offer, including benefits, from a wireless phone company. After much reflection and discussion with family, my advisor, and professionals I decided to take the part-time job with the parks and recreation agency. The full-time job (with the wireless phone company) was a dead-end job with no opportunities for promotion and I felt the parks and recreation job could help me 'get my foot in the door' in the field and improve my marketability in the future. In the end, it worked out for me. After eight weeks of part-time work, I was offered a full-time job with the agency!"

5. Keep abreast of opportunities available to you in your current position. Perhaps your position has training programs available to you that could assist you in reaching your career goals and objectives. For example, some agencies might provide incentives such as paid time off or financial assistance to pursue continuing education opportunities (i.e., workshops, conferences, graduate school, certification programs, etc.). It is your responsibility to be aware of these opportunities and target those that can assist you with your career plan.

6. Be an open, honest, and critical assessor of your performance. Routinely ask yourself, "How do I see myself, and how do I think higher management sees my performance? Am I in the right internship or job? Are my skills of real value to my agency? What other positions might fit my needs and skills well?" (Waterman, 2000).

7. Once in a job, you should recognize when you and your agency have outlived your utility for each other (Cascio, 2006). Although this issue may not arise with every job and agency, you need to be honest with yourself (and the agency) by recognizing the potential for this to occur. It is important to note that this is not an admission of failure, but rather an honest reflection of the fact that there is little more the agency can do for you and, in turn, that your contribution to the agency has reached a point of diminishing returns. Some common signs that the time has come include (a) your job ranks low on a "joy and meaning scale;" (b) requests for advancement or new opportunities are ignored consistently or only half met; (c) your job does not adequately

meet your needs in areas you care about, such as work–family balance, work location, and compensation; (d) your standing in the office has been diminished (i.e., key participants/members, sponsors, vendors, staff, etc. no longer deal with you); or (e) you are no longer fulfilling your dreams (Fisher, 2001).

8. In addition to recognizing when you have outlived your position, it is also important to leave your current job (and agency) on good terms and not under questionable circumstances (Cascio, 2006). The recreation, sport, and tourism industries are relatively small that include very connected networks of professionals. You want your experiences to work for you, and by leaving an agency on good terms you will create positive work references that could help you later in your career.

9. Finally and if at all possible, avoid leaving your current job until you've secured other employment. It is generally much easier to find a new job when you are currently employed.

Career Choice and Interest Inventories

A career in the recreation, sport, and tourism industries is filled with diverse opportunities. From working in the public sector to employment within a private setting and from jobs in aquatics to jobs working with professional sport organizations, the recreation, sport, and tourism industries encompass a variety of experiences. Although some similarities exist within the scope and nature of these varied positions within these service sectors, each job comes with its own unique qualities and responsibilities.

As an aspiring professional, you have the opportunity to identify and pursue jobs that are most closely aligned with your background and interests. Arguably one of the most important career decisions you will make, the selection of a specific career path within the field of parks and recreation, can be an enjoyable, yet difficult decision. To assist young professionals with this process, some psychologists who specialize in career counseling have proposed and researched theories of (vocational) choice. One of the most widely recognized experts in the field, John L. Holland, has suggested that the choice of a career path is an expression of personality and not a random event, though chance can play a role (as cited in Ivancevich, 2007). Holland (1994) contends that what an individual accomplishes and derives from a career depends on the congruence between his/her personality and the job environment. Furthermore, Holland (1994) believes that each individual to some extent resembles one of the six personality types: realistic, investigative, artistic, social, enterprising, and conventional.

- The *realistic individual* prefers activities involving the manipulation of machinery or tools; desires working with tools, mechanical and/or electrical drawings, machines, plants and/or animals; values practicality; and generally avoids social activities such as teaching, healing, programming, and so forth.

  Examples: Stadium operations coordinator, operations manager, park ranger, special projects coordinator, and so forth

- The *investigative individual* prefers to be analytical, curious, methodical, and precise; has interests in scientific and mathematical problem solving; and typically avoids leading, selling, or persuading others.

  Examples: Convention manager, banquet coordinator, grants and research supervisor, park planner, environmental coordinator, and so forth

- The *artistic person* is expressive, nonconforming, original, and introspective; likes to engage in creative activities; is independent; and generally avoids repetitive activities.

  Examples: Convention planner, cultural arts supervisor, sports, marketing manager, and so forth

- The *social person* enjoys working with and helping others and purposefully avoids systematic activities involving tools and machinery; oftentimes, these individuals are good at teaching, programming, leading, and counseling.

  Examples: CVB manager, recreation supervisor, professional sports agent, day camp director, senior supervisor, and so forth

- The *enterprising person* enjoys activities that permit him/her to influence others to accomplish goals; and generally avoids experiences or activities that require careful observation and/or scientific reasoning.

  Examples: Enterprise facility manager, professional sports general manager, country club manager, resort director, executive director, and so forth

- The *conventional individual* enjoys the systematic manipulation of data, filing records, or reproducing materials; values success in business, orderly behaviors, and planning; and typically avoids ambiguous or unstructured activities.

  Examples: Accountant, finance director, office supervisor, and so forth (Ivancevich, 2007)

According to Holland (1994), the more an individual resembles any given type, the more likely he/she is to display some of the behaviors and traits with that personality type. Researchers have also suggested that although one personality type predominates, many strategies and actions fall within the boundaries of two or more types. Holland uses a hexagon to describe this potential for overlapping personality types. Holland's research has found that the closer two orientations are in the hexagon arrangement, the more similar the personality types are (Ivancevich, 2007). Drawing from these findings, Holland suggests that the adjacent personality types (i.e., Social–Artistic, Integrative–Realistic, etc.) are similar, while nonadjacent types (i.e., Realistic–Social, Artistic–Conventional, etc.) are dissimilar (see Table 10.1) (Holland, 1996). Subscribing to Holland's logic, it could be argued that if your predominant and secondary personality types are similar, you will have a relatively easy time selecting a career. In contrast, dissimilar predominant and secondary orientations may result in difficulty in choosing a career (Ivancevich, 2007).

To determine one's predominant and secondary personality type, a variety of quantitative instruments have been developed. Instruments such as the *Vocational Preference Inventory* and the *Strong Interest Inventory* can be completed to assess your resemblance to the six personality types. Completing these personality inventories can provide you with some insightful information about your personality and job preferences. In turn, this information can then be used to assist you with your career planning and future direction.

Another inventory that can help you with your career direction is the *Campbell Interest and Skill Survey* (CISS). The CISS measures both your interests and skills and has been widely utilized by agencies to help employees review their career paths. The CISS uses a 6-point response scale and 200 items to assess your interests and 120 items to measure your skills. Your scores are then translated into seven orientations: (a) influencing, (b) organizing, (c) helping, (d) creating, (e) analyzing, (f) producing, and (g) adventuring (Campbell, 1992). These seven orientations are further subdivided into 29 areas, such as leadership, writing, risks/adventure, supervision, child development, and forestry. As shown in Figure 10.2, an individual's interest is displayed as a black diamond; a skill is a white diamond. The interest score designates an individual's liking or preference for an activity while the skill score indicates how confident the individual is about performing the activity (Ivancevich, 2007).

If an individual scores high on interests and skills, it is recommended that he/she seriously considers integrating the orientation or activity within his/her career plan. Someone who scores high in interest but low in skill is encouraged to develop his/her skills, while a low interest score combined with a high skill score suggests that exploration is needed. Finally, a low interest score and a low skill score suggest the individual should avoid the orientation or activity within the career plan (Ivancevich, 2007).

Table 10.1

What is Your Career Personality?

Career Personality Type	Relationship with Other Personality Type(s)?
Realistic – prefers to work with things/objects rather than people; enjoys working outdoors and being physically active	Typically works well with Investigative and Conventional personality types; is often in conflict with Social personality types.
Investigative – embraces scientific and mathematic experiences/processes; is drawn to abstract and/complex challenges and the use of logic.	Typically works well with Realistic and Artistic personality types; is often in conflict with Enterprising personality types.
Artistic –often original, intuitive and imaginative, and enjoys creative activities; prefers flexiblilty in working arrangements; and is comfortable with ambiguity.	Typically works well with Investigative and Social personality types; is often in conflict with Conventional personality types.
Social – desires to help others; enjoys counseling, training, and developmental activities with a strong interest in fostering human relationships.	Typically works well with Artistic and Enterprising personality types; is often in conflict with Realistic personality types.
Enterprising – displays high levels of energy, ambition, self-confidence; enjoys adventurous activities/projects; gravitates toward activities allowing them to use persuasion (i.e., sales & marketing); and seeks out leadership roles.	Typically works well with Social and Conventional personality types; is often in conflict with Investigative personality types.
Conventional – desires efficiency, organization, and systematic activities; skilled in and often enjoys maintaining and manipulating data, organizing schedules, and operating office equipment.	Typically works well with Enterprising and Realistic personality types; is often in conflict with Artistic personality types.

Orientations and Basic Scales

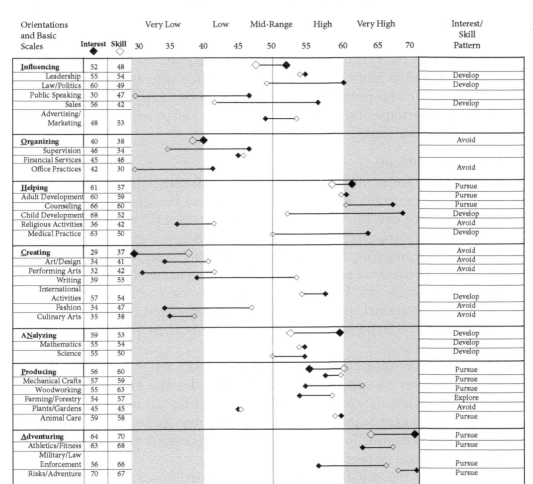

Orientations and Basic Scales	Interest	Skill	Very Low	Low	Mid-Range	High	Very High	Interest/ Skill Pattern
			30 35	40 45	50 55	60	65 70	
Influencing	52	48						
Leadership	55	54						Develop
Law/Politics	60	49						Develop
Public Speaking	30	47						
Sales	56	42						Develop
Advertising/ Marketing	48	53						
Organizing	40	38						Avoid
Supervision	46	34						
Financial Services	45	46						
Office Practices	42	30						Avoid
Helping	61	57						Pursue
Adult Development	60	59						Pursue
Counseling	66	60						Pursue
Child Development	68	52						Develop
Religious Activities	36	42						Avoid
Medical Practice	63	50						Develop
Creating	29	37						Avoid
Art/Design	34	41						Avoid
Performing Arts	32	42						Avoid
Writing	39	53						
International Activities	57	54						Develop
Fashion	34	47						Avoid
Culinary Arts	35	38						Avoid
ANalyzing	59	53						Develop
Mathematics	55	54						Develop
Science	55	50						Develop
Producing	56	60						Pursue
Mechanical Crafts	57	59						Pursue
Woodworking	55	63						Pursue
Farming/Forestry	54	57						Explore
Plants/Gardens	45	45						Avoid
Animal Care	59	58						Pursue
Adventuring	64	70						Pursue
Athletics/Fitness	63	68						Pursue
Military/Law Enforcement	56	66						Pursue
Risks/Adventure	70	67						Pursue

Source: Campbell Interest and Skill Survey (CISS). Copyright 1992 David Campbell, Ph.D. Reproduced with permission of the publisher NCS Pearson, Inc.

Figure 10.2. Campbell Interest and Skill Survey Test (CISS®)

Career Management for New Professionals

Oftentimes, the early career stages faced by new professionals are the most tumultuous. Regardless of whether the new professional is employed in his/her first job or searching for an internship in the field, new entrants into the workforce often feel a certain degree of uncertainty and apprehension about their job and chosen career path. Thus, an important starting point for new professionals who are interested in more effectively managing their careers is to understand some of the early career problems that they might encounter. The following sections will identify some of these early career issues and provide suggestions for managing these challenges.

Early Career Problems

It is common for newly hired interns or professionals to encounter a number of potential problems during their first weeks on the job. One of the most common problems new hires face is the dynamics associated with the initial job and expectations associated with this new experience. For example, when college students are preparing for a career in recreation, sport, and tourism, they often envision themselves performing high-profile, challenging, exciting tasks in beautiful environments. However, in reality, most new hires start at the bottom of the organizational chart, and may be performing tasks that are relatively tedious, menial, and far below what they perceive to be their level of competence and capability.

These potential disappointments with initial job assignments have been shown to spill over into negative workplace attitudes and job satisfaction. In particular, professionals working at lower levels of the agency with relatively short tenure often express low levels of job satisfaction. These low levels of satisfaction, in turn, are a function of unmet expectations regarding the kind of work the individual might be performing (Hall, 1996).

In addition to the initial shock associated with the job or internship's scope of work, early career professionals also encounter problems with the initial performance appraisal. Depending on the agency, the performance appraisal may be completed on an annual, semiannual, quarterly, or even monthly basis and is used to evaluate the employee or intern's performance. Regardless of the appraisal schedule, many new hires are surprised and disappointed at the results of their initial performance review. This can be particularly shocking for a student intern who is accustomed to high performance ratings in the classroom and learns that his/her performance does not "Exceed Standards," but merely "Meets Standards." Although anxious about the nature of the job, the student intern feels he/she is doing high-quality work. This shock is often compounded by those supervisors who tend to focus a lot of their initial performance appraisal reviews on those areas most in need of improvement. Thus, the student intern's first performance appraisal review may tend to be somewhat more negative than originally envisioned.

Coping with Early Career Challenges

There are a variety of techniques you can employ to reduce the impact of these early career issues. These strategies can assist you in making your early career experiences more productive and positive. A list of the more popular strategies for managing your early career experiences is provided below.

Obtain a realistic job preview. A realistic job preview (RJP) informs applicants about all aspects of the job, including both its desirable and undesirable facets (Bohlander & Snell, 2004). RJPs are premised on the notion that applicants who are given realistic information regarding a position are more likely to remain on the job and be successful, because there will be fewer unpleasant surprises. Furthermore, research has found that RJPs have improved employee job satisfaction, reduced voluntary turnover, enhanced communication through honesty and openness, and provided realistic job expectations (Bretz & Judge, 1998). Most often, a RJP can be obtained from the agency and/or its supervisor. However, if the agency or the supervisor is unwilling or unable to provide a RJP, new professionals can obtain RJPs from a variety of outside sources, including faculty, advisors, recent graduates, previous job incumbents, and so forth.

Seek out initial job projects that are challenging. Work with your supervisor to tackle an initial job assignment that is a challenging and fulfilling task. By completing this task, you are able to demonstrate your capabilities to your supervisor, which could lead to more exciting tasks to perform.

Search for supervisors that have a demonstrated track record of mentorship and support. Spend considerable time reviewing the job placement rate of former interns as well as the mentorship qualities of supervisors to identify those who have the ability to mentor and to challenge new hires. Some supervisors are more astute than others at understanding the needs, motives, and aspirations of professionals and at taking a stronger, more beneficial interest in their careers. These are the supervisors you should seek out early in your career to help you address some of the early career problems. Careful consultation with the university internship coordinator can also be helpful as, over time, they become familiar with the practices and traits of certain supervisors.

"INITIALLY, I REALLY STRUGGLED to find full-time employment in this job market. I probably applied to more than 50 jobs. I really opened my search as I applied to jobs near my hometown in Central Illinois to several states throughout the country—Maine, Texas, California, Kansas, and Alaska just to name a few. I had a few interviews, but regularly heard they went with someone who had a bit more experience which I think was easier for them to find in this job market. It was depressing. I always thought I had the tools to be a successful professional—strong academic background with grades that reflected my strong understanding of the content coupled with what I felt was a solid amount of professional experience for a new graduate. Since my freshman year in college, I had worked every summer with a park and recreation agency where I was a camp counselor, staff trainer, and even a camp director! I also led several corporate and school retreats during the fall and spring semesters of my junior and senior years. My internship site was a very reputable site as well. However, six months after my internship I was still struggling to find a full-time job. Eventually, I had to take a job outside of my field for financial reasons. As time went by, I felt like I reached a transitional period in my career path and needed to decide what to do. Do I stay with my current job (outside of the field) and invest time and energy into trying to work my way up the ladder OR do I give my field another chance? After some reflection, I decided to seek advice from my former mentors. I reached out to a few of my college professors and professional mentors. Wow, did this pay off! When I spoke to my former internship supervisor, she indicated her agency had a part-time opportunity for me. Based on my background, the opportunity was right up my alley and I decided to take it. The experience put new life into my passion for the field and revitalized my job search! I began applying for full-time jobs (in my field) again and after sending out four applications I interviewed and was offered full-time positions at three of the four agencies! I accepted one of the positions and have been working there for more than a year. I love my job! It is a great fit for me, my interests, and my overall career plan. I often wonder what would have happened to me and my career path if I hadn't reached out to a few of my former mentors. Without making that phone call, I would have missed out on that great part-time opportunity and might not have applied for my current job. Certainly, a pivotal experience in my career."

Create an Action Plan

1. Review the three strategies for coping with early career challenges (see "Coping with Early Career Challenges" section).

2. Prepare an action plan for addressing each of the three strategies during your internship. In particular, your action plan should include a vision statement and goals and objectives.

    a. Imagine yourself working at your internship site. What do you do? What makes you happy? How will this experience help you with your future career? Be as specific as possible. Your vision is the umbrella for all your goals; it's a compass to consult every time the everyday circumstances change and goals need to be adjusted.

    b. Guided by your vision and the three coping strategies, develop goals and (measurable) objectives that are aligned with your vision and will ensure you complete each of the three coping strategies. Specifically, how/where will you obtain a realistic job preview? How will you seek out challenging job projects? How will you determine if your supervisor has a proven track record of mentorship, and what role will this play in achieving your future career goals? Your goals and corresponding objectives should be designed with specific action statements and timelines to allow you to more effectively monitor your progress.

3. Share your action plan with a friend, mentor, or faculty member. Discuss your plan and how you will address potential roadblocks in completing the action plan.

Summary

As a student in his/her final years of undergraduate education, you are at a transitional period in your life. In particular, you are actively engaged in an internship experience that will hopefully catapult you into your first full-time job. The consequences of the opportunities and activities you experience during your internship will be closely linked to your career successes or challenges. To be better positioned for future success and to avoid unnecessary career pitfalls require careful career planning. Career planning is not something that should be left to chance; instead, in the evolving field of parks and recreation it requires the completion of an individual assessment; well-developed career goals and objectives; performance management and feedback; and ongoing communication with career counselors, supervisors, coworkers, mentors, and advisors. As mentioned in Chapter 2, the individual assessment needs to be revisited and updated on a regular basis. This ongoing assessment shapes your career goals and objectives and is likely in a constant state of flux as the profession and your career interests evolve over time. To keep pace with these changing trends and needs requires ongoing planning that can be used to map out your career path while helping you avoid those frustrating career roadblocks and setbacks that are associated with inadequate career planning.

Chapter 10 Essentials

- When considering your professional future, academic and work experiences are important elements of this process.

- An equally important element of your professional development process is the set of activities and experiences that constitute career planning and management.

- Despite its importance, many students and professionals are surprisingly uninformed and uninvolved in the planning and management of their own careers.

- Career planning requires a careful review of your interests and abilities and typically involves completion of an individual assessment, development of goals and objectives, ongoing communication, performance feedback, and career counseling.

- The working world has shifted from long-term employment environments to strategic, competitive, global environments that are quick to respond to changing conditions. For the professional, this shift has caused a change in career mindsets from that of job security (the belief that an individual will retain employment with the same agency until retirement) to a focus on employment security (having the kinds of skills that employers in the labor market are willing to pay for) (Cascio & Aguinis, 2005).

- As an aspiring professional, you have the opportunity to identify and pursue jobs that are most closely aligned with your background and interests.

- It is common for newly hired interns or professionals to encounter a number of potential problems during their first weeks on the job, and there are a variety of techniques that can be utilized to reduce the impact of these early career issues.

Discussion Questions

1. It is common for young professionals to have unmet expectations on the job. This, in turn, leads to low levels of satisfaction and usually high turnover. What are some things you can begin doing now to be sure you have a realistic understanding of the career you are preparing to begin?

2. Holland's Occupational Orientation lists six different personality types. Clearly, most of us do not fall into a single category. What combination of these three best fit you, and what are the implications for your upcoming internship or career?

3. The chapter clearly indicated the importance of maintaining employment security, not job security. What steps are you taking, or should you take, to be sure you are developing, enhancing, and learning the skills that will be desired by employers in the years to come?

They Say It's Your Birthday

Megan was just hired as an assistant facility manager of an indoor recreation facility for a park district in the Midwest. The recreation facility is about 90,000 square feet and contains aerobic studios, fitness center, basketball/volleyball courts, ice rink, concession area, child care area, banquet/meeting rooms, and a climbing wall. As the assistant manager, Megan has been exposed to the various aspects of facility management—scheduling, personnel management, marketing/communications, maintenance, registration software, security, operational procedures and policies, and programming.

One of Megan's primary roles is part-time scheduling and supervision of the facility and its programming during evenings and weekends. One day during the summer, a park district board commissioner and her grandchildren stop by unexpectedly to use the facility. The commissioner indicates she has brought a group over for a birthday party, and they want to use the climbing wall. Facility policy requires all birthday parties to be scheduled in advance (with a deposit) to ensure the proper personnel are available to assist with the party (i.e., climbing staff, maintenance, set-up crew, etc.). The board member has brought her own food (which is also forbidden). Megan is qualified to provide the necessary climbing services and has additional staff available. However, Megan is concerned about the message it will send her staff. Megan also knows that this commissioner has done this before to other departments (i.e., golf, arts, child care, etc.) and failing to accommodate her could be problematic for her.

1. How would you respond to this request? Be specific.

2. What led you to your decision? What elements of the situation were most helpful for you in making your decision?

3. What factors, if any, would change your proposed response?

References

Barrett, A., & Beeson, J. (2004). *Developing business leaders for 2010.* New York, NY: The Conference Board.

Bohlander, G., & Snell, S. (2004). *Managing human resources* (13th ed). Mason, OH: Thomson South-Western.

Bolles, R. N. (2005). *What color is your parachute? 2005: A practical manual for job hunters and career changers.* Berkley, CA: Ten-Speed Press.

Bretz, R. D., & Judge, T. A. (1998). Realistic job previews: A test of the adverse self-selection hypothesis. *Journal of Applied Psychology, 83*(2), 330–337.

Campbell, D. K. (1992). *Campbell interest and skill survey.* Minneapolis, MN: NCS Assessments.

Cascio, W. F. (2006). *Managing human resources: Productivity, quality of work life, profits* (7th ed.). Boston, MA: McGraw-Hill Irwin.

Cascio, W. F., & Aguinis, H. (2005). *Applied psychology in human resource management* (6th ed.). Upper Saddle River, NJ: Pearson Prentice Hall.

Daniels, C., & Vinzant, C. (2000). The joy of quitting. *Fortune,* 199–202.

DeNisi, A. S., & Griffin, R. W. (2001). *Human resource management.* Boston, MA: Houghton Mifflin.

Fisher, A. (2001). Surviving the downturn. *Fortune,* 98–106.

Hall, D. T. (1996). Protean careers of the 21st century. *Academy of Management Executive, 10*(4), 8–16.

Holland, J. L. (1994). *The self-directed search.* Odessa, FL: Psychological Assessment Resources.

Holland, J. L. (1996). Exploring careers with a typology. *American Psychologist,* 397–406.

Ivancevich, J. M. (2007). *Human resource management* (10th ed). New York, NY: McGraw-Hill.

Noe, R. A. (2007). *Employee training and development* (3rd ed.). New York, NY: McGraw-Hill.

Waterman, J. A. (2000). Informed opportunism: Career and life planning for the new millennium. In J. M. Kummerow (Ed.), *New directions in career planning and the workplace.* Palo Alto, CA: Davies-Black.

Chapter 11

Preparing for the Next Step

Overview

As you prepare to begin your internship, it is also important to think about life after the internship. Specifically, where do you want to be after the internship? What type of employment do you want? To answer these questions requires careful planning.

Planning for your first job in the field of recreation, sport, and tourism should begin well before the start of your internship. From your academic experiences and individual assessment to the development of professional goals and objectives, your work to securing employment is an ongoing process. The internship experience, although important, is just one step in the process. Thus, you need to be planning your next professional step before and during your internship experience. Too often, students will view the internship as the final, capstone experience and will hold the assumption that full-time employment will "fall into place" once the internship (and undergraduate degree) has concluded. In reality, securing full-time employment can be a much more time-consuming and detailed process when compared to the work associated with securing the internship. Thus, careful planning is needed to ensure you are positioned to best market yourself to land that first full-time job. This chapter will discuss steps and strategies associated with career development to assist you in successfully managing this transition.

Planning for Your Career: Definitions and Responsibility

Career planning is the process by which you formulate career goals and develop a plan for reaching those goals (Byars & Rue, 2004). This process is not something that should be left up to your supervisor, mentor, or simple chance; instead, it should be shaped and managed by you. Successful planning requires you to be alert to available job opportunities (both inside and outside your current agency) in relation to your abilities. For example, you might be interested in being a ranger for the country's most popular national park until discovering that more than 200 current rangers working for other national parks are available and interested for every ranger position opening at the popular national park. As a result, you may need to focus more energy on "getting your foot in the door" at another national park. Once you have acquired some years of experience as a park ranger within the national park system, you could increase your efforts on landing your dream job at the popular national park.

Clearly, planning for your next job is an ongoing process that should be a significant focus point both before and during your internship experience. It is also clear that you play an important role in planning your career. However, what are your specific responsibilities? Can your internship agency assist you with this process? What about your internship site and academic supervisors? What role, if any, do they play in your career planning? The answer to these questions is all of them should play a role (see Table 11.1 for the responsibilities of each role). In particular, a successful career plan benefits from the involvement of you, your internship agency, and your supervisors. A description of responsibilities commonly associated with each source is provided in the following paragraphs.

Noe (2007) has identified the following intern, supervisor, and agency responsibilities associated with the career management process:

Intern/Employee (You)
- **Self-assessment.** As the intern/employee, you must systematically engage in an individual assessment (see Chapter 2 for details on the individual assessment) to maintain alignment between your career path and short-and-long-term goals.
- **Self-developed action plan.** Most recreation, sport, and tourism agencies do not have a program for organization centered career planning; thus, you will likely need to develop and implement your own individual-centered career plan.
- **Create visibility through good performance and relationships.** The best approach to getting recognized is through positive (job/internship) performance.
- **Seek challenges.** When possible and aligned with your career plan, explore new opportunities for development and professional growth.

Supervisor
- **Communicating.** Effective communication is a core competency for any supervisor.
- **Coaching.** Ensures staff have the resources needed to be successful.

- **Appraising.** Consistently evaluating staff and examining these results against future development needs and career paths.
- **Mentoring.** Provides formal and informal guidance and assistance to staff as they navigate their careers.
- **Advocating**. Staff's biggest supporter.
- **Request information from other agency resources.** Serves as a clearinghouse of career information and job opportunities.

Agency
- **Develop systems to support career management.** Establishes a formalized program or platform to assist staff with their career development.
- **Develop culture that supports career management.** Oftentimes, in the form of training and development activities.

Internship Agency and Academic Institution Responsibilities

Your career plan and the development of the plan is, ultimately, your responsibility. However, your academic institution and internship agency provide support for your plans development. Both sites (academic and internship) provide formalized opportunities that assist you in developing and enriching your knowledge, skills, and abilities in the field of recreation, sport, and tourism. These institutions have the primary responsibility for instigating and ensuring you are exposed to opportunities to enhance your overall professional development. For example, many of these institutions will develop and communicate career options with their students or interns. They will work closely with the individual to provide insight and support concerning job opportunities both within and outside of their agencies as well as counsel individuals on the possible career paths that will be supportive of the individual's long-term career goals. Working closely with the student or intern, the academic and internship institutions ensure that accurate information is conveyed and that the interrelationships among different career paths are understood (Byars & Rue, 2004). Thus, rather than bearing the primary responsibility for preparing your career plan, these institutions promote the conditions and create the environments that will facilitate the development of your career plan.

Supervisor's Responsibility

Randolph (1981) once stated, "…the critical battleground in career development is inside the mind of the person charged with supervisory responsibility." At the core of Randolph's message is the need for supervisors to take an active role in their interns' career development. However, it is also worth mentioning that the supervisors are not expected to be professional counselors for the interns; rather, they are a facilitator of the interns' professional development.

Simply put, the supervisors' role is to educate the interns on the importance of developing career goals and plans, guide them in this process, and assist the interns in evaluating their actions and the impact these actions have on their career plans. In describing the supervisor's role in the job search and career development process, researchers havedeveloped a list of responsibilities and roles many supervisors perform to assist their staff (Kidd & Smewing, 2001; Leibowitz &Schlossberg, 1981) (see Table 11.1).

Table 11.1

Responsibilities and Roles of the Supervisor

Role	Responsibilities
Role 1 – "Communicator"	Holds formal and informal discussion with staff
	Listens to and understands staff's real concerns
	Clearly and effectively interacts with staff
	Establishes an environment for open interaction
	Structures uninterrupted time to meet with staff
Role 2 – "Appraiser"	Identifies critical job elements
	Negotiates with staff to establish a set of goals and objectives to evaluate performance
	Assesses staff performance related to goals and objectives
	Communicates performance evaluation and assessment to staff
	Designs a development plan around future job-related goals and objectives
	Reinforces effective performance
	Reviews and establishes development plan on an ongoing basis
Role 3 – "Coach"	Teaches specific job-related or technical skills
	Suggests specific behaviors for improvement
	Clarifies and communicates goals and objectives of work group and agency

Table 11.1 (cont.)

Role 4 – "Manager"	Arranges for staff to participate in high-visibility activity either inside or outside the agency
	Serves as a role model in staff's career development by demonstrating successful career behaviors
	Supports staff by communicating staff's effectiveness to others in and out of the agency
Role 5 - "Advisor"	Communicates the informal and formal realities of (career) progression in the profession
	Suggests appropriate training activities that could benefit individual staff
	Suggests appropriate strategies for career development
Role 6 – "Broker"	Assists in bringing staff together who might mutually help each other in their careers
	Assists in linking staff with appropriate educational (i.e., workshops, conferences, certification classes, etc.) or employment opportunities
	Helps staff identify obstacles to changing present situation
	Helps staff identify resources enabling them to land a new job or manage a career change
Role 7 – "Referral Agent"	Identifies staff with problems (i.e., career, health, personal, etc.)
	Identifies resources appropriate to a staff member experiencing a problem
	Bridges and supports staff with referral agents
	Follows up on effectiveness or suggested referrals
Role 8 – "Advocate"	Works with staff in designing a plan to address a specific job or career-related issue
	Works with staff in planning alternative strategies if specific job or career-related issues are unresolved
	Represents staff's concern or issue to upper-level management when necessary

Your Responsibility

As mentioned earlier, the primary responsibility for developing and implementing your career plan rests with you. Searching for your first post-internship job as well as future career opportunities are tasks that another person cannot do for you; it has to come from you. You are the one who knows what you really want out of a job and career.

In summary, you are responsible for your own career plan. From the job search process to managing career transitions, the onus for successfully navigating these experiences rests with you. Your supervisors and internship agencies can provide assistance during your professional journey in the form of mentorship, networking, educational opportunities, support, and overall guidance, but you must take a leadership role in developing and acquiring this assistance. In short, you must seek out and take advantage of these resources. In describing how to take advantage of these opportunities, Sherman (1993) suggests interns do the following:

- Be proactive as initiative represents a key element in the individual-centered career plan. Unfortunately this can be problematic as one of the most frequently cited areas of concern for student interns on their performance appraisals is "lack of initiative." This deficiency must be addressed if the intern is to engage in successful career planning. In addressing this concern, interns should ask for feedback from supervisors and peers regarding their skill strengths and weaknesses.

- Be cognizant of the job search process and their stage in this process. Interns should map out their plans, including the various stages (i.e., prepare resume/cover letter, submit application materials, interview preparation, etc.) of the search process, in relationship to their career development needs and timeline(s).

- When feasible, interns should take the initiative to pursue new challenges. Several positive outcomes can result from these experiences, including competency development, new professional networking opportunities, and exposure to a variety of new learning experiences.

- Network, network, and network some more. Interns should seek out opportunities to meet and connect with professionals from different divisions or departments, inside and outside the agency.

- One of the best ways to get noticed is through solid performance.

Searching for that first full-time job and developing a career plan require well-developed strategies and hard work. It is also unlikely that the desired results of your time and efforts spent developing and implementing your plan will happen automatically (Byars & Rue, 2004). In achieving your career-related goals, you must be persistent and patient with the process, as research has repeatedly shown that while most professionals recognize the value in having a sound career, they often fail to make time to develop such a plan (Byars & Rue, 2004). Strategies to successfully manage your plan are presented in the later sections of this chapter.

Common Myths Associated with the Job Search Process

One of the first steps in the job search process and overall career plan is to distinguish fact from fiction. Specifically, which job search and career development strategies are valid tools that can foster growth and career success and which strategies are inaccurate myths? In addressing this issue, it is necessary to recognize the most common myths related to the job search process in particular and an individual's overall career plan in general. Oftentimes, these myths can pose problems for students by restricting personal and professional growth. To assist you in avoiding these potential career pitfalls, some of the most common myths are provided below.

Myth #1: The Key to Success Is Being in the Right Place at the Right Time (Byars & Rue, 2004)

Probably one of the biggest myths to the job search process, this one has just enough truth to make it believable (Byars & Rue, 2004). One can always find a highly successful person who attributes all of his/her success to being in the right place at the right time. People who adhere to this myth are rejecting the basic philosophy of planning: that a person, through careful design, can affect rather than merely accept the future. Adhering to this myth is dangerous because it can lead to complacency and a defeatist attitude.

Myth #2: The Job Search is Difficult, Boring, and No Fun at All (Wallis, 2002)

If you use effective job-search techniques, you won't be stressed at all; you'll be excited (Wallis, 2002). Attitudes and behaviors carry over into other spheres of life. Thus, if you are unhappy and frustrated searching for a job, these attitudes and behaviors are likely to show up in all phases of the process (i.e., searching, applying, interviewing, etc.). One way to avoid getting "stuck in a rut" with your search is to visualize yourself in the job of your dreams and giving yourself of pep talk whenever you feel discouraged (Wallis, 2002).

Myth #3: All Good Things Come to Those Who Work Long, Hard Hours (Byars & Rue, 2004)

Individuals guided by this belief often spend 10 to 12 hours a day trying to impress their supervisors and move ahead rapidly in the agency. However, the results of these extra hours on the job often have little or no relationship to what the supervisor considers important, to your effectiveness on the job, or (most important in this context) to your long-range career growth. This myth can be challenging to manage and avoid, as it has become common practice for supervisors to design activities to "keep staff busy." Despite this challenge, you need to be able to strike a balance between working hard and working for the sake of trying to impress your supervisor.

Myth #4: A Majority of the Jobs are Listed in the Want Ads, Job Bulletins, and the Classifieds (Medinsky, 2012)

Data has indicated only 15% to 20% of the job openings are listed on these market platforms. Although these sources can be very helpful during your job search process, phone calls, personal visits to agencies, and professional conferences/workshops are encouraged to help make that initial connection.

Myth #5: Job Seekers Should Not Have to "Sell" Themselves to Potential Employers (Hansen, 2012)

As discussed in Chapters 5 and 6, the application process is all about articulating your fit for the position of interest. Successful applicants must market and sell how their skills and experiences match the position. The job seeker must utilize many of the same marketing and sales principles companies use to sell their products to showcase their intangible qualities, their fit for the position, and their positive contributions to the hiring agency.

Myth #6: A Cover Letter's Primary Purpose is to Introduce the Résumé (Ryan, 2007)

The cover letter is an opportunity to showcase your personality, intangible qualities, and written communication skills. It is used to articulate the connection and fit between you and your experiences and the needs of the agency. Furthermore, it conveys three fundamental items: (1) you understand the agency's mission and direction, (2) you've got the skills and experience to meet the challenge, and, (3) you're a smart person and solid writer (Ryan, 2007).

Myth #7: Always Do Your Best, Regardless of the Task (Byars & Rue, 2004)

This myth stems from the puritan work ethic. The problem is that believers will ignore the fact that different tasks have different priorities. Because there is only a limited amount of time, you should spend your time according to priorities. Those tasks and jobs that rank high in importance in assisting you with your career goals should receive your best effort. Those tasks that do not rank high should be done, but not necessarily with one's best effort. The idea is to give something less than your best effort to unimportant tasks in order to have time to give your best effort to the important ones.

Myth #8: The Internal Candidate Always Gets the Position Over the External Ones (Ryan, 2007)

Not true. Just because you interned for the agency doesn't automatically translate into you landing that job opening with the agency. It certainly helps to have a positive work history and references within the agency, but you also have to deal with the fact that your colleagues already know your weaknesses (Ryan, 2007). In contrast, the external candidates are starting with a cleaner slate and by the time their weaknesses are identified, he/she may already be hired. The key is for you to treat all of your experiences with the agency (i.e., part-time, seasonal, internship, etc.) as part of the interview. Simply put, be aware of your environment and your behaviors at all times while working for the agency.

Myth # 9: There are No Jobs/No One is Hiring (Medinsky, 2012)

Although the job market has tightened since 2008, there are opportunities available. Current professionals are switching jobs and careers, moving, receiving promotions, retiring, etc. These constantly changing times create domino-like effects, leading to new job openings on a regular basis. The key is stay focused and prepared because at any moment, that dream job might present itself.

Myth #10: It is All About Networking (Wallis, 2002)

Networking is an important competency to possess in recreation, sport, and tourism industries, but it is not the only way to get a job. An effective job search requires a combination of strategies and you should make a list of ALL job search methods and how they can help you secure employment (Wallis, 2002).

Understanding the Job Search Myths Exercise

1. Review the myths in the job search process.

2. Identify which myths are most surprising to you. Why?

3. Meet with a mentor and discuss these myths. Discuss how you will avoid the challenges associated with these myths. What strategies will you employ? What advice does your mentor have to help you avoid these career pitfalls?

Planning for the Next Phase: The Job Search Process and Your Career

In addition to recognizing potential pitfalls and myths related to the job search and your career planning, it is equally important to be aware of the productive steps and strategies associated with the career management process. Although each job search and overall career plan may vary in its level of sophistication, intensity, and emphasis placed on different elements in the process (i.e., résumé development, networking, geographic location constraints, etc.), most plans include the following components: individual assessment, performance history, goal development, and action planning. Each of these components will be discussed in the following sections.

Self-assessment

As discussed in Chapter 2, the individual or self-assessment refers to the use of information (by you) to determine your career interests, values, aptitudes, and behavioral tendencies (Noe, 2007). The self-assessment process often involves career interest tests, such as the *Campbell Interest and Skill Survey*, *Vocational Preference Inventory*, and/or the *Strong Interest Inventory* (discussed earlier in Chapter 2). Self-assessment exercises can help an individual consider where he/she is now in their career, identify future plans, and gauge how his/her career fits within the current situation and available resources (Noe, Hollenbeck, Gerhart, & Wright, 2003).

Taken collectively, the information obtained during the self-assessment can assist you in identifying areas in need of improvement as well as areas of strength. Once identified, these areas of strength can be more easily matched and marketed toward the available opportunities (i.e., full-time job openings) in the current job market. At the same time, action can be taken to address the areas in need of further development (i.e., workshops, classes, increased work assignments, etc.).

Performance Audit

The performance audit is the process of obtaining performance-related information from your internship supervisor and agency. Oftentimes, this information is found in the form of performance appraisals. During these appraisal reviews, many supervisors will also take time to discuss how you fit into the agency's plans (i.e., future employment opportunities within the agency, upcoming job opportunities outside the agency, career path advice, etc.). However, it is ultimately your responsibility to seek out these opportunities for career development discussions with your supervisor. For example, many interns will develop a list of job search and other career-related questions prior to the scheduled meetings with their supervisor. During these meetings, the intern can draw from his/her list of questions to share his/her goals and interests while also using this time as an opportunity to communicate career development needs with his/her supervisor.

Goal Development

Goal development refers to the process of developing short- and long-term objectives related to the job search (Noe, 2007). These goals usually relate to desired positions (i.e., to become a facility manager for an entertainment arena within two years), level of skill application (i.e., to use your marketing skills to improve the department's revenue stream in the area of youth programming), work setting (i.e., to acquire a position in a resort-based enterprise within two years), or skill acquisition (i.e., to obtain the Certified Park and Recreation Professional credential) (Noe, 2007). These goals are usually developed over a period of time and are a by-product of your previous experiences, future interests, and discussions with mentors and supervisors. The result of this process is a written plan that contains a list of strengths and weaknesses, job search goals, timelines, and development activities (projects, assignments, training, etc.) for reaching the job search goals. To illustrate, consider Figure 11.1.

Name: John Smith
Current Job Title: Intern
Agency: XYZ Parks and Recreation Department

Current Short- and Long-Term Career Goals:
- *Long-term* (3-5 years)—Acquire competencies and experience necessary to obtain a mid-level management position in the field of public parks and recreation. Competencies requiring development include personnel management, public relations, finance and budgeting, marketing and communication, and planning.

- *Short-term* (immediate to 2 years)—Obtain a full-time recreation supervisor position with a public park and recreation agency within eight weeks following my internship. Review career plan and identify opportunities to develop my professional competencies, including regional workshops, state and national conferences, and professional certifications.

Competency Development:
- *Strengths:*
  - Time management and organizational skills as evidenced by my performance on my previous academic coursework and feedback from my part-time summer camp director performance appraisals.
  - Leadership as evidenced by my executive-level roles in the department's student majors club and honors society.

- *Concern Areas:*
  - Budget and financial management—limited professional experience in this area; struggled with budgeting content in several of my academic (management and finance) courses.
  - Oral and written communication—instructor feedback (from three courses) indicating problems with projection and pace when delivering oral presentations; limited experience writing technical reports or other professional-based writing styles.

Development Activities:
- *Immediate (within next six months)*
  - Meet with internship supervisor to discuss career goals and employment aspirations within first two weeks of internship.
  - Review job announcement databases to obtain list of recreation supervisor (or related) positions. Communicate list and application plans to internship supervisor. Although ongoing, these tasks will be initiated by week four of the internship.

Figure 11.1. Goal Setting

cont.

- Submit application materials for recreation supervisor (or related) positions by week six of the internship.
- Build network of professionals within public park and recreation sector during internship.
- Obtain Certified Park and Recreation Professional certification by conclusion of internship.

- *Longer Term (1–5 years):*
  - Attend workshops and conferences that will allow me to enhance my network and practice and improve my personnel management, public relations, finance and budgeting, marketing and communication, and planning skills (ongoing).
  - Pursue a masters degree. The degree will allow me to obtain an advanced understanding of park and recreation management theory while improving my written and oral communication skills. Complete degree requirements within four years.
  - Attend executive development school to enhance knowledge in areas of personnel management, public relations, finance and budgeting, marketing and communication, and planning within five years.

Figure 11.1 (cont.)

Action Planning

Action planning involves you determining how you will achieve your short- and long-term goals (Noe, 2007). During this phase, you may engage in any one or combination of activities, such as workshops, networking events, seminars, meetings with supervisors or HR specialists, obtaining additional assessments, seeking additional assignments, or finding a mentor or coach (Summers, 1994). The specific activities and approach adopted depends on the specific needs and goals associated with your plan. What works for one person, may or may not work for you. Simply put, you must develop your own strategies to achieve your own goals.

Despite the diversity of approaches to achieving your goals, there have been two activities that have been consistently linked to success in finding that first job. First, research has highlighted the need for ongoing job search (and career development) discussions between the intern and his/her supervisor (Otte & Hutcheson, 1992). Second, interns must develop (in writing) and adhere to a timeline in the job search process. An overview of each of these activities is provided in the following paragraphs.

Communicating job search (and career development) options. To increase your chances of finding a full-time job following your internship, you and your supervisor must sit down and discuss the job search process.

Otte and Hutcheson (1992) identified the following characteristics of successful job search (and career) discussions:

- Your supervisor gains a stronger awareness of your work-related goals and interests.

- You and your supervisor agree on the next steps in the job search process.

- You understand how your supervisor views your performance, developmental needs, and career options.

- You and your supervisor agree on how your job search skills and interests can be addressed during the current internship.

- Your supervisor identifies resources to help you accomplish your job search goals that were developed during your (ongoing) discussions.

These regularly scheduled discussions can help you clarify your job search interests and overall career goals to your supervisor. This process enables your supervisor to become more informed and better positioned to help you reach these goals. For example, an intern might express an interest in securing employment as a special event coordinator for a professional sports organization. Recognizing this interest, the intern's supervisor could provide additional opportunities (during the internship) to improve the intern's skill sets in the areas of personnel management, marketing, and special event programming. In addition, the supervisor could also make sure the intern understands the relationship between his/her job performance and its applicability to the desired special event coordinator position. There may be times during the internship when the intern's performance is acceptable in the intern's current position as an intern, but would be a concern in the role of a special event coordinator for a professional sports organization. Because the supervisor is aware of the intern's career interests, the supervisor can communicate these performance issues while working with the intern to improve in these areas.

Develop timeline in writing. Developing a timeline for the job search process saves time, improves organization, and clarifies the sequencing of tasks associated with the process. Coupled with discussions between you and your internship supervisor, a written timetable can help you stay on task while clearly understanding your next move (i.e., develop résumé and cover letter for position announcements). Sharing the timeline with your supervisor can also allow your supervisor the opportunity to give advice concerning the correct timing for the various activities and tasks on your timeline. Furthermore, your supervisor might be able to let you know about resources available within the agency to assist you in completing your timeline (i.e., workshops on cover letter/résumé development, interview strategies, networking opportunities, etc.).

Tips for Managing Your Career (Walker, 2009)

- *Keep your career goal(s) realistic.* Following your heart toward a career in which you have little qualifications could yield months of frustration as you find yourself competing against numerous candidates who are more qualified. Spend your time focusing on positions that match your qualifications.

- *Landing that new position can be time consuming.* Be patient. Job searches can take several months so prepare yourself accordingly. At times, you may feel you are the perfect candidate for the job opening and yet you do not receive a response. This can be tiring and frustrating, but be optimistic; the right agency and job will come your way if you remain patient, calm, and focused. Stay positive!

- *Write a better resume than your competition.* Spend time crafting your resume. Tailor it to the position you are applying for to further articulate the "fit" between you and the job.

- *Sharpen your interview skills.* Don't just "wing" the interview. You finally got your foot in the door, now it is time to outshine the competition! Research the organization, prepare for the interview, and practice. Know your accomplishments well enough to weave them into your interview responses to showcase your skill sets.

Summary

This chapter presented an overview of planning in this process, identified common myths associated with the job search experience, and discussed the typical steps in the job search process. To be successful, interns need to plan their next professional step before and during the internship experience. Too often, students become overwhelmed during the internship and lose sight of the next step—getting a full-time job. However, securing full-time employment can be a much more time-consuming and detailed process when compared to the work associated with securing the internship. Thus, careful planning is needed to ensure the intern is positioned to market themselves to land that first full-time job. The primary responsibility in seeking employment following the internship rests with the intern, and although each job search process is likely unique, most will include the following components: self-assessment, reality check, goal setting, and action planning.

Chapter 11 Essentials

- Planning for your first job in the field of recreation, sport, and tourism should begin well before the start of your internship. Too often, students will view the internship as the final, capstone experience and will hold the assumption that full-time employment will "fall into place" once the internship (and undergraduate degree) has concluded.

- Planning for your first full-time job is a process by which you formulate goals and develop a plan for reaching those goals. This process is not something that should be left up to your supervisor, mentor, or simple chance; instead, it should be shaped and managed by you. Successful planning requires you to be alert to available job opportunities (both inside and outside your current agency) in relation to your abilities.
- Your career plan and the development of the plan is, ultimately, your responsibility.

- Your academic and internship institutions promote the conditions and create the environments that will facilitate the development of your career plan.

- Your internship supervisor's role in the job search (and career development) process is to educate you on the importance of developing career goals and plans, guide you in this process, and assist you in evaluating your actions and the impact these actions have on your career plans.

- One of the first steps in the job search process and overall career plan is to distinguish fact from fiction. In addressing this issue, it is necessary to recognize the most common myths related to the job search process in particular and an individual's overall career plan in general.

- In addition to recognizing potential pitfalls and myths related to the job search and your career planning, it is equally important to be aware of the productive steps and strategies associated with the career management process.

- Although each job search and overall career plan may vary in its level of sophistication, intensity, and emphasis placed on different elements in the process (i.e., résumé development, networking, geographic location constraints, etc.), most plans include the following components: self-assessment, reality check, goal setting, and action planning.

Discussion Questions

1. Recognizing that no one supervisor will likely embody all the career development roles presented in the text, which of the eight are most important to you? Why?

2. The text presented several common myths associated with the job search process. Select two, and tell us, do you really think they are myths? Why or why not?

3. All of the steps in the career management process (self-assessment, reality check, goal setting, and action planning) are important. Perhaps one of the most overlooked is action planning. Unfortunately, this is the stage that holds you accountable for achieving that which you have set out to do. How will you approach this critical step, and what strategies can you employ to be sure you are accountable for accomplishing your goals?

Help!

Justin is an intern with an independent league semiprofessional baseball organization. The particular team he has been assigned to work for is in its second year of existence, and Justin is their fourth intern. Justin's primary responsibilities include team marketing, ticket sales (individual and season), game day promotion, and stadium operations.

Justin has been learning a great deal about the administration of sport enterprises and is already into week nine (of 12) of his internship experience. His workload has been extensive, as he is spending over 50 hours each week at the stadium completing his tasks and responsibilities. In addition, he is putting in another 10 hours per week during his time off to complete the required academic projects/activities for his internship. Justin has communicated to his academic supervisor that he is truly enjoying the experiences, but it is also one of the busiest times of his life.

Justin's academic supervisor has also asked Justin about his future plans following the internship. Justin indicates he will explore his options at the conclusion of the internship, as he wants to focus all of his energy on successfully completing his experience with the semiprofessional baseball organization.

At the conclusion of the internship, Justin is required to complete a reflection paper to share his insight on the experience. In his paper, Justin reflects on the valuable opportunities and knowledge that he obtained. Justin also states that he was "unbelievably busy" and looks forward to taking "some time off to relax and enjoy his accomplishments."

Six months have passed, and Justin contacts his academic advisor. Justin is frustrated as he has spent that past two months looking for full-time employment and is having limited success. He has applied to more than 25 positions and has completed only one (preliminary) phone interview. Because of his struggles, Justin is contemplating a career move. He loves the sport industry but feels he is not marketable enough to "get his foot in the door." He has begun questioning his internship choice as well as his undergraduate major and is looking for some assistance and direction.

1. If you were Justin's academic advisor, what would you do? How would you respond to Justin's phone call? Be specific.

2. What are some strategies Justin could have considered when exploring internship opportunities that might have helped him avoid some of his current frustrations?

3. What are some strategies Justin could have considered during his internship experience that might have helped him avoid some of his current frustrations?

4. Justin is contemplating a career change as he has been unemployed for six months and is confronted with financial obligations (i.e., bills, rent, car payment, etc.). What are some ways Justin might be able to remain connected to the field he loves (i.e., the sports industry) while still managing the realities of his life (i.e., bills, rent, etc.)?

References

Byars, L. L., & Rue, L. W. (2004). *Human resource management* (7th ed.). New York, NY: McGraw-Hill Irwin.

Kidd, J. M., & Smewing, C. (2001). The role of the supervisor in career and organizational commitment. *European Journal of Work and Organizational Psychology, 10*(1), 25-40.

Leibowitz, Z. B., & Schlossberg, N. K. (1981). Training managers for their role in a career development system. *Training and Development Journal, 7,* 74.

Medinsky, M. (2012). Job search: Busting the myths. *School Library Journal, 58*(5), 60-65.

Noe, R. A. (2007). *Employee training and development* (3rd ed.). New York, NY: McGraw-Hill Higher Education.

Noe, R. A., Hollenbeck, J. R., Gerhart, B., & Wright, P. M. (2003). *Human resource management: Gaining a competitive advantage* (4th ed.). Boston, MA: McGraw-Hill Irwin.

Otte, F. L., & Hutcheson, P. G. (1992). *Helping employees manage careers.* Englewood Cliffs, NJ: Prentice-Hall.

Randolph, A. B. (1981). Managerial career coaching. *Training and Development Journal, 7,* 54–55.

Ryan, L. (2007). Scuttling some job-hunt myths. *Business Week Online,* 1, 16.

Sherman, S. (1993). A brave new Darwinian workplace. *Fortune, 1,* 50–56.

Summers, L. (1994). A logical approach to development planning. *Training and Development, 48,* 22–31.

Wallis, T. J. (2002). Top 10 job-hunting myths. *Career World, 30*(4), 22-25.

Walker, D. (2009). Career coaching tips from Deborah Walker, CCMC. *Information Executive, 12*(6), 15.

Chapter 12

Negotiating the Salary

Overview

Very few students are afforded the luxury of negotiating a starting salary for their student internship. In fact, a significant percentage of student internships are unpaid or paid as a stipend or at a low hourly wage. At this stage in the semester, however, you have likely secured your internship placement and are rightfully thinking about the next stage in your professional career—full-time employment. Many young professionals are beginning to feel more confident in their interviewing skills, but many, due to their personality, are terrified at the prospect of negotiating their starting salary once the offer has been advanced (Divita, 1994). Although the process of salary negotiation can be uncomfortable for certain people, there are some basic steps you can follow to feel more confident in this trying stage of securing employment. And with current research showing a significant increase in starting salary for those who negotiate effectively, it is a topic soon-to-be college graduates should familiarize themselves with (Marks & Harold, 2011; O'Shea & Bush, 2002). Some analysts have even suggested that negotiating your initial starting salary could result in over $1 million dollars in additional earning over the course of your career (Rinke, 2009). Recognizing that most employers do not make their first offer their "best" offer, there is generally some room to improve the offer if you are bold enough to begin the process. While there may be significantly less leeway in negotiating your salary when you are applying for entry- or junior-level positions, or when you don't have a great deal of experience and specialization, it is important to understand and participate in the process. Although there is significant ambiguity and stress associated with negotiating a starting salary, this chapter will outline several strategies that will help you enter negotiations more relaxed, prepared, and confident .

Recessions Come and Go

At the time of this writing, the economy is in severe depression. Unemployment is hovering just above 9% and the stock market is on a roller coaster ride. Many people have been laid off, taken on additional responsibilities without compensation, or taken a voluntary pay cut simply to hold on to their job. But the recession will not last forever, and the economy will rebound. Wise managers know that they will have difficulty holding on to valuable employees after the recession ends if they do not fairly negotiate with and compensate their employees (Porter, Conlon, & Barber, 2004).

Negotiation Background and Basics

The process of preparing to negotiate your salary has become significantly easier in the past decade. Traditionally, many organizations keep employee salaries a tightly held secret, fearing that exposing these figures would lead to distraction in the workplace, reduced morale, and elimination of the company's competitive advantage in the salary negotiation process (Pentilla, 2009). For this reason, some companies have even required employees to sign a nondisclosure agreement that prohibits the employee from sharing salary information with any third party. While nondisclosure agreements are most common in the private sector, public and nonprofit agencies may have salary disclosure rules as well. These rules may require full transparency of employee salaries to the general public or may restrict salary disclosure to board members or oversight committees. Regardless of the sector, it is safe to assume that most employers prefer to keep open discussion of salary ranges at a minimum for fear of creating a negative culture. Equity Theory has clearly demonstrated that when employees sense a lack of equity in their salary, the impact on their attitude and job performance can be significant (Huserman, Hatfield, & Miles, 1987).

This period of secrecy, however, is giving way to a new era of transparency. The advent of salary comparison websites such as Salary.com, SalaryExpert.com, and PayScale.com have given prospective employees access to information that has historically been hard to find, significantly complicating the salary negotiation process. These sites provide access to salary ranges for similar positions in the geographic region or salary ranges among competitors. These sites effectively answer the long asked question of job seekers: "What am I worth?" While the information on these websites has been accused of being dated, inflated, or otherwise distorted, they provide the job seeker with a loose benchmark to reduce the chances of undervaluing their services.

Now that you understand why discussion of salary is a sensitive matter, there are a few other basic facts to keep in mind as you prepare to negotiate your salary. First, most aspects related to salary negotiation are highly variable and will require you to carefully assess your needs, wants, long-term goals, personality type, and the relative strength of your capabilities. Beyond this, you must understand the unique characteristics of the hiring agency. The sector (i.e., public, private, nonprofit), size, organizational culture, and geographic location will all play a role in determining how flexible the organization can be in negotiating your salary. Understanding the dynamic interaction of these personal and organizational variables will help you establish realistic expectations. Second, salary negotiation is not about taking advantage of one party or the other, but rather it is about finding an agreeable work situation for both the employee and the employer (Huller, 2009). The needs and wants of the prospective employee and the hiring agency must be considered, and give and take should be expected. Third, salary negotiation is not always about negotiating salary, as your compensation is much more than your monthly paycheck. Entering the process understanding that everything is negotiable is extremely important. In organizations where salary ranges are highly restricted (many public and nonprofit agencies), you may still be able to negotiate on your commission structure, working hours, vacation time, office location, job title, supervisory responsibilities, travel and training budget, office equipment, benefits packages, a shorter review period, starting date, or other nonmonetary rewards such as laptops or a Blackberry.

Young professionals may wonder when the discussion of salary should take place. As mentioned in Chapter 6, with very few exceptions, you should not discuss salary with a prospective employer until the employment offer has been made (DeLuca & DeLuca, 2007). Inquiring about the salary range prior to the interview or at the conclusion of the interview may send the wrong signal to the employer, many of whom are looking for employees who believe in the "vision and the dream" (Pentilla, 2009). There may be two possible exceptions to this rule. First, while not common in the recreation, sport, and tourism fields, some employers may use a headhunter or recruiting agency to find or screen initial applicants. Such agencies are likely to inquire about your salary expectations in preliminary conversations. You need to be prepared to give a very open salary range when requested, or you may not be included in the final applicant pool. Likewise, some employers very candidly inquire about salary expectations in the very first interview. This means you should probably do some basic research about salaries before you go on your first interview. In the remainder of this chapter, we will give you some basic tools to help you prepare for effective salary negotiations.

> ## Note from the Author
>
> One of the most uncomfortable interview moments of my life came during an interview with Marriott International. As the interview was concluding, the HR manager abruptly closed his folder, looked me in the eye and said, "So, Ryan. What should we pay you for this position?" I froze. I had no idea what to say. I remembered my internship coordinator told me not to talk about money during the interview, but he never told me what to say if they asked me so directly. I stammered around for a moment and finally threw out a number that was a bit higher than what I would have been willing to work for. I never heard back from Marriott International, and I've always wondered if it was because I threw out too high of a number or just wasn't the best candidate for the position.

Negotiation Essentials

There are a number of excellent books on salary negotiation, and we will not pretend to encompass all the nuances and subtle tactics presented in these works in one short chapter. Instead, we will present five essential practices that will give you a solid start. At the end of the chapter, we will provide a "suggested reading" section referencing several comprehensive resources for job seekers.

Negotiation Essential #1: Embrace Your Discomfort

Research suggests that a number of different variables, including personality and gender, likely influence our comfort level or willingness to engage in negotiations with a prospective employer (Divita, 1994; Wade, 2001). One of the first steps in preparing yourself for this process is to embrace and welcome the feelings of unease that you may have. Stepping out of your comfort zone will be necessary if you want to be sure you are not underselling your services. While the economy is currently in a downturn, many job seekers feel it is foolish to negotiate the offered salary. Shouldn't you accept any offer and be glad to have it? While it is true that the depressed economy and your relative lack of experience may significantly limit your ability to negotiate large increases, you will certainly not get what you do not ask for. Embrace the discomfort and commit yourself to negotiate anyway.

Negotiation Essential #2: Know Your Value

As we have already mentioned, there are a number of resources available to help job seekers get a general idea of what the going rate is for those in similar positions and industries. Referencing sites like Salary.com, PayScale.com, and SalaryExpert.com are a good start. Depending on the agency to which you have applied, salary information for all employees may be public information. Many park districts and other public organizations openly include this information in their annual budget. You should also boldly use any and all members of your professional network. Your peers can give insight on offers they, or their friends, have received. College professors, academic advisors, and career counselors can identify salary ranges that previous graduates have reported. Remember to keep in mind cost of living differences in the figures that your peers and professors share with you. If a friend in Naperville, Illinois, got a starting salary of $38,000 doing something similar to the job you are exploring in Colorado Springs, Colorado, your starting salary is likely to be very different. Colorado Springs is approximately 25% less expensive to live in than Naperville, meaning a comparable starting salary might be $28,000. There are a number of excellent online cost of living calculators available if you do a simple Google search.

A Word of Caution

Everyone seems to know someone who heard from someone else that a friend of theirs got a starting salary $10,000 higher than your offer. While those people may exist, they are clearly not the norm. That is why everyone is telling you about them. Be sure you maintain realistic expectations.

In the event that these resources don't provide the information you need, a more basic approach may be helpful. Exploring the basic demographic information for the community in which the organization is housed is a good starting point. Websites such as www.census.gov (look for QuickFacts or the Fact Sheet) can provide valuable information about the education and median income level in a particular community.

What's a Fair Salary?

Assume you have applied for and been offered an entry-level position in Champaign, Illinois. You have had no success using salary websites or your professional network to discover a benchmark to use to guide your salary expectations. Visit www.census.gov and search for "Champaign, IL"—be sure to click on the Fact Sheet. Based on what you see here, what might a reasonable starting salary for an entry-level position be in this community?

Tips:

1. Look at the economic data and see if you can find an average income for the community. Do you know the difference between median household income and median family income?

2. Look at the demographic information related to race and gender. As unfortunate as it is, how might these numbers influence your starting salary?

3. Look at the percentage of people holding a bachelor's degree or higher. How might these figures change how you determine your starting salary for an entry-level position?

Negotiation Essential #3: Know the Sectors

In the recreation, sport, and tourism industries there is a great deal of variability in the flexibility employers will have in adjusting your salary. For example, municipal and government jobs have tightly defined salary ranges. Small increases are possible, but you might more effectively negotiate nontraditional rewards or increased job responsibilities that will improve your ability to attain your longer term career goals. Likewise, nonprofit organizations typically have a small budget for payroll, but are frequently willing to accommodate requests for flextime, remote working, and cross-training for career progression and improved marketability. The private sector is highly variable depending on the size and nature of the organization. While they do not have the same pressures as public and nonprofit agencies to keep salaries equitable or low, they frequently have high demand for open positions. Let's face it. If you won't take that job working for the Chicago Cubs at $20,000 per year, hundreds of other people will. In these environments, entry-level positions frequently relate to sales, and you might be best advised to negotiate based on performance. There is a great deal of difference in commission structures, and if you are not familiar with "base plus commission," "residual commission," or "variable commission" now might be the time to do some exploration. If you are entering the sport, event, commercial recreation, or hospitality industries a change in your commission structure can significantly improve the amount of money you take home.

Negotiation Essential #4: Know Your Needs

By now you know there is a difference between wants and needs. In a depressed economy, this distinction is all the more important. Although this is Negotiation Essential #4, in all honesty you should not apply for, negotiate for, or accept a position until you have a firm understanding of your personal financial situation. While you may want to direct 5% of your income to savings each month, you need to cover housing, transportation, and other financial obligations. If you haven't already, now is the time to develop a comprehensive personal budget. Knowing your basic needs is fundamental to the next negotiation essential. Remember, there are areas of your personal budget that may need trimming as you transition from having financial support of family to being an independent adult. Eating out three nights a week or giving gifts to all your friends on their birthdays may not be feasible in the early stages of your career.

Microsoft has a fantastic personal budget template available at http://office.microsoft.com/en-us/templates/TC062062791033. aspx?CategoryID=CT101172321033. It likely includes some important categories that you might have forgotten otherwise.

Negotiation Essential #5: Determine Your Range

Several authors and analysts suggest developing three numbers to keep in mind as you prepare to negotiate.

The "no" number. This is the salary level below which you cannot meet your basic living needs. If you have been honest and comprehensive in your approach to Negotiation Essential #4, you will know exactly what this number is. Emotions and stress could cloud your judgment, so be clear on this number from the onset. No matter how badly you need a job or like the culture of the agency, it may not be wise to accept a position that does not enable you to meet your most basic financial obligations. Remember, you don't get many opportunities to negotiate over the course of your career, and research suggests that those who are open about their issues and constraints have more success in the negotiation process (Marks & Harold, 2011). If you simply can't accept a lowball offer, be honest with the employer and explain why. What have you got to lose?

The "acceptable" number. This number might actually be a range instead of a hard dollar amount, but should represent the salary at which, based upon what you know of your value, the sector, the community, and your needs, you feel you are being compensated equitably. If the initial offer from the organization falls within this range, you may forgo negotiating salary and instead look for other perks that would enhance the quality of your working experience there.

The "wow" number. This number represents your "dream" offer and is the dollar amount that you should share when asked about your salary expectations. This number should not be a ridiculously unreasonable one and should have some basis in fact, which you can share with the employer. But recognize it for what it is—ideal, but unlikely. Research, however, does suggest that starting with a high, but supported, starting number can in fact pull up counteroffers from the organization (DeLuca & DeLuca, 2007). Be prepared to accept an offer significantly below this number.

Negotiation Essential #6: Be Honest

In the negotiation process, honesty is critical. First, you must be honest with yourself at all times—honest about your level of experience and the value you currently bring to the organization; honest about availability of entry-level positions in your industry and the salaries they bring; honest about the constraints that the current market puts on your employment aspirations; honest about your needs, recognizing the things you want become attainable after you have proven yourself in the workplace.

You must also be honest with the would-be employer. If you have had previous employment, do not inflate your previous salary in hopes of driving up the offer from your would-be employer. A simple phone call to your current or previous employer is all it takes to verify your salary. Dishonesty will only result in a missed opportunity.

We have spent a considerable amount of time discussing the negotiation of your starting salary. It is important to note that all aspects of your employment are negotiable at the time you receive an offer. Have you considered the following:

1. Vacation time?
2. Sick leave?
3. Flextime?
4. Compressed workweek?
5. Parking?
6. Professional development? (i.e., conferences, travel, subscriptions to trade magazines)
7. Commission structure?
8. Electronic resources? (i.e., certain programs to help you be more efficient/effective on the job?)

When it comes to negotiating, everything is on the table. Take your time and be creative. The agency may be highly restricted in what they can do in terms of salary, but may be more than willing to offer other incentives to make their offer even more attractive.

Summary

Salary negotiation is often seen as a distasteful process and may be fraught with dialogue and exchanges that make young professionals uneasy. There are, however, very few opportunities in your career to negotiate your salary, and even modest increases can have a significant impact on your lifetime earnings. While you must carefully prepare and always use your best judgment, salary negotiations need not be the ambiguous or awkward experience that young job seekers fear. Using the information presented in this chapter, you will be well on your way to being sure that you are being compensated fairly for the value you bring to the organization. If you are interested in learning more about this topic (and who shouldn't be?), consider reviewing the following texts:

DeLuca, M., & DeLuca, N. (2007). *Perfect phrases for negotiating salary and job offers.* New York, NY: McGraw-Hill Companies.

Dawson, R. (2006). *Secrets of power salary negotiating: Inside secrets from a master negotiator.* Pompton Plains, NJ: The Career Press, Inc.

Chapter 12 Essentials

- Salary negotiation often makes young professionals uncomfortable. Embrace the discomfort and press ahead.

- While cycles in the economy (and even seasonal cycles in industries) might limit the leeway companies have in negotiating with prospective employees, you will certainly never get what you don't ask for.

- Even modest increases in your entry-level salaries can have a big impact on your lifetime earnings.

- Knowing your value, knowing the industry, knowing the community, and knowing your personal limitations are all critically important if you are to negotiate successfully.

Discussion Questions

1   Recognizing that the unemployment rate of college graduates is still hovering at an all-time high, what do you think a fair salary range is for someone with your level of education and background? Share this with a trusted practitioner or educator and see what they think.

2.   Outside of your salary, what are other things you might negotiate with a prospective employer over? How important are these compared to your salary?

3. In the early stages of your career, there might be things you have to "give up" due to a lack of income. What are some things you have enjoyed as a college student that you might have to give up on, or scale back your consumption of, as you transition to the professional environment?

4. What is the difference between a "want" and a "need"? List your most basic needs. Use these as a baseline for your "no" number.

All Is Fair?

Sandy just completed an interview for a recreation supervisor for a municipal park and recreation department. The interview went well. Sandy connected with staff; she was confident and excited about the responsibilities associated with the position; and she liked the community. Sandy is optimistic about her chances and was told all interviews would be completed by the end of the week with a final decision being made within the next few weeks.

Three weeks later, Sandy receives a phone call from the recreation director of the municipal park and recreation department. The director informs Sandy that she was selected as the top candidate for the position. The director offers Sandy the position at an annual salary of $41,000 with the city's standard benefits package and a municipal vehicle with gas card to use for travel to and from the various programming sites.

Sandy knows the position announcement stated the salary range would be between $40,000 and $47,000 per year and is dependent upon qualifications. Sandy has one year of part-time supervisory experience, which is near the bottom of expected qualifications listed in the position announcement ("position looking for one to three years supervisory experience"). Sandy was also not expecting the offer to include a municipal vehicle and gas card. As a result, Sandy accepts the position at the $41,000 annual salary level.

Six months later, the other recreation supervisor takes a position with another agency and leaves the department. The recreation director initiates a search process and eventually hires Barbara as the new recreation supervisor. Sandy really likes Barbara and is eager to work together as the two positions share many of the same programming responsibilities.

Shortly after Barbara begins working for the department, Sandy offers to take Barbara out to lunch to celebrate her new position. During lunch, Sandy learns that Barbara followed a very similar career path as Sandy and the two have about the same amount of work experience (i.e., about one year of previous part-time supervisory experience).

When the bill for lunch arrives, Sandy offers to pay for lunch as a way to welcome Barbara and congratulate her for securing the position. Appreciating the gesture, Barbara responds, "That is very nice of you, but Sandy you don't need to do that. A few years ago, when I was constantly pinching pennies to pay bills and rent each month I would have gladly accepted your offer. But, now that I finally got a full-time job, with benefits, a car, gas card, and more than $46,000 per year, I feel uncomfortable accepting your offer. Just you taking time out of your schedule to visit with me and welcome me to the department is more than enough. Thank you!"

While Sandy is flattered by the kind words, she is stunned to learn Barbara is earning more than $5,000 per year than she is. They both share similar responsibilities with similar amounts of previous experience. How did Barbara secure more money?

1. If you were Sandy, what would you do? Would you meet with the recreation director to discuss your concerns? If you did, what do you think would be the recreation director's response?

2. In your opinion, why did Barbara receive a salary that was near the top of the salary range? Why did Sandy receive a salary that was near the bottom of the range? What could Sandy have done to receive a higher salary?

3. Many municipal agencies are required to provide public access to compensation records of their employees. How might this information been helpful to Sandy during her job search and salary negotiation phases?

References

Bottos, L., & Coleman, B. (2002). The new salary negotiation. *Compensation and Benefits Review, 34,* 22–28.

DeLuca, M., & DeLuca, N. (2007). *Perfect phrases for negotiating salary and job offers.* New York, NY: McGraw-Hill Companies.

Divita, S. (1994). Why be intimidated by negotiating salary? *Marketing News, 28,* 15.

Huller, K. (2009). *Negotiate, but know your value first.* Pennsylvania CPA Journal, 80,1–2.

Huseman, R., Hatfield, J., & Miles, E. (1987). A new perspective on Equity Theory: The Equity Sensitivity Construct. *Academy of Management Review, 12,* 222–234.

Marks, M., & Harold, C. (2011). Who asks and who receives in salary negotiation. *Journal of Organizational Behavior, 32,* 371–394.

O'Shea, P., & Bush, D. (2002). Negotiation for starting salary: Antecedents and outcomes among recent college graduates. *Journal of Business & Psychology, 16,* 365–382.

Pentilla, C. (2009). The salary secret is out. *Entrepreneur, 37,* 23–26.

Porter, C., Conlon, D., & Barber, A. (2004). The dynamics of salary negotiations: Effects on applicants' justice perceptions and recruitment decisions. *The International Journal of Conflict Management, 15,* 273–303.

Rinke, W. (2009). Negotiate salary; it could mean $1 million. *Sales and Service Excellence, 9,* 14.

Wade, M. (2001). Women and salary negotiation: The costs of self-advocacy. *Psychology of Women Quarterly, 25,* 65–77.

Index